STORM CENTER

A Personal Account of Tragedy and Terrorism by

WILL AND SHARON ROGERS
with Gene Gregston

STORM CENTER

The USS *Vincennes* and Iran Air Flight 655

Naval Institute Press   Annapolis, Maryland

Library of Congress Cataloging-in-Publication Data

Rogers, Will (Will C.)
    Storm center : the USS Vincennes and Iran air flight 655 : a personal account
of tragedy and terrorism / by Will and Sharon Rogers with Gene Gregston.
        p.   cm.
    Includes index.
    ISBN 1-55750-727-9
    1. Rogers, Will (Will C.)   2.   Rogers, Sharon (Sharon L.)
3. Vincennes   (Cruiser) 4. Iran-Iraq   War,   1980–1988—Naval   operations,
American. 5. Aeronautics—Persian Gulf—Accidents—1988. 6. United States.
Navy—Officers—Biography. 7.   Terrorism—United States—History—20th century.
I. Rogers, Sharon (Sharon L.)   II. Gregston, Gene, 1925–   III. Title.
DS318.85.R64R63   1992
955.05′4—dc20   92-9202
                                                                                      CIP

Printed in the United States of America on acid-free paper ∞

9 8 7 6 5 4 3 2

First printing

For all who sail in harm's way,
and for those who wait . . .

Contents

Preface

This account of the tragic destruction of Iran Air Flight 655 by the cruiser *Vincennes*, the subsequent bombing of our van, and the events surrounding both of these incidents is not an attempt to replow old ground. Our intent rather is to tell the reader the personal story of two ordinary people catapulted into the center of extraordinary circumstances. We have attempted to correct numerous errors that found their way into the public perception of these events. Some errors arose simply because we chose to restrict access to ourselves. Others were flights of fancy that ignored published facts.

Our goal has been to portray an accurate account without drawing on classified information or divulging data that would affect our personal security. Conclusions and opinions, unless clearly attributed to others, are our own. The contents reflect our views and not necessarily those of the Department of Defense, the Navy Department, or any agency involved in the events described. Although it was often impossible to reconstruct dialogue exactly, we have striven to represent it as accurately as possible. If a comment is directly quoted, it is based on at least one participant's recall, supporting notes, recorded tapes, or sworn and witnessed testimony.

For us this book serves as a vehicle to express our gratitude to the multitude of people who encouraged and supported us. We hope the effort represents an accurate footnote to the historical events.

Acknowledgments

Many people played important personal roles in this story. To recognize all of them is, unfortunately, impossible. We wish, however, to specifically acknowledge those persons whose concern, support, and courage enabled us to weather the storm: our families, who rode the whirlwind with us and whose love was a deep well from which we drew constantly; Vice Admiral Bob Kihune, USN, and his wife, Hope, whose support never wavered no matter how dark the moment; Vice Admiral Tony Less, USN, who understood the point of the spear; Captain Ted Atwood, USN (Ret.), a friend, confidant, and vital link; the crew of the "Checkmate Cruiser," Team 49, simply the best; Captain Dennis McCoy, JAGC, USN, a craftsman at his trade and the right choice; Rear Admirals Guy Zeller and F.C. "Fox" Johnson, USN (Ret.), who made difficult choices and shared with us their understanding; the USS *Vincennes* Association and the people of Vincennes, Indiana, who offered instant and continuing support; the parents of Sharon's fourth-grade class at La Jolla Country Day, who stood up when the moment to be counted arrived, and their children, forever special students; the lower-school faculty, who protected and comforted a friend and colleague; Congressman Bill Lowery, who was willing to pay the professional cost of steering a supportive but rocky course; Karl Higgins and Linda Hansen, who helped open some welcome doors; the FBI and NIS agents assigned to the bombing case, who in many instances were willing to work around a stifling bureaucracy to get the job done; and the NIS personal security detachment, who were flexible and understanding and made a difficult situation bearable.

The assistance of others was invaluable. Captain Jerry Hull, Commander Doug McDonald, and Lieutenant Commander Mike Scharf, USN, gave generously of their expertise and advice. Commander David L. (Matt) Dillon, USN (Ret.), filled many critical holes with his vast files and detailed recall. Captain and Mrs. Bill Bokesch, USN (Ret.), provided a valuable critique of most of the manuscript. Our editor, Constance Buchanan, improved the text with skill and sensitivity and ensured the integrity of our story.

And finally we thank Gene Gregston, whose enormous assistance in organizing the mass of clippings, tapes, and notes showed us the way through numerous false starts. His patience in suffering through our various drafts and rewrites was remarkable. Without his help, professional skill, and gentle, continuous prodding, this effort would have evaporated.

Will and Sharon Rogers

STORM CENTER

1

COMMAND DECISION

War is a mist through which the keenest eye cannot always
discern the right path.
—Sir William Napier, *History of the War on the Peninsula*, 1840

"Trinity Sword this is Oceanlord two-five, we're taking fire . . . Executing evasion, clearing!"

It was hard to believe: The Iranians were firing at our helicopter. I punched into the radio circuit and asked Oceanlord to confirm. "Two-five, this is Trinity Sword Actual, is anyone hurt? Confirm hostile fire!"

The command pilot quickly replied, "Sword, no injuries, we confirm eight . . . ten rounds . . . air bursts, returning!"

I immediately ordered the helicopter back within our protective cover, told the bridge to close the helo at best speed, notified commander, Middle East Force, of the attack, and ordered general quarters. When general quarters sounds, the noise of nearly four hundred people racing to their battle stations carries throughout the ship. In the combat information center (CIC) we could hear the thunderous clatter of running feet, aluminum ladders rattling, heavy watertight hatches being dogged down, and joiner doors slamming shut.

Then over the internal communications circuits came the voices of station supervisors checking in: "Engineering, manned and ready!" "Mount 52, manned and ready!" "Bridge, manned and ready!" All stations reported manned and ready within six and a half minutes.

I had told the crew before we arrived in the Persian Gulf that should the general alarm sound it would not be a drill, it would be for real. On 3 July 1988, it turned out to be very, very real.

In the preceding days we had received numerous intelligence reports warning us that Iran might "do something" to embarrass the United States over the Fourth of July weekend. That something was about to take place: a deadly game of tag, played in pewter bowl visibility, in which we appeared to be It.

On the third I was shaving when the phone buzzed in my sea cabin at 6:33 A.M. It was the CIC watch officer.

"Skipper, you better come down. It sounds like the Montgomery has her nose in a beehive."

The Montgomery, a fast frigate operating in the western approaches to the Strait of Hormuz, had sighted thirteen Iranian gunboats with weapons manned breaking into three attack groups and menacing a Pakistani merchant ship. This activity was odd on several counts. Iranian Revolutionary Guard (IRG) boats normally preferred to operate at dusk or during the cover of night; this was an unusually large number of boats operating in concert, and they were boldly maneuvering in the proximity of a U.S. warship. The harsh lessons of the Persian Gulf were in the process of repeating themselves.

The IRG boats were 40-foot Swedish-made Boghammers, smaller American-built Boston whalers, and Gulf dhows, all armed with an assortment of mortars, heavy machine guns, rocket-propelled grenades, and 107-millimeter rocket launchers. Under most circumstances they were a combination not capable of sinking a large ship but more than able to exact extensive damage and personal injury.

I had started the day looking forward to arriving in Manama, Bahrain, where we were going to celebrate the consecutive birthdays of our ship, the USS Vincennes, and our country. The Vincennes is one of the U.S. Navy's newest and most technically advanced ships, an antiair-warfare (AAW) cruiser equipped with the world's finest battle management system, Aegis, named after the magic shield of the Greek god Zeus. In the hands of a well-trained crew, Aegis is capable of simultaneously processing and displaying to systems operators several hundred surface and air radar tracks. Its great tactical advantage is the speed with which it determines course, speed, and in the case of air contacts, altitude. While this information is displayed visually, targeting data is automatically provided to the ship's missile battery. Conse-

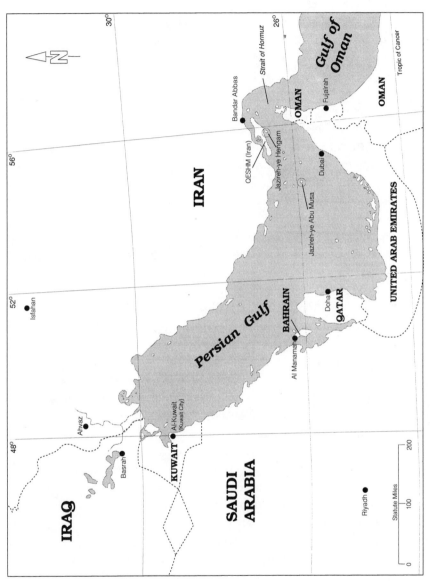

The Persian Gulf (Map by James Burnett)

quently, the system can react to potential threats with incredible speed. In this era of high-speed aircraft and missile threats, Aegis provides an additional bit of a precious commodity—time.

Despite Aegis's capability of almost instantaneously reacting, caution was our constant byword and companion. The USS *Stark* had been hit by two missiles mistakenly fired in the Gulf by an Iraqi pilot little more than a year earlier, killing thirty-seven sailors and wounding dozens more. Vivid memories of a blackened hulk and flag-draped coffins were never far from our minds.

Summer in the Gulf is marred by abysmal weather. Daytime temperatures in excess of 120°F and 95 percent humidity are common. A hot desert wind, the Shamal, always threatens to kick up, carrying with it dust the consistency of talcum powder. Even when the wind subsides this grit remains in the air, drastically reducing visibility and coating any exposed surface with a brown film. The rising sun soon renders metal surfaces untouchable and the intensely reflective surface of the water appears greasy from the settling dust. This day was no exception.

At 7:11 A.M. (all times indicated are local—Greenwich Mean Time + 3) the *Montgomery* heard a series of explosions north of her, but there were no calls for assistance. Within minutes of receiving her report, we had orders from commander, Destroyer Squadron 25, aboard the USS *John Hancock*, to proceed to the vicinity of the *Montgomery* and assist in investigating the small-boat activity. The *Hancock* and the USS *Coronado*, flagship for Rear Admiral Tony Less, commander, Joint Task Force, Middle East, were dockside in Bahrain about 325 miles northwest.

One of our embarked helicopters, Oceanlord 25, was airborne, returning from a normal dawn patrol. The aircraft landed aboard, quickly refueled, and vectored to the *Montgomery*'s position to monitor the situation. At 7:49 A.M. Oceanlord informed us that four of the IRG boats were approaching a German merchant vessel. I ordered general quarters at 8:18. One minute later the IRG boats began circling the German ship. An Omani patrol boat warned the IRG craft to clear the area and the small craft appeared to comply. At 8:46 I requested and received orders to return to our assigned transit to Bahrain. We secured from general quarters.

At 9:09 we challenged and, following his reply, began monitoring an Iranian aircraft that had appeared on our radar and was slowly orbiting to the west of Qeshm Island. This was a P-3F Orion, a four-engine turboprop maritime patrol aircraft and one of six sold by the United States to Iran during the reign of the Shah. Originally built for antisubmarine warfare (ASW) and reconnaissance, the Iranian P-3s had been modified as ship-killers able to carry sea-skimming Harpoon missiles.

This one was not following the normal patrol pattern, which on alternate days was either a route south and east along the coast and return, or north and west and return. We had observed this numerous times. Today the P-3 looked to be maintaining a position capable of providing aircraft or vessels with information useful for coordinated attacks. Whatever its purpose, we would watch it closely.

By 9:15 Oceanlord was orbiting at slow speed about eight to ten miles north of the Montgomery, observing the small craft from about 1,200 feet and providing information on their activity to us, the Montgomery, and the USS Sides, a guided-missile frigate coming through the strait after completing an outbound escort. Suddenly the aircraft commander, Lieutenant Roger Huff, and the pilot, Lieutenant (j.g.) Mark Collier, radioed the startling information that eight to ten air bursts had detonated a hundred or so yards from them. Over bridge-to-bridge radio an Arab voice exulted, "We have destroyed the great Satan Blackhawk!"

The voice was wrong on two counts. The helicopter was not a Blackhawk, nor was it destroyed. Oceanlord was a Sikorsky SH-60B Seahawk designed for ASW and carrying a crew of three. Other than 0.38-caliber pistols carried by the air crew and a door-mounted M-60 machine gun, the aircraft had no defensive capability and certainly no offensive system effective against surface craft. The helo was thin-skinned and vulnerable to any sort of projectile, so the crew, to put it mildly, was concerned.

The klaxon sounded general quarters again and we turned north to close the helicopter. I could not possibly have guessed what the next hours would bring before we stood down from general quarters once again. Within minutes we closed within seven or eight miles of the IRG craft. Oceanlord was back in proximity to us, and we had taken tactical command of the Montgomery as directed by Admiral Less. In view of the increasingly bizarre behavior of the IRGC, the admiral and his staff were now in continuous radio contact with us.

This much was certain: The Iranians' unprovoked attack and unclear intentions called for institution of a longstanding procedure for requesting air support from the carrier group operating in the north Arabian Sea. I directed Lieutenant Commander Scott Lustig, my AAW coordinator, "Set Fury Fez! Tell *Forrestal* to launch the alert package now!" This request was transmitted and acknowledged, but it would take time before the aircraft could reach the ingress point to the strait.

I ordered the *Montgomery* to take up position 4,000 yards on the port quarter of the *Vincennes* and directed that Oceanlord be vectored to a holding pattern off our aft starboard quarter. The *Sides,* about 18 miles from our position, received orders from commander, Destroyer Squadron 25, to proceed at maximum speed to our area. Admiral Less directed us to take tactical control of the *Sides.* I radioed her: "I am assuming tactical command of you." The *Sides* acknowledged.

I could not believe the IRG had acted in such an overtly hostile way in daylight and in the clear presence of U.S. naval combatants. At my console in the CIC I watched the maneuvers of the small boats on one of the four 42-square-inch video screens called large screen displays (LSDs). These show the radar symbology of surface and air contacts being tracked by the Aegis system.

The small Iranian boats were represented in white relief dots on a dark blue background, each dot within a diamond, the computer-generated symbol for a hostile surface ship. Aircraft also appeared as white dots, but in half-diamonds for hostiles, half-circles for friendlies. White lines projecting from the dots indicated course and the relative length of the lines, speed.

In addition to the LSDs and the console screens, smaller track displays provided alpha-numeric information pertaining to individual targets, including assigned track number, speed, course, distance from ship, altitude, and identification friend or foe (IFF) if applicable.

The Aegis combat system's elaborate array of sensors and computers feeds information to the displays and weapons systems in many cases automatically, or as quickly as you can push a button. Operators were recorded making button depressions four to six times a second during the intense activity that followed. The system records virtually every button pushed, every switch thrown, every keystroke made, and almost every status report. Aegis cruisers are called Star Wars at Sea, and the *Vincennes* had been noted in the international press as the "supership" of the Persian Gulf.

CG 49 CIC Stations (Drawing by James Burnett)

In the past, the commanding officer's battle station was always on the bridge of the ship. With the advent of sophisticated electronic sensors and complex weapons systems, information necessary to fight and control a ship effectively is concentrated in the CIC. Accordingly, my station at the command console was three platforms below the bridge, in a space bathed in soft, pale blue light surrounded by the hum of air-conditioning and electronics.

Sitting to my left in the CIC was Scott Lustig, responsible for alerting me to any potential air threats against the *Vincennes* or the *Montgomery*. To my right was my tactical action officer (TAO), Lieutenant Commander Vic Guillory, who was directing the surface tactical picture and monitoring the watch team's performance. Vic and Scott were two of my best and most experienced officers. Scott, slight and balding, is a Citadel graduate and New York native with a quick sense of humor and great enthusiasm for his job as combat systems officer. Responsible for the maintenance, operation, and readiness of the Aegis system and its associated weapons batteries, he was one of the officers originally assigned when the *Vincennes* was commissioned. Vic, my operations department head, is a physically imposing graduate of the Naval Academy and a dynamic officer blessed with an innate grasp of complex tactical scenarios. Bright and eager, he could always be counted on to stay ahead of any problem. I had great faith in both of these men. We understood one another, worked well together, and had spent untold hours shoulder to shoulder in the CIC's dim confines.

I felt just as strongly about the rest of the officers and crew. I considered them a slice of the best the United States has to offer. A logo affixed to the back of their ball caps proclaimed Team 49, and they were just that—a team dedicated to ensuring that hull number 49 was the best. They had established an enviable record and were proud of it. I knew every man personally and was proud to be their skipper. I was fortunate to have had two previous commands at sea, but command of the *Vincennes* was the ultimate assignment in my twenty-three-year naval career.

In the event of my incapacitation or absence from the command console, the TAO as my direct representative would assume complete authority to fight and defend the ship. Commander Rick Foster, my executive officer, was on the bridge. His primary responsibility was to ensure safe navigation, respond instantly to the demands of the CIC, and see that the ship was battle ready.

Information was fed constantly to Scott and Vic by various console operators, other ships, and commander, Middle East Force. From the command console I monitored this flow of information through a headset, scanned the LSDs, and interjected orders as necessary.

In view of the attack on Oceanlord, at 9:24 I told Vic to make sure the 25-millimeter deck guns of the *Vincennes* and the *Montgomery* were "covering" the two groups of IRG boats. Targeting solutions for the 5-inch batteries were developed, but the guns remained centerlined so as not to display an overtly threatening posture. This was a standard defensive operating procedure in the Gulf whenever there was potential for hostile surface action.

Five of the southernmost group of six craft broke off and appeared to move away toward the throat of the strait. The remaining unit slowed and drifted down our starboard side about 1,000 yards away. Carrying a bow-mounted recoilless rifle, it was watched closely by our 25-millimeter-cannon crew. The patrol boat's crewmen did not man the weapon but rather prostrated themselves as the boat disappeared astern.

However, the other group, seven boats identified as those that fired at Oceanlord 25, had by now closed within four miles of the *Vincennes* and the *Montgomery*.

At 9:39 I requested permission to engage the small boats with the 5-inch guns, as they continued to close us on erratic courses. Admiral Less asked us to verify that the boats were not leaving the area. We reported that, to the contrary, the craft were approaching and increasing speed.

At 9:41 the order came, "Take Boghammer group with guns. I say again, take Boghammer group with guns."

Simultaneously, the bridge reported over the intercom, "They're shooting at us!" Shell splashes began to fall close aboard, spent bullets and shrapnel ricocheted off the starboard bow and the ablative coating behind the forward missile launcher. At 9:43, with the small craft at a range of slightly less than four miles, mount 51 forward and mount 52 aft, in concert with the *Montgomery*'s single 5-inch gun, commenced fire.

I fully expected our first salvo to persuade the IRG boats into retiring. Instead, they continued to close and fire. Although visibility in the dusty haze was limited to about 4,000 yards, the boats had to be aware of what they were engaging.

The IRG was a major, semiautonomous military organization assumed to be under the control of Tehran, but according to much informed speculation it was capable of independent operations. Members were absolute fundamentalists, loyal only to the Ayatollah Khomeini. They called themselves the Sword of Allah and were pretty unpredictable.

The gun mount crews were rapidly feeding heavy projectiles and powder cans into ammunition carousels, their guns continually changing targets among the fast-moving craft. In the next two minutes mount 51 expended twenty rounds and mount 52 fired nineteen. High-speed small boats are difficult targets, as both their range and deflection can change almost instantly.

The seven approaching boats had split into two groups and I was concerned about a possible Iranian tactic called the "swarm." A group of craft under the tactical control of a master boat forms two attack units to make high-speed firing passes along both beams of a ship. This move concentrates the attackers' firepower and dilutes the defensive efforts of the target. Nor did I want my ship within range (about 2,500 yards) of the boats' rocket-propelled weapons, as they could severely damage the superstructure and certainly kill or injure crew members. We continually maneuvered ourselves to stay outside this envelope, and I ordered the *Montgomery* to follow our movements.

I told Lieutenant Commander Guillory that if the boats should break out of the haze, our two 25-millimeter Bushmaster cannons, fitted to the main deck at midship, both port and starboard, were to engage without further orders. I was concerned with the consequences of a toe-to-toe firefight at close range: The men manning the deck cannons had no protection outside of sandbags stacked along the lifelines.

The rules of engagement under which we operated influenced my every decision. Following the *Stark* incident, the rules applicable to the Gulf had been extensively reviewed and revised. The upshot of this process underscored the responsibility of the man on the spot to take positive action to defend his ship if in his judgment hostile intent was demonstrated. Specifically, any aircraft or surface ship maneuvering into position where it could fire a missile, drop a bomb, or use gunfire against a ship was considered to be displaying hostile intent. Through diplomatic channels the United States had issued to airmen and mariners of all concerned nations a series of notices called NOTAMS, which highlighted this inherent right of self-defense. A thorough understanding of the ramifications of the rules was critical, and we had spent a great deal of time studying, reviewing, and committing them to memory.

"Don't take the first round" was engraved in the decision-making procedure of all American ships in the Gulf.

The Iranians contributed in broken English to the increasingly convoluted bridge-radio transmissions. At times the bridge heard them calling each other children. Following one outbound salvo from our guns, a voice was heard saying, "Child Allah has departed." This rhetoric was interspersed with curses and expressions of hatred for the "great Satan": "Son of bitch, we kill all . . . Kill them in the name of Allah. . . ."

At 9:47 we took the Iranian P-3 under close control, as it had changed course and was heading toward us. "Under close control" means that the console operator brings up and displays the following information: track number, geographical coordinates, course, speed, altitude, bearing, range, and IFF modes. Aircraft are equipped with transponders that respond to the coded signal of another IFF system. The reply is displayed as a digital readout and can assist in identifying aircraft as civilian or military. Transponders operate in three basic modes: I and II, which identify military aircraft, and III, civilian aircraft. U.S. military planes are also capable of responding to mode IV queries.

The P-3 became Scott Lustig's top priority. He knew what the aircraft was, but not what it was doing. He was also aware that in response to our request, the carrier USS *Forrestal* had launched an E-2C Hawkeye early-warning radar plane and at least two F-14 Tomcats. These aircraft were en route to holding points over the northern Arabian Sea approaches to the strait.

At 9:47 and 35 seconds, the *Vincennes*'s SPY-1 radar picked up an aircraft coming out of Bandar Abbas on a southwesterly course of 210°. The aircraft was immediately labeled "unknown, assumed enemy," standard procedure in the Middle East Force for any aircraft departing that field until its identity is determined and intent defined.

Scott informed me of the new contact and added that it was on a closing course and climbing. I knew Iran had added F-14 fighter planes to the F-4s and other military aircraft at Bandar Abbas, an airfield shared with commercial aviation. On 18 June we had been advised of the changing patterns of F-4s operating from the airfield and cautioned "to be alert for more aggressive behavior." We were also told, "The F-14 deployment represents an increased threat to allied forces."

Between 13 June and 2 July seven F-14s were challenged. Iranian military aircraft had been repeatedly observed squawking multiple IFF modes and codes, at times following commercial air routes and tracking closely behind airliners. Even known Iranian commercial air carriers had been observed changing IFF modes and codes while crossing the Gulf. The bottom line was that IFF in the Gulf only served to indicate an airborne aircraft.

Our CIC "air alley" was now monitoring four aircraft: the *Forrestal*'s E-2C, which appeared on our radar on the northern portion of its orbit, our helicopter, the P-3, and the unidentified plane departing Bandar Abbas.

Petty Officer Richard Anderson, whose job was to identify radar contacts, used his remote-control indicator to check the transponder squawk of TN 4474 bearing down on us from the north. He received two replies, a civilian mode III and a military mode II with a four-digit code known to have been used by Iranian F-14 fighters. He broke into the internal communications circuit and warned "all stations" that TN 4474 squawked a mode II IFF and "breaks as an F-14." For the first time the aircraft came up labeled F-14 on the LSD in front of me.

The new contact was challenged on both military air distress and international air distress frequencies: "Unidentified aircraft on course two-zero-one, speed 303, altitude 4,000 feet, this is United States naval warship [USNWS] bearing two-zero-five 40 miles from you. You are approaching USNWS in international waters. Request you state your intentions. Over."

All messages were in English, the international language for communications in the air and at sea. There was no response.

The *Sides*, moving northward out of the strait, noted the new contact almost simultaneously and was the first to assign a radar track number (TN) 4130, to the aircraft. Moments later the *Sides*, attempting to gain an altitude reading on the track, dropped out of the radar link. So the *Vincennes* assigned TN 4474 to the unidentified plane. The electronic tactical data system allows all participating units to share radar information and thus obtain an expanded picture beyond normal radar horizons, an obvious tactical benefit.

Not until much later would we learn how a bizarre set of circumstances—a fourth ship 180 miles away, atmospherics, errors in protocol, and duplicate numbers—would be a factor in the decisions made in those few volatile moments.

We put the new track under close control while the identification supervisor checked the commercial aircraft schedules available at his console. Nothing matched.

Scott challenged the P-3: "Iranian P-3 on course zero-eight-five, speed 270, this is USNWS bearing zero-eight-five at 64 miles. Request you state your intentions. Over."

"USNWS, this is Iran P-3. Our intention is search mission. We keep clear of your unit."

"Iran P-3, this is USNWS. Stay 50 miles from my unit. Over."

The P-3 was compounding the problem but as yet did not appear to represent a direct threat. The aircraft acknowledged. It was now 9:48. TN 4474 continued to close from Bandar Abbas. Another challenge was issued. Again, no response. Tension mounted in the CIC. For most, it was the crew's first taste of combat. Adrenalin was flowing. People focused on the jobs they had been trained to do. Extraneous thoughts vanished.

Our challenges to TN 4474 continued. We requested the aircraft to change course to 270°. No answer. Most certainly the P-3 heard our warnings on the military distress frequency—it had been in communication with us on that channel.

At 9:50 the spent shell extractor malfunctioned in our forward gun mount, jamming the weapon. To bring the aft gun to bear on the attacking boats, I directed a full-rudder turn swinging the cruiser's stern around. We were now steaming at close to 30 knots, and the ship heeled dramatically as we made the turn. Lights in the CIC flickered with every concussion of the deck gun. Books and equipment spilled from shelves and racks and men who were standing scrambled to keep their footing.

The smell of expended cordite from the guns permeated our extensive filtering system. The young sailor sitting next to me on the damage-control net said, "Captain, Sonar 1 reports shell hits on the starboard side forward. They don't see any damage." I squeezed his arm to acknowledge.

Before we had completed the turn I ordered Lieutenant Commander Guillory, "Bring the aft gun to bear, now!" Anxious voices filled the internal communications net and Vic directed a shift to an alternate circuit to get rid of the chatter.

Scott radioed Captain Dick Watkins, Admiral Less's chief of staff in the *Coronado*, that we had a possible Iranian F-14 bearing 025° at a range of twenty-eight miles. I told him to indicate that I intended to engage the contact at twenty miles unless it turned away. Scott asked Watkins if Admiral Less concurred. Less did, but ordered us to warn the aircraft again before engaging with missiles. The time was 9:51.

I ordered continuous challenges to TN 4474 on both military and civilian channels, each time requesting the aircraft to change course to 270°. The only response heard was an intermittent keying of a radio microphone on the civilian frequency.

The CIC officer, Lieutenant William Montford, standing behind me monitoring the circuits and writing the time line of events, looked over Scott's shoulder at his console readout and saw a mode III at an altitude of 8,000 or 9,000 feet and rising slowly. He stepped forward and said, "Possible commair [commercial airliner]." I extended an arm over my head and acknowledged him. In the Gulf the presence of commercial air traffic was always a major concern and no less so in this case, despite the fact that the heading, altitude, and silence of this aircraft didn't smell commercial.

The small craft continued to close and in no uncertain terms I was urging Lieutenant Commander Guillory to increase our firing rate and order the bridge to go to maximum speed. The high, pitched whine of the main propulsion gas turbines churning out 80,000 shaft horsepower was a partial response to these demands.

"Iranian aircraft . . . fighter on course two-one-one," another warning went out on the military distress band, "speed 360 knots, altitude 9,000 feet, this is USNWS bearing two-zero-two from you, request you change course immediately to two-seven-zero, if you maintain current course you are standing into danger and subject to USN defensive measures, request you change course two-seven-zero, repeat two-seven-zero, over."

These warnings were standardized, and everyone in the Gulf had been directed to use them verbatim. However, hoping to obtain a response, the young sailors on the circuits were adding every scrap of information they could think of.

It was now 9:52 and the aircraft's range had decreased rapidly to twenty-five nautical miles. As the aircraft closed to approximately twenty miles, I asked, "What is 4474 doing?" Over the comm net came the response, "TN 4474 descending, speed 450 knots."

Admiral Less gave permission for "weapons free," and the procedures for missile launch commenced.

Scott asked and I gave permission to illuminate the inbound track with weapons fire-control radar at a range of twenty nautical miles. Then he asked if I wanted to engage at twenty miles. I answered negative, I wanted to be sure of this character's intent. I directed warnings to continue. Comfortable with the reaction time of the Aegis system, I felt I could hold off a few moments longer.

Turn! Turn! I pleaded silently. But the steady flow of information and the aircraft's relentlessly closing attitude confirmed to me that he was, in fact, a major threat.

The Montgomery reported sinking one of the IRG gunboats. And reports from the bridge indicated the Vincennes had taken out at least one of the craft. We couldn't be sure from watching the radar screens, for we were still shifting targets rapidly and the tracks were fading in and out in sea return.

I was confident of our accuracy but more concerned with staying out of the IRG crafts' effective range. In the CIC we could hear and feel mount 52 at its maximum rate of fire. Chatter from the gun-control modules as crewmen exchanged correction information was continuous.

Another challenge from someone other than the Vincennes was broadcast to TN 4474, and I assumed this was being transmitted by either the Montgomery or the Sides. About this time, amid all the sound and activity, I learned that when the Sides had rejoined the radar network a new TN of 4131 had been assigned to the outbound Bandar Abbas contact. The Vincennes's system automatically adopted the Sides's newly assigned number and retrieved 4474, electronically "hoarding" its assigned block of numbers for later use.

The silent aircraft symbol on the screen was now on a bearing of 018° at a range of sixteen nautical miles. It was 9:53. Again I requested verification that the IFF mode and code that we had received were, in fact, indicative of Iranian military aircraft; this was reaffirmed. Neither the *Montgomery* nor the *Vincennes* had intercepted any electronic emissions from TN 4131, and I asked once again for the operators manning the electronic warfare consoles to verify this. "Negative, negative, Captain. We've got nothing!"

Give me a signal of some kind, talk to me! You've always done it before! I kept repeating to myself. Despite a rising sense of urgency in the CIC, I continued to withhold permission to engage.

Meanwhile, my senior chief air controller, Charles Nolan, was in contact with the E-2C and keeping track of the Fury Fez alert package launched by the *Forrestal*. Still far to the south, these aircraft would have no bearing on the unfolding scenario.

The *Vincennes*'s air-distress operator transmitted another challenge: "Iranian aircraft on course two-one-one, speed 385 knots, you are approaching USNWS operating in international waters. If you do not change course to two-seven-zero immediately you are subject to U.S. defensive measures." The urgency in his voice was unmistakable. The past experience of naval forces in the Gulf had been that aircraft operating in the area invariably maintained a guard on air-distress frequencies. I simply could not understand why this particular airplane did not heed nor respond to multiple warnings. Someone muttered over the internal net, "Goddamn it, he's getting close."

When TN 4131 was ten miles away I felt I could wait no longer, it would soon be within minimum range of our missiles. I was now convinced, beyond doubt, that the aircraft was supporting the surface engagement in progress, and that my ship and crew were in imminent danger.

I reached over my head, and with a turn of the key granted firing permission. At his console the missile systems operator, Petty Officer Timothy Ryerson, saw his fire-authorization light flash. He paused and asked his supervisor, "Do I have a take order on TN 4131?" He was told, "Yes, take."

At 9:54 and 22 seconds, Ryerson hit the fire authority button, launching two missiles in succession from the forward rails. He estimated that missile time of flight would be twenty-five to thirty seconds before intercept. I kept my finger on the hold-fire button so I could destroy the missiles in case of any response from the aircraft. As the missile and track symbols approached merge point, I lifted my finger.

Intercept came at 9:54 and 43 seconds. This was immediately

reported to commander, Middle East Force, at Bahrain. The target symbol disappeared from the screen.

The bridge reported seeing the flash of missile detonation through the haze. There was a spontaneous cheer, a release of tension from the men. But this subsided quickly with the sobering realization that someone had died.

Meanwhile, the surface battle continued. Less than two minutes later, at 9:56, another aircraft departing Bandar Abbas was detected by both the *Vincennes* and the *Sides*. The latter radioed that she had "birds affirm"—her fire-control system was locked on to the target and an intercept solution developed—and that she intended to engage this new track, 4133, which was flying the same course as TN 4131. I responded negative after a quick consultation with commander, Joint Task Force, Middle East (Captain Dick Watkins, speaking for Admiral Less), who felt the track was too slow and did not appear as an immediate threat.

We challenged TN 4133 on both distress frequencies but received no response. Two minutes later we illuminated the track with missile fire-control radar. The aircraft turned northwest, away from us. As we would later learn, it also played an odd role in the sequence of events.

By 10:03, there were only two IRG boats still painting on the gunfire-control screens. These two broke off and departed to the north, whereupon I ordered the *Vincennes* and the *Montgomery* to cease fire. The gun battle had lasted twenty minutes. We had fired seventy-two rounds, the *Montgomery* forty-seven.

At 10:19 we confirmed to commander, Middle East Forces, that the aircraft had been destroyed. "Give us battle damage assessment," was the message back. "Are you okay? Is *Montgomery* okay? Report ASAP."

At 10:20 two F-4s were detected departing Bandar Abbas. They appeared on our radar as soon as they were airborne. About thirty miles away they started circling and made several attempts to lock us up with their fire-control radar. Every time they turned nose toward us, our electronic warfare operators engaged them with active countermeasures and broke their attempts.

After several tries they ceased illumination, broke off, and made no more feints toward us. Our relief in the CIC when they dropped that game was practically visible.

There appeared to be no other immediate threats and I directed

Lieutenant Commander Guillory to recover Oceanlord. I stepped out of CIC to clear my head, but when I returned, traffic on both warning frequencies and the bridge-to-bridge VHF (very high frequency) radio was increasing. At 11:10 an Iranian hovercraft approached the Montgomery and the Vincennes at about 50 knots. A challenge was transmitted, and we prepared to fire a warning shot with the 5-inch aft gun when the vessel turned away.

Some of the radio transmissions were confusing. A slowly orbiting aircraft well to the south and west identified itself as an Iranian search and rescue helicopter. After repeated efforts to communicate, the following exchange took place with considerable interference and static.

"Iranian helicopter on course one-seven-zero, speed 110 knots, this is USNWS operating in international waters. We bear one-nine-two from you. Request you identify yourself and state your intentions."

"USNWS this is Iranian search and rescue helicopter, if you talking to me I am searching for the pilot on the . . . We be clear of you . . . ah, ah, we just looking for search and rescue."

After about twenty minutes radio contact was again made.

"Iranian aircraft this is USNWS. Over."

"USNWS this is Iranian helicopter SAR [search and rescue]. I am searching this area. What do you need?"

"Iranian SAR this is USNWS. Request information on personnel that you are searching for and downed aircraft. Over."

"This is . . . ah . . . this is Iranian . . . ah . . . international Iran air . . . Iran air . . . Airbus . . . Airbus with . . . ah . . . two hundred ninety persons."

"Iranian SAR aircraft this is USNWS. Copy all."

This SAR helicopter was orbiting around Darax, a checkpoint on the A59 commercial air route that was well south and west of us. We kept trying to get a fix on the location of the missing aircraft the Iranians seemed to be seeking. Following a conversation with his controlling authority, the Iranian helicopter pilot quit talking to us.

In the meantime, Admiral Less's headquarters received a report that an Iranian airliner was overdue at Dubai. SCANNER, the AWACS aircraft that covered the southern half of the Gulf, was not in the air, and no one seemed to know what the fragmented radio talk meant. The VHF radio on the bridge covers international ship-to-ship frequencies. We had placed a small recorder next to it to tape transmissions but had no way of timing their recording. Sometime during this period the tape recorded the following:

"This is Iranian speedboats. This is Iranian speedboats. We are ... [garbled] ... to damage United States. Damage United States. We are ... [garbled] ... kill you.

"Yankee, Yankee, We are ready to answer your actions. We are ready to answer your actions. Damage United States of America.

"United States, you shot a passenger air.

"You shot a passenger air.

"... [garbled] ... United States.

"United States, we are ready to answer your actions. We are ready to answer your actions.

"United States, you shot an airplane of passengers. You are not human and your government is some kind of animal."

Then an interruption from an unknown source: "Get the fuck off the radio!"

"Bandar Abbas, port control. Please send a chart for helping passengers of the airplane which was shot down by United States animals.

"... [garbled] ... you have any bodies ... [garbled] ... for us.

"Damage United States of Americans. Damage United States of Americans. United States, we are ready to answer your actions."

This was obviously disturbing, but the SAR helicopters were far to our south and not searching where the engagement had taken place. We had nothing definite. Over the next hour and a half reports of a continuing search for an overdue civilian carrier continued to filter in. We had launched two missiles, and there was an aircraft missing. It was painful but not difficult for me to put the two facts together.

The inbound track had not been an aircraft carrying a helmeted figure leaning intently over his weapons panel or positioning for a terminal dive, but rather a civilian airliner packed with dozens, perhaps hundreds, of innocent and uninvolved souls. Although I was desperate for another answer, deep inside I knew there wasn't one. With that fateful turn of a key, I had created a horror that I would never escape.

About midafternoon in the now subdued atmosphere of the CIC, I sat down and penned the most difficult message I would ever write. I recapped the events of the day for transmission to Admiral Less and up the chain of command to the Pentagon, closing with the statement, "I and I alone am fully responsible for the actions of the *Vincennes*."

2

—◇◇◇—

ON THE BACK
OF THE TIGER

Hurled headlong flaming from the . . . sky
With hideous ruin and combustion down. . . .
—Milton, *Paradise Lost*, 1667

During the brief minutes of intense and violent combat everyone in the *Vincennes* was running on adrenalin. Now in midafternoon, about five hours afterward, that rush had faded. I felt drained and had a splitting headache. Admiral Less had directed us to remain in the area and assess the situation. The radio circuits on the bridge and in the CIC were filled with incoming and outgoing traffic as we tried, again and again, to raise the Iranian SAR craft. Nothing. Less called again and relayed an order from General Crist, commander in chief, Central Command, McDill Air Force Base, Florida, for us to close the aircraft-impact site.

We had a good idea of where the aircraft had hit the water, but that was within Iran's declared exclusion zone. There were Iranian military aircraft operating in the area along with a number of small craft and helicopters. Involving the ship in that mess would be begging for trouble. I mulled this over and finally called Admiral Less, strongly recommending that we keep our distance. A short time later he called back and concurred.

Oceanlord 25 was back on deck, refueled with the aircrew strapped in and ready to launch. Less wanted to know whether I felt safe sending the helicopter out for a reconnaissance and damage-assessment flight. I discussed the issue with Huff, the commander of Oceanlord. The flight profile would have taken the helo inside what the Iranians called the line of death twelve miles from their coast. Huff might have learned something, but I did not feel it was worth the risk. Roger agreed. We were both torn by the decision; it would have helped to have some facts. Again, Admiral Less agreed with my decision. We secured the helicopter.

We moved a little farther south but were still within surface-radar range, and we just sat there for awhile. The ship was very quiet.

I asked Vic; Scott; Rick Foster, my exec; and Lieutenant Bill Johnson, my navigator, to meet me in the operations office one deck above the CIC and sum up events as they had seen them. I was trying to get as much information as I could, something we all wanted. "Boss," said Rick, "with the visibility we could barely see the *Montgomery*."

The CIC officer called and said, "Hey, the international air-distress talker raised an Iranian SAR helicopter, and they say they're looking for a pilot."

That tracked with the F-14 attack scenario as we had seen it. Scott kept saying, "He didn't talk, he didn't talk, he wouldn't talk to us."

"Look, Scott," I said, "we did what we had to do, let's just leave it at that right now. We don't have any more to go on, let's see how things sort themselves out. We'll hope for the best, if it turns out to be the worst, we did what we had to do and I made the decision and it's my responsibility. So let's stop the hand wringing right now until we get more facts."

It was obvious to me that this was going to warrant an investigation, and I directed the CIC officer, Lieutenant Mike McClellan, to sequester all records and start taking verbatim statements from all the players in the CIC. I told Johnson to do the same for the bridge personnel and get all the statements authenticated by the executive officer.

I got on the radio and called the skippers of the *Sides* and the *Montgomery* and told them I needed their logs and records sequestered and verbatim statements taken from their bridge and CIC personnel. I got a "Roger out" from the *Montgomery*, but the commanding officer of the *Sides* did not seem willing to cooperate. I was in no mood to put up with that nonsense. "The events of today are going to warrant an investigation, and you are directed to comply," I told him.

Admiral Less, monitoring this byplay, came up on the circuit and in no uncertain terms directed compliance.

One reason for the heavy radio traffic, of course, was the pressure to get more information for Admiral William J. Crowe, chairman of the Joint Chiefs of Staff, in Washington, D.C. Central Command, to which Admiral Less was reporting, had awakened Crowe at 3:18 A.M. Washington time (4:18 P.M. in the Gulf) to inform him of the engagement with the Iranian speedboats. He was awakened again at 4:00 A.M. with the information that we had shot down an F-14. An hour later he was called and told there was now some question about the type of aircraft destroyed.

This sort of fragmented information is not unusual in combat. First reports are quick and dirty, you pass on what you've got, and later as details become available you fill in the holes and correct errors. Admiral Crowe had gone to the Pentagon and needed any information we had before he met the press.

The *Vincennes* received orders relieving her of tactical command of the *Sides*, then somewhat later of the *Montgomery*. We were detached at 2:00 P.M. to resume our transit to Bahrain. We still didn't have much in the way of information, but it had become fairly certain what had happened. As we cleared the scene I secured the *Vincennes* from battle stations and set the condition III steaming watch. The ship had been at general quarters for almost seven hours. I was reluctant to leave the area, as I kept thinking we could find something to put the puzzle in order.

The ship was absolutely quiet. Not a tomb, just quiet. You could hear the subdued whine of the electric blowers, footsteps, but no conversation. That's very unusual: You always hear voices, the clatter and bang of people working, moving things, going about the hundreds of tasks it takes to operate a ship.

I went up to my sea cabin and splashed some water on my face. The cabin, two platforms up from CIC and one down from the bridge, is located on the facing part of the superstructure. It has a porthole in the forward bulkhead looking over the bow of the ship, another porthole in the sleeping quarters looking out to port. In both the sleeping quarters and the head the bulkhead is angled on the port side. Because of that angle, when the sun is beating directly down, particularly in a climate like the Persian Gulf, the air conditioner really has to work to keep it cool. If you removed the light cover over the porthole—you can't open the glass to get fresh air—the sun pours through and the temperature climbs out of sight.

Cruisers give the skipper an option of dining either in the wardroom or by himself in his cabin. Normally I did not take my meals separately unless there was something requiring my full attention. Then I might eat in the sea cabin or up on the bridge. I liked the close association of the wardroom, being able to share thoughts and laugh with the other officers. It was an opportunity for everybody to let their hair down.

There is a fairly extensive communications system wired into the sea cabin. By dialing a rotary switch I could listen to radio or the internal circuits, and if I wanted to speak, a small toggle switch put me on the line. Holding with tradition, there was a brass speaking tube, a device that's been in the navy since Noah. You lift a brass lid and blow into it—whuff, whuff—and that alerts people on the opposite end to listen. If somebody has been smoking and you open the tube, whew! This extensive phone and radio system ensured that even in my sea cabin I was never out of touch with any area of the ship. While in the Gulf I never strayed far from the bridge, the CIC, or the sea cabin, except to make tours of the ship.

The U.S. Navy has been in the Persian Gulf since 1946, when a small support force was sent to the tiny island nation of Bahrain. As Great Britain withdrew all of its forces east of the Suez Canal in the 1960s, the United States took over piers, radio transmitters, warehouses, and other vacant facilities. Over the years the American presence inside the Gulf remained pretty much minimal until the 1979–81 Iranian hostage crisis, when nearly thirty U.S. ships were put on patrol in the area, with a carrier group in either the Indian Ocean or the North Arabian Sea.

In 1987 a series of Iranian missile and mine attacks was launched against Kuwaiti tankers moving vital petroleum through the Gulf. Following requests for assistance from the government of Kuwait, President Reagan made a decision to reflag a number of these vessels under U.S. colors. This action, designated Operation Earnest Will, provided American convoy escort and defensive protection to ships transiting in and out of the Gulf. As a result, U.S. naval presence dramatically increased in the crowded, volatile waters where Iran and Iraq had been waging a costly war for eight years.

On 14 April 1988 the guided-missile frigate USS *Samuel Roberts* struck an Iranian mine while on patrol. If not for her crew's heroic efforts, the ship would have been lost. In response, the United States mounted Operation Praying Mantis, a retaliatory strike against Iranian naval units and militarily occupied offshore oil facilities. Executed on 18 April, this rapidly planned operation was successful. Several Iranian naval units, including one guided-missile frigate that had conducted particularly vicious attacks against unarmed merchant shipping, were destroyed, along with a number of gas/oil platforms.

Although Praying Mantis set back Iranian political attempts to force the United States from the Gulf, American intelligence had strong indicators that Iran intended to deploy and use Chinese-made Silkworm missiles in an effort to close the vital Strait of Hormuz to shipping. As part of the U.S. response, my ship, the USS *Vincennes*, was ordered to detach in late April from exercises off the California coast and deploy immediately to the Gulf.

Our normal patrol speed was 6 knots, very slow. We'd go down along the Omani coast and back up near the entrance to the Strait of Hormuz. This was the Southwest Patrol Area, the most active in the Gulf. There was always an enormous amount of surface shipping, oil platform activity, and news media helos, not to mention voluminous air traffic. The British, French, and Italian navies, like the U.S., were very active in the Gulf, serving as escorts for ships flying their national colors. The Soviets were performing the same role.

We would escort vessels through the strait in daylight and make a night transit back, always at general quarters. Our solo passages were made quickly, usually at 20 knots. The strait looks narrow on a chart, but the passage is about twelve miles wide, plenty of room to separate the traffic going back and forth. On a reasonably clear day we could see the Omani peninsula on one side and the Iranian coast opposite, no green, just brown and yellow desert shimmering in the heat.

When the ship operates at conditions of heightened readiness for long periods, maintenance suffers and you do a lot of creative things to keep her up. We divided the day into thirds, so that a third of our stations and half our weapons were fully manned all the time. Every day, all stations completed a long checklist to ensure that every system was operational and that crud hadn't fouled up the weapons or electronics. With this system, we could ratchet our battle readiness up or down quickly.

Twenty-four hours a day, a mine watch was posted in the bow of the ship. It was blistering hot duty during daylight hours, and even though shade was provided for the station we had to relieve the men there every half hour. All hands were trained to look for and report anything floating in the water. We took anything we saw seriously until we determined absolutely that it was not a mine. Even tin cans were reported. Of course, not all mines are floaters. If they aren't, you can't see them. The mine strike on the *Samuel Roberts* was a vivid lesson. The force of an underwater explosion is tremendously powerful, easily able to break the back of a ship.

Fortunately we encountered no mines, just sea snakes. These creatures are three to four feet long, relatives of the cobra, ugly, yellow-brown things and poisonous. During the summer months jelly fish by the thousands blanketed the water surface. These, mixed with oil, debris, and a coating of dust made the water less than inviting.

On 3 July 1988, though, it was the IRG boats that demanded our attention. When we were directed to change course to monitor the situation of the *Montgomery*, my first thought was, "Hell, we're going to be late for the ship's birthday party." We had made all the arrangements, reserved the swimming pool for the crew, ordered a ton of food, everything.

That afternoon I sat down on the edge of my bunk and put my head in my hands. I was absorbing the day in bits and pieces. The human mind has a unique ability to prevent shock, assimilating events at a staggered pace. Now I felt the full impact. It was devastating. I couldn't believe the speed with which everything had happened and the outcome. I sat there trying to collect my thoughts, reaching for a solitude that wasn't there.

The phone rang. It was the CIC officer asking me to come down. There was a misunderstanding up the chain of command about us being able to extract data from the ship's computer system. This is something you cannot do on board. The Aegis system is capable of recording complex events on computer tapes for reconstruction and analysis, but the tapes have to be sent back to the Naval Weapons

Center in Dahlgren, Virginia, for interpretation, an exacting and tedious task even in a laboratory environment. I had some bright young men who were doing the best they could to get into the system and extract information. They were making headway, but it was laboriously slow. The command in Bahrain wanted the data off the tape as rapidly as we could get it, and I was trying to explain that we did not have the onboard capability to do much other than poke at the problem.

The requests and replies were wending through a chain of authority from the ship to commander, Joint Task Force, Middle East (Admiral Less) to commander in chief, Central Command (General Crist) to the secretary of defense (Frank Carlucci) via the chairman, Joint Chiefs of Staff (Admiral Crowe) and the national military command center. There was a lot of conversation about the complexity of the system. Still, we were asked to develop a time line, down to the second.

The radio circuits were recorded on audio tape, so we had people spinning them back, crowded around tape recorders and transcribing verbatim the conversations from the bridge-to-bridge radio and command circuits. What the system is not capable of doing is recording internal voice communications. All of that reconstruction had to be based on individual recall. The operators, everybody sitting at the consoles, were absolutely sure of what they'd seen: The aircraft was at such and such an altitude, flying a closing profile, with a belligerent IFF code showing.

The senior air-intercept controller, who had no other job than preparing to take control of U.S. aircraft sent to assist us, and who wasn't occupied at the time of action, wrote down on his scope face the altitude of the aircraft when it was engaged, 7,800 feet, which we later photographed for the investigative board.

After about an hour I went back up to the sea cabin. All of a sudden I was overcome by a feeling of being absolutely alone. There's no one here but me, I thought, and I am 100 percent responsible for everything this ship has done. The magnitude of events was pressing down on my shoulders, the thought of all those lives lost constantly rolling around in my mind. I went to the cabin's forward porthole, pulled up the light shield and looked out over the bow, put my forehead against the glass and cried.

This emotion was cathartic, though I felt drained. The crew, I realized, had to be told that they had performed as they were trained to do. It was critical, because they too were walking a fine edge. Suddenly these well-trained, proud men had found themselves in the middle of a firestorm. I thought, "They're young kids, they don't understand what's happened." For that matter neither did I; we were on the tiger's back with no way off.

I wanted to get a message off to San Diego, because I knew before long this would hit the streets. So I penned a message to Rear Admiral Bob Kihune, commander, Cruiser-Destroyer Group 5, my administrative boss, and explained to him the events of the day as best I could. I repeated the majority of the information I had sent earlier to Admiral Less. I also sent a personal message to Captain Ted Atwood, our chaplain in San Diego, telling him the crew was fine and to please contact Sharon, my wife, and let her know that I was all right. I sent both of these messages "immediate precedence": I needed to get the information to everybody in my immediate chain of command, and I wanted to make sure the crew's families were informed as soon as possible.

After I got those messages off, I called another conference in my cabin with Guillory, Lustig, and Foster. I wanted to review the events again. Had we missed something? Had we, any of us or all, dropped the ball? I had a thousand questions and very few answers. I stood by my desk and said, "Now guys, there is going to be an investigation, there must be an investigation, it is right and just that there is one. We need to understand what we have done today was right under the circumstances, and nothing will be held back. There will be no attempt to cover up anything, and every scrap of information, every bit of data we have will be made available. I want that clearly understood." I underscored that there was no blame being laid, they had reacted to my command, my decisions, and the outcome was my responsibility. I wanted that clearly understood. Then I told Commander Foster to assemble the crew on the flight deck in thirty minutes.

I needed that time to collect my thoughts so I could stand before the crew and make them understand that they had done the right thing, regardless of the outcome. I needed to put on the right face, what the Japanese call *masko*. The crew must not see into my soul.

It was about 4:30 P.M. and still very warm when everyone except those on watch gathered on the flight deck, where one of our helos was still sitting. I walked out through the hangar and Foster, using a portable loudspeaker system, called the men to attention. I told them to be at ease and sit down if they wished. I recapped the events of the day and reiterated to them that they were without a doubt the finest group of people I had ever had the privilege to sail with, that their reputation as Team 49 was second to none. We had been involved in a high-pressure, time-compressed situation and they had reacted as they had to, precisely when they had to. They had performed magnificently and I was proud of them. I wanted them to know that.

Then I explained in some detail the fact that anytime an event like this occurs, a full and thorough investigation must be conducted. We were going to be forthright and do everything possible to reconstruct exactly what happened. Anyone who had any piece of information, anything to add, was to contact his department head or the executive officer and get it down in a sworn statement while it was fresh in his mind. They were quiet and attentive. When I finished speaking they stood in spontaneous applause. I felt a flood of warmth from them. I couldn't bottle it up any longer: The tears flowed and I turned on my heel and left.

I remember looking at Scott as I was talking. He was obviously in a state of shock—functioning but unwilling to accept what we now knew. So was everyone else, for that matter.

A short time later, I went up on the bridge and looked out. Scott was standing on the forecastle between mount 51 and the forward launcher where the blast marks were. He stood there head down and then slowly wandered off. Although concerned about him, at that point I had just about expended all the psychological coin I had. I went back up to my sea cabin to write another message to Ted Atwood. I was waiting for word that he had contacted Sharon. Shortly I received a response from him that Sharon had been reached, that she and my son Bill sent their love and all was well on the home front. Of course, I knew all was not well, they had been thrust into the eye of a storm without much information and were immensely concerned. But knowing that she and Bill were okay, I could begin to deal with anything else.

I didn't feel like eating, but it seemed important to resume the ship's routine, so I went down to the wardroom. We had a rather

The crew of the USS *Vincennes* gathers on the helicopter deck as I address them, 3 July 1988. (Photograph by Lieutenant Roger Huff, USN)

subdued meal, rehashing the events of the day, then drifting into talk about inconsequential things. That was the most difficult meal I ever ate in my life.

After chow I took a walk around the weatherdeck. It was still light. I tried to see as many of the crew as I could. Stop, grip an arm, say hello, pat them on the back. I went through the whole ship, down to engineering, combat systems, out on deck, ending up on the forecastle. There was a petty officer standing with a hose and washing down the blast marks and cordite burns. I went over to him and put my arm on his shoulder and let him know that he had done the right thing, they had all performed magnificently. He looked at me briefly and shook my hand.

It's never quiet in the Gulf. There's always the sound of wind across the superstructure, sea gulls calling. Now, however, we seemed to be sailing in a void. All I could hear was the water lapping against the hull.

The USS *Vincennes* en route to Bahrain after the Persian Gulf action, 3 July 1988. (Photograph by Lieutenant Roger Huff, USN)

I went back to the cabin. I wanted to take a shower but I couldn't muster the energy to do it. My head was splitting.

The ship moved back into her routine. Reports were made and received. I went up to the bridge at sunset and sat in my chair. I could hear the low hum of voices. Everybody seemed lost in their own thoughts. I made another tour of the ship. I didn't feel like doing anything, I didn't want to see anybody, I didn't want to talk, but I wanted the crew to know I was there for them.

The officer of the deck read from the navy prayer book just before taps every evening, a short nondenominational prayer. This evening I felt the devotional should come from me and I went up to the bridge just prior to taps and prayed.

"Lord, this has been a long and most difficult day. We have found ourselves in the crucible and lives have been lost. We ask for your strength and guidance now and for the days ahead. Watch over the men of the *Vincennes* as we go about the tasks we must complete, provide them with the assurance that they have performed their duty to the best of their ability. Be with our families and keep them safe and encouraged and comfort those who sorrow this night. Amen."

It was dark, but I could sense numerous people in the pilothouse and clustered on the bridge wings. Unusual. I stayed up there a few minutes, chatted with the officer of the deck, went over my night orders with him, then went back to the cabin and lay down fully clothed on top of the rack. I could not get undressed.

At about eleven that evening we started getting telegrams from people in the United States. People just went to Western Union and sent a telegram to the *Vincennes*. The radio man came to my cabin with a sheaf of them and said, "Captain, I think you'd like to see these." There were maybe five or six of them. One read, "Well done." Another, "Hang in there, *Vincennes*." Another, "The nation is with you." This would prove to be the trickle before the flood.

The rapid turnaround in information surprised me. At that time we didn't know what Admiral Crowe had said to the press or much of anything else that had happened back home.

I was so exhausted I couldn't sleep. My mind was spinning like a kaleidoscope, snapshots of the day racing by. I could see the LSD, that symbol coming down, hear the voices, the guns going off, the commands being given, the responses, the scream of the missiles. Events kept replaying themselves. At about one I went to the wardroom about four decks down and got some ice water. About half the officers were still up. We said hello and talked a little. Back in my sea cabin, the kaleidoscope started again.

Throughout the night a stream of high-precedence traffic came in asking when we were going to arrive in Bahrain, passing information on what was happening in Washington, asking for more information, a review of the time line, answers. Over and over again. A couple of times I had to get on the radio and explain that we were doing the best we could. Finally I made all concerned understand that we did not have the on-board capability to extract data so quickly. They had what we had. The stone had been squeezed.

There was a ladder just outside my sea cabin. Usually I could hear people going up and down but this night it was very quiet. The footsteps sounded as if they were made by felt overshoes, and they were coupled with pauses and muffled conversation.

The next morning I was up early. The floor looked covered with snow. There were fifty or sixty folded notes that had been slipped under the door, scrawled messages from crew members: "Hang in there, Skipper," "We're with you, Boss," "Good on you, Captain," "We are always together, Team 49," "Thanks, Skipper."

I opened the door and there hanging on a stanchion by the ladder was one of our ball caps with the Team 49 logo. That lone hat hit me hard. But its display assured me the crew was okay. And today there was sound.

I could hear the wind, I could hear the gulls calling, people moving around and talking. It was as if we had been steaming in another dimension but now were leaving it, there was sound and heat. I could taste the dust in the air, I could smell the stack gases. The *Vincennes* had returned to the world.

3

UPHEAVAL AT HOME

Chaos of thought and passion, all confused.
—Alexander Pope, *An Essay on Man*, 1773–74.

My mother-in-law was standing at the foot of the circular staircase, calling up to me. "Sharon, there's someone from San Diego on the phone for you." I could see her in my mind's eye, probably already dressed in casual slacks, cotton shirt, and tennis shoes—maybe the cute ones decorated with strawberries and bright red laces. At five feet, Gran fit perfectly the old expression that special treats come in small packages.

I had just spent a peaceful night in the upstairs room we always use when visiting Will's home in San Antonio. It is a small, warm room filled with a large antique brass bed and a three-drawer mahogany chest that had been my in-laws' first furniture purchase, the chest that had held Will's baby clothes. Facing the bed are floor-to-ceiling bookcases with a number of dog-eared books read by the family over the years, books I'd always enjoyed rummaging through before turning off the lights. For me, this room had always represented a retreat.

Just steps away in the adjoining room our son Bill was sleeping in his dad's old bed. How special it was that Bill could be surrounded by his father's childhood memories: the crazy hats Will had collected, which hung from each corner of the small four-poster bed, the shadow boxes that held his model airplanes and soapbox derby miniatures, the highboy that hid old school reports that we'd giggled over as we discovered them.

Connections . . . so many!

As I passed through the kitchen on my way to the phone, the pine clock on the wall registered seven o'clock. It was Sunday morning, 3 July 1988.

"What's happened?" I asked no one in particular. "Who's calling at this hour from San Diego?"

I immediately recognized the voice of Debbie Pipkin, one of Will's ship's ombudsmen. We captains' wives were relieved and overjoyed when the ombudsman program was initiated during the Vietnam era by Chief of Naval Operations Elmo Zumwalt. Up until then, the skipper's wife bore most of the responsibility for acting as liaison between the command and all the ship's dependents. Too big a task for any one person.

Debbie, married to a missile-fire-control chief, was one of the two *Vincennes* ombudsmen Will had selected the previous year. A friendly, energetic young woman, she performed the duties with zest and sensitivity. We were lucky to have her and Carmella Lutz, whose husband was a gas-turbine technician.

Before her departure, the *Vincennes* had purchased an answering machine upon which Debbie would record Will's weekly message received via the Dependents Assistance Board (DAB). Dependents, families, and friends could call the unlisted number as often as they wished to keep abreast of ship's news. In fact, so many calls came into her home, Debbie kept the machine in a closet to muffle the incessant ringing.

"Sharon," she said, "a yeoman from DAB called me at five this morning with a message from the captain. Something's happened in the Gulf but the captain says everyone's okay."

"What more can you tell me?"

"That's all I know, but it's just scary. I'm going to be swamped making a lot of telephone calls notifying other wives and families. If I hear anything more I'll call you."

This system of networking among relatives of a ship's crew was designed for use in situations just like this, to inform as quickly as possible and avoid unnecessary worry that might be caused by rumors or misinformation from other sources.

I later learned that Will had sent his message immediate precedence. Knowing, because of the time difference between the Gulf and San Diego, that it would arrive in the middle of the night, he wanted to make sure Captain Ted Atwood recognized its urgency. Ted had been officer in charge of the DAB for six years. Sensing the need for an organization that could immediately react to dependents' problems, especially when servicemen were deployed, he had proposed to the commander, Naval Surface Force, Pacific, that it be formed as a direct, personal, immediate-response link with commanding officers at sea. It was soon established.

Overhearing my conversation, Gran turned the television on to NBC. I could hear the matches of Wimbledon in the background as I finished my conversation with Debbie. I sat down on the edge of Gran's daybed and quickly recapped the conversation. Will's dad—Dos, as we called him—turned to me. His slight posture was a reminder of his open-heart surgery two years earlier. I was aware that Will's deployment worried him and hoped that this information wouldn't affect him.

"Sharon, there's fresh coffee in the kitchen," he said.

I needed some and a moment or two to collect my thoughts. As I poured the coffee into one of Gran's delicate china cups, my thoughts drifted to the brief seventy-two hours Will and I had experienced in April as he and his crew worked around the clock to prepare the Vincennes for her sudden early deployment. Will and I had lived in San Diego for fifteen years and in our present home for less than three in April of 1988. A white two-story stucco with a brown-tile roof, common in southern California, our house was only twenty minutes from the 32nd Street Naval Station. We were still having fun arranging and rearranging furniture, pictures, and rugs. Three years is a long time for a navy family to live under the same roof. A standing joke among us wives is that our cabinets get cleaned every eighteen months owing to transfer orders. Anyway, this was home to the Rogers. Upstairs, in the middle room, hung Will's ships' plaques, the oil painting of his first command, the minesweeper Exploit, and various memorabilia of a successful twenty-three-year naval career.

"Five days, Will. Less than seventy-two hours. This has never happened before." So many things to do, mainly routine tasks that all service people are encouraged to see to before any long deployment: update the power of attorney and will, review insurance, make a navy exchange run for uniform items, pack, meet the demands of the ship . . . and just simply be together. We had thought there would be five weeks left to us.

I was also teaching full time, and I wanted to make sure that these pressures didn't adversely affect my fourth-graders.

"I haven't really worried about you since Vietnam," I said. "Is everything going to be okay?" How many times did I ask that question during those five days? And how many times did he assure me that there was nothing to worry about?

"What about the *Stark*? It could happen to you."

"Sharon, stop worrying. The *Vincennes* is a capable platform. We can take care of ourselves."

Amazing how two people so close in thought can ease one another's concerns, all the while knowing that reassurances cannot control events.

Gran's voice interrupted my thoughts. "Sharon, come here! There's something about the *Vincennes*."

Garrick Utley broke into the tennis match with a news bulletin about an action in the Persian Gulf. The *Vincennes* had shot down an Iranian F-14.

I stared at the screen. Oh my God! "What did he say? An F-14?"

But hadn't Debbie told me that they were okay? Hadn't she received word from Will? Gran, Dos, and I kept repeating what we'd just heard, trying to make sense of it, trying to remember every word. While Dos and I talked, Gran phoned Dick, Will's brother. It was early, but Dick had cable TV service and she wanted to hear the news from CNN.

Bill was still sound asleep. I walked upstairs and entered his dark, quiet room. How could I break this to him? I didn't even know what was happening. Bill had been at Baylor University in Waco, Texas, completing his freshman spring semester when his dad had to deploy so suddenly. He hadn't been able to see him off, give him that important embrace, that special note we always place in his stateroom for later discovery.

"Bill, wake up. There's something about the *Vincennes* on TV. They're saying an F-14's been shot down. But Debbie Pipkin called and has received a message from dad that the ship's okay. Get dressed and come downstairs."

People have accused me of being stoic, and I must have been particularly measured in this instance. But then, Bill's a deep sleeper and often needs an additional five minutes to wake up. Whatever the reason, he routinely rolled over and with the wave of a hand gave the signal that he'd get up. There was no conversation. I hurried from the room to get back downstairs.

The phone rang again and it was Dick. Nothing new on CNN. He'd keep us informed.

My attention was again drawn to the TV. It seemed so unreal, the coverage of Wimbledon's international sporting match conducted in genteel surroundings interspersed with reports of violent conflict in which my husband stood on center stage.

I had mixed feelings about where I should be. I was relieved to be here with Will's folks during this surprise turn of events but felt the tug toward San Diego, where the *Vincennes* family was. It was just a coincidence that Bill and I were in San Antonio. After Will's departure in April, we began making plans for the upcoming summer. We had decided to fly to New York to visit Colgate University, the college Bill would be transferring to in the fall. It was a last-minute decision to include a side trip to Will's family for the Fourth of July.

Showered, shaved, and dressed in khaki shorts and a T-shirt, his usual summer attire, Bill walked into the room. Taller at five feet, eleven inches, than his dad or grandfather, he'd grown into a handsome young man. Tanned from California beaches, he trimmed his black hair short in what we used to call an Ivy cut. His hazel eyes, large and expressive, reminded me of my dad's.

Again, Wimbledon was interrupted. The commentator now started waffling about whether it was an F-14 that had been shot down. Apparently Iran was claiming it was not an F-14 but a commercial airliner. This new bulletin caught us all by surprise and made us angry.

Soft-spoken, calm, unflappable—if friends were to describe me those would probably be some of the catch phrases they'd use. Maybe the stresses of the last few months were beginning to take their toll, maybe I'd reached my "Plimsoll level," as Will would say. I could feel my back arch, and every muscle in my body seemed stretched and tight.

"The Iranians are making this up." I said, shaking my head. "No. I can't believe it." Gran and Dos were confused, too. They hadn't realized that commercial air traffic continued to fly in the Gulf.

Dick called. CNN was running the same information. Now, it seemed, they were breaking into the telecast with news bulletins every fifteen minutes. Each one leaned more and more to the conclusion that it had been an airliner shot down.

I couldn't take it any longer. "Dammit! Dammit!" I jumped to my feet, startling everyone, and disappeared into the kitchen. It was too much for me to comprehend. I stood leaning against the tile counter, gripping it for dear life—as if it alone were holding me up. I wanted to break free of my body that stood so stiff, I needed to scream, to punctuate the stillness, but this five-foot frame held my emotions hostage and wouldn't react. I don't know how long I stood like that.

Finally, walking back into the family room, I sat down at the built-in desk and once again picked up the phone. Debbie had given me the number of the DAB and I dialed it. The naval station officer of the day told me the DAB office was not open yet. I later learned that Ted was at the naval station pier to greet a returning destroyer squadron. So I phoned our friend and neighbor, Commander Mick MacDonaugh, commanding officer of the destroyer *Cushing*, the ship Will had commanded from 1981 to 1984. I knew Mick could transmit a message from his ship to the *Vincennes* quickly.

"Hello, Mick, this is Sharon Rogers and I'm calling from San Antonio. I need to ask a favor of you. Can you get a message to Will?"

"Sure. What is it?"

I was aware that he could hear the anxiety in my voice and from his reaction realized he hadn't heard the news. I filled him in with the little bit I'd heard. He relayed the following message to Will: "Bill and I are all right. We love you. Contact us when you can."

I continued to sit at the desk. I looked up at the large oil painting of Will in his dress blues commissioned when he was commanding officer of the *Cushing*. The face reflected the Will I knew: broadly smiling, confident, at ease with the mantle of command. It was comforting to sit and gaze at it.

Jarred by the phone's ring, I answered and was not surprised to be talking with Will's boss, Rear Admiral Robert Kihune. Both he and his wife, Hope, are two of the warmest, most genuine people I've ever known. When Admiral Kihune speaks before a group he always stresses the importance of the navy family.

"How are you, Sharon?"

Lying through my teeth, I responded, "I'm okay, Admiral."

"I'm calling to say we've received a message from Will about the Gulf incident and just wanted you to know that he acted correctly. All the commanding officers who have served over there have been worried that something like this would happen. So I wanted to tell you this, Sharon, and find out if you were okay."

"Thank you, Admiral, I really appreciate your call. Bill and I will be flying home soon."

"Let me know if there's anything we can do from here."

"I will, Admiral, and thank you."

NBC was just introducing Admiral William J. Crowe, chairman of the Joint Chiefs of Staff, a large, imposing, but fatherly looking figure. His shoulderboards reflected his significant four-star rank. He stood in front of a map of the Persian Gulf holding a pointer in his hand, the kind I've used so often in my classroom. Again, I sat down on the edge of Gran's daybed to listen. The four of us were all stationed around the television, each of us silent and focused, trying to catch every piece of this frightening, complex puzzle.

Crowe reported the facts as he knew them regarding the surface battle with the IRG boats, saying that reports indicated two were sunk and a third heavily damaged, and confirmed that the downed airplane was an A-300 Airbus. The media pool that covers Department of Defense matters began aggressively questioning Crowe. One reporter kept honing in on how such a sophisticated ship could misidentify the aircraft. Another questioner asked if Will had been "a little impetuous."

These two questions rolled around in my mind as the press conference continued. What stupid questions, I thought. I was shaking and unable to think clearly. How dare they imply that Will was not professional! What did they know of the problems in the Gulf or the capability of this Aegis cruiser? God! I was furious. But all the while Admiral Crowe stood his ground, trying to explain the physical conditions and limitations of the Persian Gulf, the time frame, electronic equipment, the capability of the Aegis system. File footage was shown later of missiles leaving a ship's bow. And then an Iranian boat with a handful of men hauling in a piece of fuselage . . . and a half dozen bloated bodies roped together floating on the surface of the water.

It was a nightmare of such magnitude that none of us could assimilate it.

"Bill, we each have to write dad a letter, now," I said. I knew it would be days, maybe weeks, before he received mail, but I had to connect with him.

Bill wandered into the kitchen and dropped into a small needle-point chair, where he stared into space and tried to gather the energy to write his dad. How many times over the last nineteen years he had sat there. My mind drifted back to when he was a baby climbing up on this chair, surrounded by all his special treasures since stored in the drawer of the pine chest not far away. Now too big for the antique, he just sat there and for the longest time didn't move.

Looking back at what I wrote, I realize that it wasn't very inspirational. I was in a state of shock. But at least I managed to convey my message:

> The news from Admiral Crowe is that you did everything correctly to protect your men and you did.
>
> I've been desperate to get a message to you. Ted Atwood was preaching a sermon, so I called Mick MacDonaugh and he said he could send that short message immediately.
>
> Debbie called the house at seven A.M. Texas time with your message that the men were okay. I want YOU to be okay.
>
> I'm pacing the floor waiting for your call to come through.
>
> I talked with Admiral Kihune and he had tried to call me earlier. I gave him the San Antonio number. He said, as well, you had of course acted correctly and that all the commanding officers who had returned from there had worried that this would happen.
>
> Please take care of yourself. If ever I need to talk to you, it's now. I know you'll get a message to me as soon as you can.
>
> I love you.

Bill's letter was straight from the heart:

> We are really shaken up by what has happened. When news began drifting in on TV, the only thing that really mattered to me is that you are okay. Knowing that you are all in one piece is the sole importance and I am forever thankful.
>
> I just thought that I would write to tell you how much I love you, how much I miss you, and how much I wish I could talk to you. Don't

worry about anything here. Everyone is holding up well. Dos seems to be a lot better and Ma and Gran are taking everything in stride.

I can't wait until you get home and you, Mom, Paddock, and I can all be together, safely.

During Admiral Crowe's press conference, the Department of Defense released to the media a short biography about Will listing his home as San Antonio. It was midafternoon before the press put two and two together and found Will's parents' house. The front doorbell rang twice, but none of us answered.

Sometime that day I made the decision to cut our visit short and return to San Diego the next day, the Fourth of July. I felt a desperate need to be back among the navy families and closer to information sources. I wanted to wrap my arms around our dependents, the wives, their children. We needed each other's support.

That evening the telephone rang. The connection was poor, intermittent and full of static, but I recognized the distant, strained voice as Will's. Shouting to make ourselves heard, he said, "I'm holding up."

"We are, too. Can you talk to your parents?"

"Sharon, I can't talk to anyone but you now. If I had it to do over again I'd do the same thing . . . but God, I'm devastated!"

Despite the rotten connection I could still hear the fatigue and despair on the other end of the line. There was no mistaking it. "We love you, Will. Can you hear me? We love you."

4

——✕✕——

AFTERSHOCKS

The night is dark, and I am far from home.
—Cardinal Newman, *The Pillar of Cloud*, 1833

THE PERSIAN GULF

As the *Vincennes* proceeded northwest I haunted the navigator's desk watching our position slowly change on the projected track lines. I knew we had to be within a hundred-mile arc to have access to the Bahrain telephone satellite relay. A short passageway aft of the sea cabin led onto the upper deck. The area behind the forward stack, protected from the wind, was relatively quiet except for the moan of intake air feeding the main engines. I crouched there with the ship's cellular telephone and repeatedly punched in the access code until, with relief, I finally heard the call ring through. Despite the extreme range and terrible interference, the brief contact with Sharon gave me an instant feeling of reassurance, of being in touch with reality.

Most of that morning—and it was no holiday Fourth of July—we had been busy on the radio. In Bahrain Admiral Less was inundated with requests for additional information from the staff of commander in chief, Central Command, in Florida, who in turn were deluged with questions from the Pentagon. At our end we were doing everything possible to supply answers.

Radio traffic remained heavy as we anchored in Bahrain's Sitrah anchorage about eleven o'clock that morning. Bahrain port control directed us to a position about six miles from the big Mini Sulman pier where the *Coronado* was tied up. For a couple of reasons we were never able to use the pier. Our draft made tying up there a little precarious, and anchored, we would draw less attention. Since our entry into the Gulf, we had been a high-visibility ship.

It was the next day before the media discovered we were at anchor in the outer harbor. The circumstances of this discovery resulted in one of the lingering public myths about the shootdown.

A navy combat camera crew had embarked on the merchant vessel *Mighty Servant* to record the *Samuel Roberts* transit out of the Gulf. We had been directed to bring the team on board after they completed their assignment and return them to Bahrain. I had given them free access to the ship and crew. From the time they arrived they had filmed much of the activity on board, and on 3 July they recorded some of the action on the bridge. At Bahrain we disembarked the camera crew and they went by boat to the pier and then to the Gulf Hotel to await a flight to the States. In the hotel bar they recounted their experiences to NBC personnel and members of the Department of Defense media pool. The NBC correspondents hastily communicated with their home office, and through the freedom of information act the network gained access to the camera crew's videotapes.

In itself, this would not have caused a problem. However, once edited to fit network time slots, the footage distorted events. Much of what was displayed on television in late August transpired long before the actual engagement. The lead sequence, for example, recorded the bridge watch manning their stations as the *Vincennes* commenced the return transit through the strait on 2 July. One particularly misleading clip showed five or six pulsating radar symbols on the bridge console and identified them as the attacking small craft. In fact, the images represented oil rigs. I later learned that the two camera crewmen responsible for this clip had been severely disciplined for their role in generating this particular bit of disinformation.

Those problems would surface later. Uppermost in my mind after anchorage was seeing that the ship's routine went forward. Since we were shut down it was an opportunity to perform maintenance that can't be accomplished under way—washing the mast and upperworks, painting the sides, taking down equipment. The key was to keep everyone busy, get them back into the routine to which they were accustomed. I didn't want men hanging around on the lifelines wringing their hands.

Anchoring in the outer harbor was a plus from the standpoint of security and enabled us to reestablish the routine quickly. However, the location obviously required that all support and supply services be brought out to us. With consistent high winds, blowing dust, and dense morning and evening fog, the weather, in the words of the navigator, was "doggy doo." As a result, scheduled services were often interrupted.

Another problem was the ship's gig. Its engine was sour. It looked as though getting to and from the beach would require a long swim or a converted commercial ferry, neither desirable. Thankfully, this situation was resolved when the commanding officer of the Coronado, Captain Robert C. "Willie" Williamson, offered me the use of his boat and its outstanding crew. They were there night or day when needed. During the afternoon of the Fourth of July, as I boarded for a run to the flagship, the young boat officer turned to me and said, "Skipper, we want you to know everyone in the Coronado is behind you guys." A welcome comment.

My visit to the Coronado was brief, for Admiral Less was not there. I exchanged greetings with Dick Watkins, his chief of staff, and arranged to return for a lengthy visit the next day. Back in the Vincennes, I took the opportunity to look at the news reports and telegrams flooding in. Gradually I was assimilating a view of the general worldwide reaction to the downing of the Airbus.

The influx of telegrams had increased significantly following Admiral Crowe's initial press conference. I was surprised at the number of people who knew you could send a telegram to a navy ship. Western Union sends the message to a navy master communications station, in our case Stockton, California, and the message is then retransmitted to the ship via the naval communications system.

Typical of the early telegrams we received was this: "Frank M. Sell American Legion Post No. 289 and its veterans of West Milford, N.J., are behind you one hundred per cent." It was signed by forty-one members. Many of the first messages were sent to us via the American embassy in London. One said simply, "You have made the right decision." Another read in part, "I have never visited your country, and I do not have any American acquaintances. However, I think you might like to know that an ordinary English schoolmaster is troubled at the unsympathetic reporting of the USS *Vincennes* dilemma. . . . I have great admiration for those who serve in your forces in the Gulf. . . ."

In a cover letter from London Captain Joseph McCleary, naval attaché to Ambassador Charles H. Price II, mentioned, "When these letters, cards and telegrams first began to arrive, I decided to send the favorable ones to you and drop the rest in the round file. Interestingly enough, I never discarded any as they were all favorable.

"The British have always been a seafaring and trading nation so that the term 'freedom of the seas' has real meaning to them. . . . I send these . . . to you to reassure you that there are a lot of people out there in the world, including myself, who have great respect for the very hard decision you had to make and support you right down to your boots."

These and other messages were posted on bulletin boards in the crew's mess for all to see.

In his press conference Admiral Crowe had stated, "The number one obligation of the commanding officer of a ship or of a unit is the protection of his own people." And President Reagan said, "The course of the Iranian civilian airliner was such that it was headed directly for the USS *Vincennes*, which was at the time engaged with five Iranian Boghammer boats that attacked our forces."

We appreciated the supportive statements from Admiral Crowe and President Reagan and the expression of goodwill pouring in from the public. All well and good. But anytime I had a couple of minutes to think, which wasn't often, the fact struck me that until the board of inquiry completed its investigation and rendered a judgment, the reputation of the finest cruiser in the navy and my personal hide were on the line.

Facts, not emotion, would decide the outcome.

SAN ANTONIO

Hanging up the phone was tough. I held the receiver in my hand and imagined Will was still there, not twelve thousand miles away. I knew the family had been hanging on my every word, trying to get a feel for what Will was saying. When I hung up I could barely face them. They'd wanted to hear his voice, too.

"He's upset but he's okay. He said if he had it to do over again, he'd do the same thing, make the same call."

"That's all I needed to hear," replied Gran.

No one else said anything. It was quiet and I could feel the stress lifting in the room. Gran called Dick and relayed our brief conversation, then Bill, looking exhausted, said goodnight to everyone. Already night . . . I wanted to be by myself too, away from the repetitive newscasts and graphic pictures. I knew as I climbed the stairs to the bedroom that I'd be calling the airline first thing in the morning. It would be rough telling Gran and Dos. What should have been a wonderful reunion had ended.

I was up early the next morning. Delta had a flight leaving around noon for San Diego. That sounded as if it would work. I mustered up my courage and spoke with Will's folks. "Gran, you know I wish I could stay here with you, but I just have to get back. I need to see the other wives and be closer to home."

"We understand," she said. "We feel so much closer to Will with you here, so just let us know things as quickly as you hear them."

As we discussed departure plans, Dos interjected, "Let me pay for your return tickets. How much are they?" This is an example of the generosity he has always displayed.

I woke Bill and told him to start packing. Then I returned to my room and did the same. It remained quiet in the house, each of us lost in our own thoughts.

Dick and his wife Marjo had asked us to lunch. Before we left the phone rang. It was Chaplain Atwood. After I told him about our return he insisted on meeting us at the airport. I hadn't even considered how Bill and I would get home, so Ted's offer was welcome. As we drove to Dick and Marjo's I was thankful that Will's folks would be with them when we said goodbye.

Bill, my in-laws, and I had been at Dick's about an hour and were just finishing a light lunch when the door bell rang. Granger, Dick's twenty-year-old son, found a reporter from the *San Antonio Express* on the other side of the door. Not knowing what to say, he called his father.

"Look, I don't have any comment other than my brother is a pro at what he does," Dick told the reporter, "and whatever decision he made was correct and for good reason."

When Dick returned to the living room he grinned and said, "If she'd known the entire family was only fifteen feet away, she'd probably have become a permanent fixture on the roof." His sense of humor was a boost to us all.

Our route to San Diego had a forty-minute layover in the Fort Worth–Dallas airport. I'd made an early morning call to my sister, Pat. She and Faris, her husband, wanted to drive from their Fort Worth home so we could see one another for those few minutes. My two nephews, John and Mark, who live in Denton, would also drive over.

It was only a fifty-minute flight, and we taxied to the gate on schedule. Entering the lounge, Bill and I saw the family. They appeared to be the only ones waiting, for the plane was almost empty. After long embraces, we moved to a sitting area and I recounted Will's earlier phone call. Seeing my sister and her family that morning was very important to me. Here we were, six people, hugging, teary-eyed, to passersby probably looking like any other family experiencing an emotional reunion.

As we walked through the airport, I couldn't escape the newspaper headlines: "*Vincennes* Downs Jet: 290 Dead!" Those words and others like them were blazoned across the front page of all the newspapers in the racks. Passing a coffee shop, I heard an anchor on television recounting the same horror. "*Vincennes* Captain Will Rogers . . ." The words were screaming in my mind.

A part of me wanted to put a quarter in the slot and read the horrible words, but I couldn't subject myself to the assault. The minute I pulled a paper from its stack, I felt, a hand would grab my shoulder and I'd be whisked around to find a microphone thrust in my face. I was in too vulnerable a state of mind to take that risk. So I bought no newspapers and I didn't read anything on the flight to San Diego. I talked a little with Bill, but for the most part we just sat, held hands occasionally, and stuck to our own thoughts.

But I could see people reading the papers about my husband and Bill's father. There was no escaping that.

As Bill and I walked up the passenger ramp in the San Diego airport and entered the terminal satellite, I was expecting to see Ted in uniform, but instead he was wearing civilian clothes. This struck me as odd. After a quick hug, I introduced Bill to Chaplain Atwood. He grinned and said in his characteristic deep Georgia drawl, "I decided to play low profile and make it look like I'm meeting my sister and nephew. We'd rather not attract the attention of any media who might be around."

"Thanks, Ted. They've already discovered Will's folks' house and his brother's. I'm not able to make a statement yet . . . if ever."

I didn't know what kind of transportation to expect, naval van or sedan. In fact, Ted had driven his own station wagon. I learned later the fifteen-year-old vehicle was one of his trademarks. He used it for hauling DAB equipment, sailors, and dependents. And whenever it was parked on the pier it was a sure sign the good chaplain was out and about.

"Let's go over to the office," he said as we placed our bags in his car. The DAB office was in the opposite direction from our house and I was eager to go home, but Ted insisted. "We'll call your neighbors from there and see if any reporters are hanging around."

It was nearly five-thirty, a typical balmy late afternoon in San Diego, as we traveled down I-5. I'd never been inside the DAB. This long one-story frame building sandwiched between the commissary and the day care center is located on the "dry side" of the 32nd Street Naval Station, that is, not on the water. The large parking lot was entirely empty.

"No one's here," I commented.

"Sharon, it's the Fourth! Everyone's off." I kept forgetting what day it was.

As officer in charge, Ted had the keys to the building. Climbing three or four concrete steps, we went through the side door and entered a long hallway with small offices opening on either side.

It was quiet. Ted led us to his office, a square space with enough room for a desk, a couple of chairs, and an old leather couch. My eyes were drawn to his family pictures hanging on the wall as he began searching the white pages, then the crisscross directory. Of the four houses on our cul de sac, ours had the only listed number.

I kept mentioning going home but Ted said he would feel more comfortable and was confident that Will would feel more comfortable if we stayed at the amphibious base bachelor officers' quarters (BOQ) that night. He was very persuasive. "Going home may be what you want," he reasoned, "but Will is over there and we want to give him every assurance we can that he'll not have to worry about your safety. Will will be glad you're in the BOQ." I didn't realize that Ted and

Captain Steve Clarey, chief of staff to Vice Admiral George Davis, commander, Navy Surface Forces, Pacific, had already arranged for a suite and that Will had been informed of this. Nor had I given much thought to safety from retaliation; avoiding the media had been my major concern.

It was nearly dark when we got to the Coronado BOQ, a high rise looking over San Diego Bay and serving as transient quarters for military personnel passing through or temporarily assigned to the area. Checking in, I learned we would be staying on the ninth floor in one of the VIP suites, Iwo Jima, and registered under a name other than Rogers. The suite consisted of a bedroom, bath, and small living/dining area. There was a refrigerator stocked with fruit juice and soft drinks and a coffee maker on a side table. The view from the room was spectacular, looking out over the amphibious base, the Coronado Yacht Club, and west to Point Loma, a promontory that forms the western barrier of San Diego Harbor.

It wasn't long before I suggested to Bill that we walk over to the officers' club. "We'll get a sandwich and come back, okay?" Once we were on the street it dawned on me again—the Fourth of July meant everything on the base was closed. So we started walking west toward a hamburger stand on Orange Avenue. Passing the yacht basin we could see holiday bunting and flags flying from the rigging of boats clustered in Glorietta Bay waiting for the annual fireworks display to begin. As we crossed a small bridge families were sitting on the sand on blankets and folding chairs, kids were waving sparklers, music was softly playing on radios. This was where we always spent our Fourth of July celebration, so I knew it well. But this year it seemed more subdued and quiet.

We entered a Wendy's just as it was beginning to close. Employees were mopping floors, wiping down tables, and we were the only two customers. We managed to choke down our sandwiches and left.

When we walked back the festivities had begun. Fireworks were erupting and rising over the bay, brightening the dark sky with bursts of color. Every explosion sent a shock wave through me, and with every sky rocket all I could see and hear were those two missiles leaving Will's ship.

With my arm linked through Bill's, I realized I had started to cry. It was a long walk back.

"Will: Captain Clarey has secured this suite for tired travelers at the Naval Amphibious Base, Coronado, in name of Captain Murray. After good night's sleep they will head for Sherlock Holmestead. Your San Diego mainbrace has been increased by two. —Ted."

Thanks to Ted I knew that Sharon and Bill were safely in San Diego. I was back aboard the *Coronado* early on 5 July. I wanted to spend some time with Admiral Less and needed a brief break from the *Vincennes*.

Captain Dick Watkins met me as I arrived. A big bear of a man with lots of sea time under his belt, he was an old friend and we had operated together extensively in the past. I put great value in his opinions; we spent the next couple of hours rehashing the events of the third. His had been the voice on the other end of the command circuit that day. Consequently, he was able to share the perspective of the flagship as events unfolded. After about two hours we were told that the admiral had returned and was in his office. As we went in he stood up, walked around his desk, and grabbed my hand with both of his. "Are you okay? Everything all right?"

"Everything's fine, Admiral. We're doing okay. I'm sorry."

"We'll sort it out," he said.

"I can't believe it."

"Well," he replied, "we'll get to the bottom of it. Anything I can do?"

I told him we were standing by, had sequestered all the logs, records, and documents, and had statements taken from all the principal players.

"Tell me about it."

I recapped everything and we had a long detailed discussion, a couple of hours or so.

Admiral Less, Dick, and the commanding officer of the *Coronado*, Captain Williamson, could not have been more understanding or supportive. Less had a luncheon scheduled for some dignitaries aboard the *Coronado* on 6 July. He invited me to attend. I accepted. That's the way he operated, trying to keep everything on an even keel regardless of unusual goings on.

"We don't know when the investigative board is arriving," he said, "but I've been told that Admiral [William M.] Fogarty will be the senior member."

"Fogarty's an excellent choice," I said. "I don't know him personally, but I do know he's a pretty straight guy."

Dick and Captain Williamson invited me to join the staff for lunch in the flag mess. As we ate we watched CNN, which didn't do much for my digestion. Dick remarked that he was arranging with the U.S. embassy in Bahrain to get tapes of Admiral Crowe's press conference and President Reagan's statement. They arrived later that afternoon and I took them back to the ship so the crew could watch them.

When I returned to the ship I witnessed a phenomenon that would persist for our entire stay at anchor. Members of the crew would filter out of the hatches and accesses onto the main deck when they knew I was en route back. They would wait by the lifelines, and when they saw me and were assured everything was all right, they'd sort of melt away. They were very quiet and subdued—not down, just watching in the knowledge that the ship was facing a crisis. They'd come up to me, put their hands on my shoulder, pat me on the back without ever saying anything. It's unusual for enlisted men to touch an officer, but their assurances felt damned good. I was really bearing the weight of the whole mess and couldn't shake a nagging feeling that no matter how things painted, I was going to be racked up.

I sent a message to Ted to remind him of the contingency plans made after the *Stark* tragedy the previous year and asked him to set up a meeting with all the *Vincennes*'s dependents. Additionally, I expressed the crew's concern regarding media interaction with their families. The crew was worried about that because when we left for the Gulf, reporters had phoned crewmen at night and hung around in their front yards. That was simply for the departure.

SAN DIEGO

Britt and Guy Zeller had been our friends for many years. Guy, now a rear admiral and commander, Cruiser-Destroyer Group 3, had just returned from the Persian Gulf on 3 July. I called Britt from the BOQ on the morning of the fifth. She invited us to dinner that night. I was anxious to talk with them both. The Zellers' quarters were on flag row at North Island, only a few minutes drive from the BOQ. Captain Steve

Clarey picked us up and drove us there. It was relaxing being with navy friends—knowing, if anyone could understand my emotions, they would. Britt served dinner on the patio. It was dusk and Guy had some steaks cooking on the grill. The view looking across the sloping lawn to the ocean, the smell of mesquite chips plus the warm feeling from the wine helped me relax for the first time since the morning of the third.

I was trying to get a better picture of what Will and everyone in the Gulf was up against. Guy and Steve answered my incessant questions with as much information as they could. They kept saying, "It was an accident about to happen, we knew it might happen, all commanding officers feared it would happen." I deeply appreciated their candor.

It was beginning to get cool and Britt suggested we go inside and look at some of the items Guy had bought while on cruise. How familiar this all was: a ship's homecoming, a husband's purchases while away. We had just begun looking at a Persian rug when the phone rang and Britt called for me.

Ted Atwood was on the line. "Sharon, get back to the BOQ. Will's trying to call you and says he'll be calling again within twenty minutes. He says he really needs to talk with you now."

The news was so upsetting I wasn't embarrassed to leave abruptly. Steve drove Bill and me back. We'd barely returned when Will called from Captain Watkins's stateroom in the *Coronado*. Bill spoke to his dad for the first time and said later, "He didn't sound all that great." I grilled Will about the events of the third, then we talked about any number of things, Bill and me going home the next day and such. But I remember only one thing Will said during that entire conversation.

"They're sending a team out," he told me, "and they're after my head."

BAHRAIN

The news correspondents had been going crazy waiting around in the Gulf Hotel for news. The Middle East Command's public affairs officer had provided only one standard comment, "We cannot confirm nor deny the movements or presence of any naval ship in and around the waters of Bahrain." The media could not get to the pier area or the administrative support compound, and certainly not onto the ship. But they finally figured out that if they went out to the commercial quay wall they could see the ships riding in the Sitrah anchorage. On the morning of 6 July they started showing up there, lined up behind binoculars and telephoto lenses. Since we were two or three miles out, however, I don't think they could read any lips.

One enterprising character hired a small boat and thought he would maneuver close enough to the *Vincennes* to yell some questions at anyone who would talk to him. But the Bahrain navy maintained a strict patrol of the anchorage, intercepted him, and quickly escorted him away.

SAN DIEGO

After two nights in the BOQ we were more than ready to return to our home. It was anything but a normal homecoming. Ted drove while we followed an NIS (Naval Investigative Service) team. As we approached the house, I could see people in the front yard and someone with a dog circling our Toyota van. I learned that the dog had been checking for bombs around the van and the perimeter of the house. Someone had planted a small American flag on the front lawn. That anonymous message meant a great deal to me. I also discovered other messages everywhere—stuck in bushes, slipped under the welcome mat, hanging from the mailbox, taped to the front door. Most of them were from the media.

"1:30 P.M., Mon. July 4. Mrs. Rogers, well, I guess you should add our name to the list. Would like to talk with you, if you feel up to it, about your feeling and get some background biographical information about your husband. Thank you for your help, Eric Bailey, The *Los Angeles Times*, (619) 544-6003."

Another read, "4 July 1988, Sharon Rogers: Please call the *San Diego Union*, 293-2228 or 193-1243. We would like to talk to you about navy wives networking and get the name of the ombudsman for your husband's ship and reaction to the shooting of Iranian plane. Are the wives planning any particular action in the wake of the tragedy?"

It was good to get home but nerve-racking. Iran had been publicly declaring its intention to retaliate, a threat the NIS took seriously. Agents briefed Bill and me on precautionary measures and also asked the San

Diego Police Department to monitor the house and make routine drive-bys. Officer Pam Smith of the North City police station was among those at our home. Later, on her own initiative, she devised a plan for evacuating us from the house in an emergency. We were not aware of this until several months later.

As the NIS agents prepared to leave I asked, "Is there anything I need to do?"

"Just be careful and aware of your surroundings and call us if you notice anything out of the ordinary." Then each agent gave me his card. All of this talk only increased my concern, and I insisted that no car be left in the driveway or at the curb. Bill found a friend in La Jolla who had room in his garage to store our pride and joy, a 1965 Austin-Healey. Additionally, we arranged to keep Bill's car at the naval base.

Eight months later, I would regret that we had dropped our guard.

With the agents gone I decided to check our answering machine. The calls were so numerous that our tape had run out. One of the most stirring was from J. W. Huff, father of the helicopter commander of Oceanlord 25, expressing strong support for Will. He said he was thankful that Will was his son's commanding officer and that under Will's command he knew his son would remain safe and in good hands.

Will says I have never been a compulsive person, but on this day I became a compulsive collector of every scrap of information and message I found. I clipped everything in print and wrote down notes on anything I heard. I decided to xerox all I could and send it to Will every day.

The tide of mail had already begun backing up in our mailbox. There were letters and notes from friends, parents of my students, students themselves, all offering their prayers and best wishes. A letter from Parkersburg, West Virginia, read, "We attended the *Vincennes* reunion last year in Indiana and met you and Will. We just want you to know that our thoughts and prayers are with you both and with the crew of the *Vincennes*. We are proud of them and behind them one hundred percent." Another, from one of my fourth-grade students, read, "I heard on the news about the incident in the Persian Gulf. When I heard the commander's name I knew it was your husband. I just want you to know my prayers are with you."

Among the first letters came one whose words revealed remarkable prescience: "Will," it read in part, "we are grateful for your courage and commitment, grateful for your bravery in taking the risks of command. Not being all-knowing is a human flaw which has brought about great tragedy. May you regain an inner peace in the assurance God works for good in all circumstances with those who love Him and are called to obey Him . . . Maybe this grave toll can be the cruel dramatic shock to quell the Iran-Iraq conflict." Indeed, numerous observers attributed the end of that terrible eight-year war later in the summer partly to those fateful events of 3 July.

The rest of the day I kept busy making calls and preparing for the dependents' meeting scheduled the next evening. Bill returned with Chinese food, the first of many carry-out meals we would eat that summer. I was exhausted. Without even throwing away the cardboard containers, I climbed the stairs to our bedroom and crawled into bed. I hoped I could steel myself for the upcoming meeting. It would be an emotional evening!

BAHRAIN

Later in the afternoon of 6 July, Commander Ron Winfrey, the lawyer assigned to Admiral Less's staff, called to say he was on the way out from the flagship and needed to see me. When he arrived we went to the in-port cabin. Although it was no surprise, he informed me that Vic Guillory, Scott Lustig, and I were to be formally named as parties to the investigation. It did come as a surprise to find that Admiral Less was also to be named. Commander Winfrey explained that as area commander Admiral Less was considered a principal party. "Real nice," I thought. "I've got the boss in the soup, too."

The point of his visit was to advise us that as formally named parties we were entitled to legal counsel. He asked if I knew anyone that I might like. Winfrey was out, for he would act as the admiral's counsel. After pondering a minute, I remembered a close friend who was also one of the top judge advocate general (JAG) officers in the navy, Captain Dennis McCoy. Dennis was currently assigned as senior JAG to the superintendent of the Naval Academy. If at all possible, I wanted him. In fact, the more I thought about it, the more I wanted him.

I called Scott and Vic to the cabin and explained the situation. Scott just went flat—he looked as if he'd just been punched in the stomach. None of us had ever been involved in anything like this before, and it was not a very happy prospect.

"Look, all I'm telling you is we're going to get the best legal talent we can," I said. "Think about it. Maybe somebody you may have worked for or with . . . They'll try to get anybody we name."

Vic looked somber as hell. "You pick him, Skipper. I don't know anyone."

I thought for a second and turned to Commander Winfrey. "Do you have any ideas, and I mean a hot shot? There is no goddamn way we are going into this thing with some lieutenant fresh out of Fred's School of Law."

After a moment he said, "If CinCPacFlt [commander in chief, Pacific Fleet] will release him, Lieutenant Commander Mike Lohr would be a great choice."

Vic answered, "Okay, whatever."

I turned to Scott. "You used to work for Vice Admiral Donnell. I'll send him a personal and see if he has any suggestions, okay?" Scott nodded agreement.

Messages started flying, and within thirty-six hours Dennis McCoy was en route to Bahrain. Admiral Donnell quickly responded, suggesting Commander Ron Swanson, whom Scott approved. Swanson and Lohr were rapidly appointed. With barely time to pack their socks, they found themselves in the air. These men turned out to be three superb legal minds with personalities to match.

That evening I was standing alone on the aft missile deck looking at the channel and watching the sun go down. The thought occurred to me, "What the hell am I doing here and how did I get here?" Over and over again, I thought, "What in the world am I doing here, with this boat at this time with this boa constrictor around my neck?"

5

———◇◇◇———

OVER OUR SHOULDER

The difficulty in life is the choice.

—George Moore, *The Bending of the Bough*, 1900

Around New Year's of 1965 Will stunned me with the question, "How would you feel about my joining the navy?"

"That's a hard question to answer. I don't know anything about the navy or anybody in it. I've never seen a navy ship much less been on one. Are you serious?"

We were both teaching school in San Antonio while Will was finishing his masters degree at Trinity University. The Vietnam war was escalating and hung like a cloud over all young men eligible for the draft. Will had been contacted and told that his deferment was about to expire. The navy was his service of choice, and after some discussion with the recruiter, he was offered a spot in the August class of the officers' candidate school in Newport, Rhode Island.

This was the biggest decision we'd had to face as newlyweds, and we both knew it was a major one that would involve extended separation from our families for the first time in our lives. What did I know about the navy? The only connection I could think of was the story Mother often told of my first tottering walk. It seems my uncle was home on leave from the navy and, attracted to his handsome uniform, I took my first steps in his direction.

I was born in Toledo, but our home was in Perrysburg, a small Ohio village located on the banks of the Maumee River and named for Admiral Oliver Hazard Perry. My family lived in a white, two-story clapboard home that Mother had inherited from her ninety-five-year-old aunt. As a girl, Aunt Margaret had traded with Native Americans from its back porch. Mother was thirty-four, Daddy forty-four, when I was born in 1939. My sister, Pat, age ten, had been anxiously hoping for a baby sister. I've often heard about the terrible storm, the snow and ice that covered the Old River Road and made driving treacherous the night Daddy drove Mother to the Toledo hospital.

Valentine's Day was approaching, and Pat remained at home cutting out hearts and thinking of names for her new sister. Sharon—Mother and Daddy must have liked the one she picked, and Pat was quite proud of her selection. Later when I began to walk, I followed Pat's every step. Sitting astride my white rocking horse next to my bedroom window, I would pass the time until she returned from school. She was good-natured and allowed me to shadow her.

Daddy's folks lived just a few miles away in the university town of Bowling Green. We visited often. I looked forward to listening to family stories, waiting for Grandpa to walk home from his office for lunch, braiding Grandma's hair and being allowed to fall asleep in Grandpa's overstuffed chair while waiting for Mother and Daddy to return from an evening out.

Grandpa had a lovely pond stocked with goldfish and carp in his backyard and I remember how very still we'd sit on the bench next to the pond, Grandpa reading and I coloring. I was fascinated by the water's movement and the brilliant sheen of the fish. Even today, nothing relaxes me more than to sit and gaze at a body of water and let my thoughts drift.

We would often go to the ice cream parlor at the day's end and I'd order a chocolate dope, vanilla ice cream smothered in chocolate sauce and peanuts, unfortunately still my favorite today. I was five when we moved to Texas, but we would continue to return to these small Ohio towns to visit with aunts, uncles, and cousins, to catch up on local news and visit friends.

I look back on my schooldays with fondness. My musical career was short-lived, but I did manage to become second chair violin in my grade-school orchestra. I also enjoyed running and was selected for the track team. Daddy had attended college on an athletic scholarship, and I'm sure he always wished one of his girls would excel in some sport. Running relays on cinder-topped surfaces proved to be a challenge. I don't remember ever breaking through the tape, but Daddy sat in those bleachers cheering me on nonetheless.

My first taste of "celebrity" occurred when I was fifteen and in ninth grade. It was the schoolwide election for Valentine Queen, and along with other girls I'd been summoned to the principal's office to have my picture taken for the Fort Worth *Star-Telegram*. Later in the week the results were announced: I'd been elected. The celebration was to take place with me dressed in white and my court in red. I didn't own a white gown. I remember Mother frantically calling friends to enlist help in locating one. I ruled over my court in a borrowed floor-length tulle formal, hair cut short and brushed back in ducktails, the style of the day.

When I entered Arlington Heights High School, I joined a service club that worked regularly in a local children's home. On my first visit I handed out sticks of gum, and when I returned a week later the children eagerly sought me out. From then on I was the "Gum Lady." Working with those sweet kids might have pointed me in the direction of teaching. I loved school, and was interested in entering a service-related profession. Speech therapy or teaching might be the path to follow, I thought.

Baylor University, located in the central Texas town of Waco, enjoyed a sound reputation in both fields, so after high school Mother and Daddy drove me ninety miles south to begin university life. At the time of my entrance Baylor enrolled around four thousand, and I had no idea that I'd meet, fall in love with, and marry someone from that number.

I roomed with my good friend, another Sharon, whom I'd attended school with from the third grade. Our fifth-floor room in the new six-story freshman dorm was compact. Two beds, two desks, two closets, and too small. But we managed for one semester until we moved to a first-floor triple. We laughed when our old room was converted into a storage and broom closet.

I was introduced to Will in my sophomore year through a mutual friend. He was one of the funniest, most clever guys I'd ever met, and I enjoyed his company a lot. He wasn't tall, five feet eight inches, and wore his black hair in a flattop. He was tan from lifeguarding in the summer and dressed traditionally in khaki pants and a button-down oxford shirt. Wearing low-cut tennis shoes, he kind of bounced when he walked and never seemed to lack for energy.

On our first date he took me to the downtown theater to see a double feature. I think the only words spoken that evening were, "Do you want a Coke?" and "How about a Snickers?" It was one of the longest dates of my life! I didn't know then that Will is a serious movie buff and at the drop of a hat he would opt to see anything in celluloid.

Neither of us owned a car and unless Will could borrow one, we walked on our dates. We enjoyed long strolls winding through the campus. Along the sidewalks stood memorial lampposts with plaques honoring Baylor graduates who had died in World War II and Korea. We would stop while he filled in details of the battle and its location. I learned more about the past on those walks than I ever did in a classroom. It was obvious Will was well read and interested in historical events, especially naval history.

Although we were never pinned or officially engaged, we seldom dated others, and it became an understanding that we would probably get married. And that we did. On Sunday, 12 July 1964, at four o'clock in the afternoon, with Will's grandfather officiating, our wedding took place in the Fort Worth First United Methodist Church, and it was a lovely and simple affair. After a week's honeymoon in New Orleans, we returned to a brand-new apartment in San Antonio. With both of us teaching and Will completing his masters, we never considered that world events would turn our little world upside down and inside out, and that our days in Texas were numbered.

Will was inducted into the navy in Houston. A few weeks later, in August 1965, he flew to Newport, Rhode Island, to enter the four-month officer candidate course. I drove to Fort Worth to spend the remaining days of the summer with Mother and Daddy.

Just before he was commissioned Will was asked to fill out a "dream sheet" stating his preferences for ship type, job description, and home port. There was room for three responses under each heading. The one ship he did not want was an aircraft carrier because of its size and long deployments. He preferred any job other than engineering, and we were both hoping for a California home port. So we were rocked back on our heels when his orders read, "SHIP TYPE: USS *INDEPENDENCE* CVA 62; BILLET DESCRIPTION: ENGINEERING; HOME PORT: NORFOLK, VA."

Will was obligated to the navy for three years. We decided to accept our good fortune that he was in his service of choice, and three years wasn't forever. At the end of his contract, we would reevaluate our circumstances and go on from there. But as the old saying goes, Will took to the navy like a duck takes to water!

My father was selling college yearbooks in Fort Worth, waiting for an opening on the Baylor faculty, when I was born in December 1938. Shortly after my birth, an instructor's position in the psychology department opened and we moved to Waco. Two years later my brother Dick was born. We remained in Waco until 1944, when the local draft board invited Dad to the party. The impact of sustained combat on individuals was beginning to be recognized, and clinical psychologists like my father were in high demand.

He was inducted, directly commissioned into the Navy Medical Service Corps, and ordered to the Oak Knoll Naval Hospital in Oakland, California. Shortly before we were able to join him he was transferred to the sprawling Shoemaker Naval Base twenty miles east of Oakland. The war was winding down and much of the base was inactive, perfect for exploration. Shoemaker had been a major processing station for replacements being sent to the Pacific, and I was fascinated with the barracks and storage areas full of things left behind.

A vivid memory was a trip into San Francisco to see the carrier *Essex*, just returned from the war zone. Even today I remember clearly her enormous hull, the wooden flight deck crowded with dark blue aircraft, and the smell of paint and oil so characteristic of navy ships.

Early in 1946 Dad, released from active duty, decided to use his GI benefits to get his doctorate from the University of North Carolina. During his tour he had done a lot of work with prisoners in the naval brig. In appreciation, they had rebuilt a wreck of a Model A Ford, painted it red, white, and blue, covered the top with a navy hammock, and presented it to him. This number took us from coast to coast and points in between without a whimper.

These sojourns were fascinating to my brother and me. The great southwestern desert, the brown, rolling eucalyptus-covered hills of California, and the pine forests of the eastern seaboard didn't look at all like Texas. I think these adventures and that little four-banger Ford aroused my wanderlust and enthusiasm for things mechanical.

Dad completed his degree in the summer of 1947 and was offered a job as a clinical psychologist with the Veterans Administration in San Antonio. This colorful and historic city was going to be home. After a couple of moves, my parents bought an old Victorian in the middle of the city's historic Monte Vista district.

It was a great place to grow up. Whenever my brother and I were not pressed into service helping Mom and Dad attempt to grow grass on Texas bedrock limestone, we were on our bicycles. Constructing rafts on the San Antonio River, camping in the mesquite breaks, playing flag football on the old Mamie Eisenhower residence grounds, or building tree forts—this was the pleasant montage of my childhood. Another plus was the city's proximity to Dilley. This tiny ranching community in the middle of the red sand flats of south Texas was my father's birthplace. My brother and I were intimately familiar with every sand hill and cattle tank. We expended hundreds of .410 shotgun shells stalking white-winged doves to little effect and chasing down the neighbors' range horses for brief wild rides.

Anything with wheels, gears or cylinders interested me—model airplanes, intricate soap-box racers, motorbikes. When the day arrived for that rite of passage to something with four wheels, I had wheedled my parents into letting me acquire the remains of a 1932 Model A. Lots of time and effort transformed this derelict into a low-slung black beauty with an engine too large and mufflers too small. I loved it!

Despite the usual teenage tribulations, for the most part my high school days at Thomas Jefferson were lots of fun. The occasional, surreptitiously acquired Pearl long-neck beer was about as adventuresome as anyone got. Our biggest concern was whether the Jeff Mustangs would defeat the arch rival Brackenridge Eagles in the annual football clash. Friday night sockhops and cruising Buddy's Burger Stand with a close circle of friends were the week's high points.

It's strange how small things can play such a central role in a person's life. An English lit assignment dealing with Herman Wouk's *The Caine Mutiny* became more than a requirement for me. I read and reread the novel, intrigued with the word pictures of life aboard a destroyer. I didn't realize just how accurate his descriptions were until I found myself pitching out of my bunk in an old World War II tin can. Although I can unequivocally state that I never served with anyone remotely resembling Captain Queeg. Another spark was my "steady's" father, an air force colonel who had flown a B-17 in North Africa during the war. I spent many hours with him discussing the military and his adventures. I even made a scale model of his aircraft, the *Bad Penny*, and gave it to him for his birthday. The combination of these things probably set the hook—I just didn't know it yet.

In my junior year my brother was involved in a terrible automobile accident. Thrown from the vehicle, he landed on his back and neck and was permanently paralyzed. For months he was near death. The emotional whipsaw nearly destroyed my father. If it had not been for my mother's enormous inner strength and faith, I'm certain the family would have unraveled. Throughout, though, Dick displayed tremendous courage and unflagging humor in the face of life-threatening and -altering circumstances. His attitude proved an object lesson to me, and I have often profited by it.

My attendance at Baylor was almost preordained. I never really considered another choice. I enrolled in the premed curriculum for reasons I've never been able to define, although my brother's accident probably had something to do with the choice. I dropped this pursuit as a junior and collected minors in more disciplines than I care to recall.

I had often seen Sharon around campus and devised several schemes to meet her, none of which succeeded. However, at the start of my junior year I happened to see her talking to one of my fraternity brothers. This was my chance, and I took it. With her sense of humor and outgoing personality packaged in a tiny frame she was much more interesting than organic chemistry. Besides, she was a whiz at helping me with my Latin sentences.

Although I enrolled in the class of '61, dropping my original major meant an additional year of courses, and Sharon and I both graduated in 1962. Two years later, surrounded by family and college friends, we were married.

The following year Sharon hosted a farewell party for me as I prepared to leave for Rhode Island and the navy. She had made a huge cake in the shape of a ship with "USS *Neversail*" emblazoned on the hull. As friends and family gathered around to cut this creation, we toasted the end of summer and the start of a new course for Sharon and me.

Will graduated from officer candidate school in December of 1965. He looked handsome and official in his brand-new blues and melton-wool bridge coat. It was a challenge to pack all his new, heavy uniforms in the small suitcases. But it was the holiday, we were together again, and we were going home.

We arrived in San Antonio on 20 December. On the twenty-second my world fell apart. Mother suffered a massive stroke and by the time we reached Fort Worth and Harris Hospital, she was in a deep coma. Even today I can see her lying still in that sterile white hospital bed. I hope and pray that she heard my words as I held her and stroked her arm and told her that I loved her. On Christmas Eve, her doctor entered the waiting room and in a flat, tired voice informed Dad and me, "I have bad news for you. Mrs. Loomis is dead." I turned to Daddy and held him tight. Exactly thirty-eight years before, on 24 December 1927, they had been married.

Will was with me during those dismal days. I recall the funeral director requesting my address and my being uncertain, now with Will in the navy, exactly what it was. And then Will responded, "Norfolk, Virginia." I stared at him and thought, But I've never even been to Norfolk.

Our drive to Virginia was a quiet, reflective one. We were heading for the home of Will's Aunt Ruth, who lived in Virginia Beach. After our arrival, Will began orienting himself to life on his floating city while Ruth and I shopped for a rental. We found a small basement apartment just a block away from the beach. We discovered just how different the eastern winter seascape was from the Gulf Coast: gray skies, tall blowing sea grass, and the rime of ice around the tidemarks kept reminding us that we were far from home.

Will enjoyed his duties aboard the Independence, liked the new responsibility and the opportunity to advance. He qualified as engineering watch officer in less than twelve months, the only ensign on board to earn this distinction. The months passed and our apprehension became reality. The Independence departed for a nine-month cruise to the Mediterranean. This development gave me the opportunity to return to Fort Worth and spend the summer with Daddy.

I returned to Norfolk in early September, having been hired as a fifth-grade teacher. I was delighted to be in the classroom again. Time passed and Christmas again rolled around. I spent most of the holidays with Daddy, working a quick trip around San Antonio so I could visit with Will's family. Those short winter days in Fort Worth were to be my last with my father. He had weathered a heart condition for a decade and that, coupled with the loss of Mother, probably shortened his days. I returned to Norfolk and only a week later was called home one more time. Daddy had suffered a fatal attack. So at age twenty-eight I experienced the ultimate loss. I came to realize how much I had been loved by two wonderful people, and I have never stopped missing them.

In February Will returned from his cruise with grand tales of Barcelona, Naples, Istanbul, Malta. He lovingly presented me with a gold charm bracelet that held a replica of every city and country he had visited.

When Will was nearing the end of eighteen months in the *Independence*, we realized that we would soon have to decide whether to commit to the navy way of life. Before this decision was made, Will wanted to explore the small-ship navy.

Following discussions with his detailer in Washington, D.C., he got his wish and was assigned to the destroyer *George K. MacKenzie*. The *MacKenzie* was home-ported in Long Beach, where I taught for another year. Then, with almost no warning, we were notified the ship would be shifted to Yokosuka, Japan, a navy base thirty miles south of Tokyo. I chose to travel there by cruise ship rather than fly since the government at that time gave dependents an option. While Will rode his pitching destroyer west I enjoyed the opportunity of a lifetime, traveling to Yokohama in the lap of luxury aboard the first-class *SS Roosevelt*.

The day before leaving for Japan I learned I was pregnant. We'd waited four years to start our family and happily called home from the pay phone on the pier to share our wonderful news. Most of the other "Mack" wives were also expecting, and I was ecstatic to be a member of the club.

In Japan we rented a small house in the seaside area of Hiyama, thirty minutes from the naval base. When it was time to deliver, two of my friends, also very pregnant, drove me to the naval hospital. We arrived after a harrowing ride over Japanese farm roads in our seventy-five-dollar Hillman Minx. The orderly's first words were, "Which one of you is delivering?" Naturally, this is an experience every husband wants to share with his wife, but our son Bill just couldn't wait for his dad's next in-port visit.

My skipper in the *MacKenzie* was Captain Sherwin James Sleeper, a demanding boss but an extraordinary seaman. Our operating schedule was intense, we were shorthanded, and he really pushed me to learn the destroyer's ropes. It was total immersion learning. Jim really knew his stuff, and if you were interested he was eager to share his skills. He was a people person as well.

It was a difficult time. We'd be in Yokosuka for a few days, then turn around and return to the gun line off Vietnam. We drew a lot of fire missions, and I was one of only three gunfire liaison officers on board. As one of us was usually on the beach working with the marines, the other two virtually lived in gun plot. We were in the middle of one of our numerous fire missions when the radioman stuck his head into the CIC and shoved a message under my nose. My son had arrived! I had just received a fire correction from the beach, giving me a right and a drop correction. In my excitement I relayed to the computer room, "Right eight pounds, drop fourteen ounces." The crusty old fire-control chief bellowed up the voice tube, "What the hell are you talking about?"

Somehow this interchange made it off the ship and the Associated Press picked it up under the caption, "New Son Eases Tensions."

Bill's birth was in February 1969, and four months later the three of us were winging our way back to the States so Will could enter destroyer school in Newport, Rhode Island. I missed Japan, but Bill was beginning to crawl and I was relieved to get back to the luxury of central heat and carpeting. This move was a real crossroads for us. After much discussion between us, Will had requested augmentation into the regular navy from the reserves. It looked like we were going to be navy blue for a while.

In December he reported as commissioning operations officer to the USS *Vreeland*, built in New Orleans and then home-ported in Charleston, South Carolina. The *Vreeland*'s skipper was Captain Dave Stefferud, a brilliant man, with a tremendous sense of humor, great fun to be with. He pushed Will hard but gave him room to run and sent some rather strong letters to the Bureau of Naval Personnel recommending him for early command.

David's efforts on Will's behalf paid off. He was given command of the ocean minesweeper *Exploit*, also home-ported in Charleston. It was as much fun as it was supposed to be. We felt as if that little ship was ours personally, and when we left to go to the Armed Forces Staff College in Norfolk it was hard to give her up.

Bill was almost four when we learned we'd be moving to Washington, D.C. We bought a modest brick home in Alexandria with a breathtaking backyard. The previous owner had planted camellia bushes, azaleas, and climbing roses on three sides of the house. The sloping yard encompassed a third of an acre and was spotted with large cherry, apple, and magnolia trees. Bill learned to climb the apple tree. My dearest memories from that time are of watching him from the kitchen window as he played fort and chased his miniature dachshunds through the grass. My unpleasant memories are of mowing that third of an acre when Will was away.

During this assignment Will had the good fortune to work closely with three respected admirals, Harry Train, Staser Holcomb, and Carlisle Trost. It was Admiral Train who had Will assigned to the secretary of defense's Weapons Systems Evaluation Group, which involved a year of travel back and forth to Israel in the wake of the Yom Kippur war of 1973. This was a real exposure to the international community and a great experience for him. I still have the string of olive beads Will brought me from Bethlehem.

The navy was building the *Spruance* class of destroyers, and Will wanted into the program. He was happy when he learned he was to be commissioning executive officer of the *David R. Ray*, his first dream sheet choice, in 1978. It was fun to repeat our *Vreeland* experience and bring a new ship to life.

In September 1981 he took command of another *Spruance* unit, the *Cushing*, based in San Diego. Halfway through Will's tour Admiral Harry Schraeder, the group commander, recommended that he be extended a year as commanding officer. He was pleased to be able to deploy her twice and I was happy for him, but those were some long months.

Just before being relieved as commanding officer, Will was told he had been selected for the Strategic Studies Group by the chief of naval operations (CNO), Admiral James Watkins. This was a proud moment. According to one of his fitness reports, the appointment marked him as "one of the best of the best of the best" in the navy. Besides, we loved Newport, had lots of friends there, and hadn't been able to wear our winter clothes in years.

Not to say that we didn't have mixed emotions. Bill was entering tenth grade and I was teaching. However, the bottom line was if we wanted to be together, we'd go and make the best of it. As it turned out, Bill made some lasting friends, I enjoyed a year's vacation, and Will, as one of the CNO fellows, had the chance to be involved in policy development beyond the sphere of the navy.

While with the Strategic Studies Group I was selected for major command. Sharon and I really wanted to return to San Diego, but my old boss, Admiral Trost, who was now head of the CNO's plans and programs shop, called me to Washington, D.C.

"Will," he said, "I need you to set up a special program. The CNO has promised the defense secretary to provide commanders in chief direct liaison to the navy staff, in order to give them an in and an understanding of the navy budgeting process. I'll do what I can to make it a short tour." He was good to his word, as always.

The job was exciting and I had a lot of leeway to make it work, but I daydreamed of returning to sea, and the ship I wanted was the *Vincennes*. When I had the *Cushing* and they brought CG 49 around on her delivery cruise, I watched her moor and said to myself, "That's her, that's the one!"

About midway through my tour in Washington, Guy Zeller called me in. "You're to be assigned as Nick Gee's relief in the *Vincennes*, but keep it to yourself until the slate is formally out."

I was ecstatic—the ship I wanted, home-ported in San Diego—and I couldn't think of a guy I'd rather relieve than Nick. I knew he would turn over a tight package. I've always felt being the second to command a new ship is the best deal of all. The first skipper has the pride of bringing her to life but also the agony of getting the kinks out. And I was fortunate in another way: A number of the crew who had commissioned the *Vincennes* wanted to stay on board; that cadre of experience would be invaluable.

The *Vincennes* was the first of the new *Ticonderoga*-class Aegis-equipped guided-missile cruisers to be assigned to the Pacific Fleet. Command of this magnificent ship was a tremendous opportunity. I knew the time would fly by, and I intended to enjoy her to the fullest.

6

———◇◇◇———

SUDDEN DEPARTURE

Joyous we too launch out on trackless seas,
Fearless for unknown shores.
—Walt Whitman, *Passage to India*, 1871

"Captain to CIC!" crackled through the wardroom speakers where I was conducting a meeting with a group of squadron commanders and the CAG (carrier air group) commander of the USS *Carl Vinson* (CVN 70). It was 11 April 1988, and we were into our third week operating as a unit of a multiple carrier battle force some four hundred nautical miles off the coast of southern California. This was our last at-sea period before an extended western Pacific deployment a month hence, and we had been tasked by the Third Fleet commander, Vice Admiral "Duke" Hernandez, to coordinate the final training event, a major surface and air missile exercise. This was to be a complex evolution. In order to review the scenario and consolidate everyone's roles, the principal players had been invited aboard to iron out the final details.

I hurried forward through the ship and up two ladders to the CIC. As I entered, the watch officer handed me a radio handset. "Skipper, Three Alpha Bravo wants to speak to you personally."

This was the fleet commander's call sign. A number of things normally result from a call from the big boss, most of them undesirable. As far as I knew, though, we had been holding up our end of the stick, so I was at a loss for the reason.

"Three Alpha Bravo, this is Tango Three Uniform actual standing by, over," I said. The response came back immediately and I recognized the voice of Captain Fritz Gaylord, chief of staff to Admiral Hernandez. "Three Uniform, this is Alpha Bravo. Will, what do you need to execute immediate detachment and deploy to the Persian Gulf?"

I dropped into the chair at the command console and after a moment to collect my thoughts replied we would need to fuel and transfer visitors back to the *Vinson*. There were sure to be additional requirements as well; we would feed them as soon as possible.

After a brief period, we were told to expedite the transfers and coordinate with the accompanying oiler for immediate refueling. The normal chatter and hum of the busy CIC had been replaced by total silence. There is an old axiom in the navy that rumors travel through a ship at the speed of light. I punched into the ship's general announcing system to inform the rest of the crew, knowing there was probably not a man on board who wasn't already chewing this one over.

As the crew scrambled to initiate the order, I had the executive officer assemble all off-watch officers and chief petty officers in the wardroom to review our requirements. Although we were all taken aback by the order to deploy immediately, I was pleased by the professionalism and flexibility of the officers and men as they hastened to review our equipment and personnel status.

Every seat in the wardroom was taken, and a number of people were standing around the long dining tables, notepads and various documents in hand. I told my department heads and the engineer, operations, combat systems, weapons, and supply officers that a quick assessment of priority needs, parts, repairs, and stores was critical. Items of lesser priority would be addressed later.

The rise and fall of voices, the sound of phones and internal communications circuits and people coming and going generated an electric atmosphere. The rattle of tie-down chains being dragged through the hangar bay above our heads indicated that the helicopter was preparing to return the carrier air wing guys back to the *Carl Vinson*.

Three of my officers were aboard the *Vinson* and I hoped they would be on our bird when it returned. They were not, and as a result had a series of adventures before they were ultimately flown back to the beach late the following day.

It rapidly became apparent that if higher authority allowed, the best course of action would be a return to San Diego to get emergency fuel and stores and load our air detachment's second aircraft. This recommendation was passed up the chain to the commander in chief, Pacific Fleet, and we were directed to proceed to San Diego at best speed. A return navigational track to San Diego was plotted. All four main-propulsion gas turbines were brought on line, at-sea refueling arrangements were canceled, and the *Vincennes* commenced her transit home.

Our expectation, based on a number of conversations over the command circuit, was that we would depart the following morning. At this point we were unclear as to the factors driving the accelerated deployment. As one of the chief petty officers put it, "Something must have hit the fan in that armpit!"

Although the rationale was obviously of some interest, our immediate concern was maximizing the limited time we would have before departure. Additional lists of requirements were produced, examined, prioritized, and transmitted to the myriad support organizations that would be preparing for our return.

The waterfront was going to look like fleas on a hot plate; no one could afford to waste time. High on the list of priorities were damage-control items above our normal allowance. A major lesson learned from the *Stark* and *Samuel Roberts* incidents was the need for additional oxygen-breathing apparatus cans and shoring materials. The damage-control officer was adamant that these items be placed on our list. I concurred; pictures of the *Stark* and the *Roberts* were worth reams of messages and reports.

Of equal importance was informing the crews' families of our unscheduled return and imminent departure. The navy, like any large bureaucracy under normal circumstances, moves at its own pace, and that can be frustratingly hidebound if the system fails to attach the priority to an issue that you feel is warranted. However, this same system has an admirable ability to metamorphose almost instantly into a well-oiled, reactive machine when the occasion demands. We were now the focal point of this sort of supportive and efficient effort.

At about ten that evening, as we approached our berth at the San Diego Naval Station, rain began to fall and we were greeted by an eerie but comforting sight. The pier was crammed with cranes, trucks, packing crates, and dependents milling about, all bathed by the light from banks of portable arc lamps. The glow was diffused by the rain, giving the scene the distinctly surrealistic appearance of a vignette from a World War II movie.

I could see Sharon, an umbrella over her head, standing between two large cranes. She looked small and alone, but as our eyes met she smiled and waved. This was going to be tough!

It was Thursday and lunchtime, but for some reason I was still in my fourth-grade classroom when a secretary brought me the message: "Call the chaplain." That's all? My first thought was that something had happened to Will. My classroom was one of the few to have its own telephone. I walked to the back counter and dialed the number. Ted wasn't in his office, so I telephoned Commander Matt Dillon, the public relations officer for the surface force commander.

"Hello, Matt, Sharon Rogers. I have a message to contact Chaplain Atwood but I can't reach him. Do you know what he wants?"

"Yes, it's probably about the ship coming in early. She's returning from the op area and should be at the pier about six tonight."

"Oh, really? What's up?"

"All I know is they'll be in less than twenty-four hours, then they're supposed to deploy."

"You've got to be kidding!"

"No, that's the word. So we're trying to get the message out to as many wives as possible."

"Thanks, Matt. I'll contact our ombudsmen and hope the phone tree's in action."

I needed a quiet place to make my calls and, noticing the lower-school director across the green, hurried over to ask her if someone could cover my class. Sensing the urgency in my voice, she told me to use her office while she took care of my students. I started making phone calls and learned that Debbie Pipkin and Carmella Lutz were notifying as many wives as they could reach. But many were working, shopping, or absent from home for some other reason. And those contacted were not at all happy about the news. All we knew was that the ship was coming in to be fueled and restocked and would leave the next morning. Even during the intense days of Vietnam I'd never heard of such a rapid turnaround.

School let out at three-fifteen and I left immediately. We lived only five minutes away and I wanted to get home. More telephoning, more dialing ship's information to get word of arrival, more concern. . . .

By the time I arrived at the 32nd Street Naval Station it was dark and difficult to find the parking slot allotted to Will. Trucks were arriving with crates. Forklifts, cranes, pier workers and wives with small children were everywhere. I spoke with as many as I could, but the rain made it difficult to chat.

From the moment we warped to the pier the ship looked like an anthill. Two gangway brows had been rigged and a steady stream of parts and supplies poured on board. A couple of high-lift cranes were positioned on the pier to load large-volume equipment and stores. Ammunition, fuel, and bulk-supply barges arrived and departed from the outboard side of the ship. Everything coming on board had to be inventoried, stored, and secured. Open-deck space was at a premium, and senior petty officers were acting as traffic wardens to prevent gridlock. Night-duty crews from the supply center, ship repair facility, and personnel support activity had been augmented. Staff personnel from commander, Naval Surface Force, Pacific (Vice Admiral George Davis), were also on hand.

The navy is pretty deliberate in maintaining operational schedules such as the thirty-day stand-down period before deployment. That time may be reduced but it is rarely cut out completely. To yank a ship out of her work-up cycle before deployment is almost unheard of. Deployments were accelerated during Desert Shield/Desert Storm, but no deployment before or since then has been as rapid as that of the Vincennes on that April night in 1988.

Sharon came on board and stopped off in the wardroom where she could visit with some of the other wives. We left the ship around midnight. At about four in the morning a message from commander in chief, Pacific Fleet, delayed our departure for twenty-four hours, welcome news. Shortly after receipt of this message a follow-on phone call indicated that our departure would be further delayed, slightly more than ninety hours from docking, to allow the delivery and installation of two 25-millimeter cannons that were being air-shipped from the Crane, Indiana, weapons depot. Departure was now estimated for 10:00 A.M. Monday, 15 April. We were to sail independently to Subic Bay, in the Philippines, making an overnight stop for repairs and then proceeding directly to the Persian Gulf. Additionally, we were directed to be prepared to transit the Strait of Hormuz no later than 18 May. It became obvious as the track was plotted that only a high transit speed would enable us to meet these requirements. Each hour we remained in San Diego forced up the speed and associated fuel expenditure necessary to meet the arrival date.

As we would not make the normal predeployment stop in Pearl Harbor, our transit of the Pacific would require at least two at-sea fuelings. The navigation team immediately went to work developing a proposed track and potential fueling points. The proposal was transmitted, commander in chief, Pacific Fleet, concurred, and both Third and Seventh Fleet commanders responded with the required fuel support.

Our on-deck coordination grew more complex with the arrival of the two 25-millimeter cannons, which had been flown to San Diego along with installers and technicians and which had to be precisely installed. Meanwhile, at HSL-43, the parent squadron of our Seahawk helicopters across the bay at North Island Naval Air Station, the lights were on continuously. In view of our pending operations, a decision had been made to swap our aircraft for two with special Mideast equipment. These birds had just returned from the Gulf and needed extensive work to restore them to condition for deployment. Our aviation detachment, with the help of squadron personnel, were in effect rebuilding two complex aircraft in forty-eight hours. The squadron's air-combat maneuvering team would embark for the duration of the transit to familiarize our aviators with situations they might encounter in the Gulf.

When our turnaround seemed to be well in hand, I isolated myself in the sea cabin to review what I knew about the tasking. The crew and their families had to be provided with as much unclassified information as possible regarding the shift in schedule.

The complete rationale was not made available to me until well after our departure. However, it was obvious that a decision such as this was serious and decided at the highest levels of government. My guess was that the Iranian threat to close the Strait of Hormuz with the Silkworm missile lay behind it all.

As a matter of policy, the United States was and is committed to freedom of navigation in international waters. Protection of U.S.-flagged shipping was being provided in the Gulf under the Earnest Will convoy concept, which called for an appropriate response to this emerging threat. The *Vincennes* was available, the right platform in the right place at the right time.

I briefed the wardroom officers on my thoughts but cautioned them to keep discussion to themselves and do what they could to squelch the rumor mill, which was in full swing. Following this, I arranged for a meeting on Saturday evening with dependents to discuss our imminent departure, allay their fears if possible, and attempt to answer their questions. The media had by now got wind of the accelerated deployment and were barraging families with questions. It was therefore important to provide the dependents with facts. I decided to couch my remarks to them in a positive light and from the broad political perspective of what the navy was attempting to accomplish in the Gulf. I also wanted to caution them that unless they heard something from an official, informed source to dismiss the comment as rumor.

Meanwhile the personal needs of the crew and their dependents had to be addressed. The list of DAB requirements was extensive. Powers of attorney, wills, and a pile of other legal documents required attention. Then there were arrangements for pay allotments, bill payments, automobile storage, and in some cases housing. Many crew members had already purchased airline tickets and made other leave arrangements; all had to be canceled and refunds obtained.

Ted Atwood, in conjunction with Vice Admiral Davis's public affairs officer, Commander David L. "Matt" Dillon, assumed the role of answering media inquiries. This removed a great deal of the pressure being brought to bear on people who could add nothing but emotion to the coverage. The efforts of this fine group went a long way toward easing the personal upheaval of our turnaround.

Will and I spent as much time together as we could during that brief weekend. We kept comparing these hours to those we'd experienced in Yokosuka during the Vietnam war. Then, Will's ship would spend fifty to seventy days on the gun line off Vietnam, returning home only for brief periods. When you have only forty-eight hours every minute must be enjoyed, and we tried to put the upcoming deployment as far from mind as possible.

There were, however, some important transactions that had to be dealt with. Sitting at our dining room table, Will and I discussed his will, my power of attorney, and carefully reviewed the monthly bills. Those chores completed, we climbed the stairs to our office to look at a navigational chart of the Persian Gulf. Unfolding the four-foot-square chart, we sat on the floor to map out our homemade system of grids. This divided the map into blocks, numbered and lettered, so that when he telephoned or radioed and said he was in H3, for example, I could look at the chart and know where he was. He would take along a small duplicate. We thought this would be a comfort to us both.

Later we changed into warmer clothes and drove to Seaport Village to walk along the cobblestone paths that wind through the charming replica of a New England seaside village. On the drive we bought four cases of A&W cream soda, one of Will's lifelong passions, for him to take on the deployment. In the village we went to a kite shop. Will has never lost his childhood fondness for kites and loved flying one from the deck of his ship. As we browsed through the shop we spotted a particularly handsome one with colors of the rainbow across its wings.

"Will, is that the one?"

"You bet. It'll be a kick to sail off the flight deck. It's so large they'll have to set flight quarters to launch it."

It was getting cooler, we were hungry, and Mexican food sounded good. We headed toward home to a favorite neighborhood restaurant.

The weekend hours flew by and before we knew it Monday was upon us. Anything not done simply had to be left undone, and shortly after six in the morning we drove to the naval base. There were numerous little things that needed our attention, but we were determined to enjoy a few more moments together.

My thoughts began to drift as we drove down the familiar southbound freeway with the early-hour commuters: I'm sitting next to my husband as we make an ordinary commute to his "office" and the people driving alongside us will be making this same drive tomorrow and the next day and the next. . . . It will be 180 days, six months, before I'll go this way again with this person by my side. What a strange, abnormal way to live your life.

At about nine-fifteen in the morning Commander Foster, my exec, stuck his head into the door of the wardroom where Sharon and I were chatting with some of the officers' wives. "Captain, all departments report ready for sea. All hands on board, request permission to set the special sea and anchor detail."

"Okay, Rick, let's do it," I replied. "I'll be on the bridge in a few minutes."

We had been repositioned over the weekend outboard our sister ship, the *Valley Forge*. Her commanding officer offered to have someone escort Sharon to the *Forge* bridge where she could watch our departure.

Hugging and giving each other one last kiss, we said our goodbyes. Will walked me to the *Vincennes* gangway where the quarterdeck watch came to attention and saluted. The command duty officer from *Valley Forge* greeted me and offered to escort me to their bridge. Walking through the ship and climbing a set of five steep ladders made me thankful that I'd worn my flat-heeled shoes. In a couple of minutes I stepped onto the wing of the bridge and Ted Lockhart, the commanding officer, handed me a huge mug of steaming coffee. It was chilly and the hot cup felt good.

I'm not overly fond of heights, and here I was three stories above the water on a small platform with see-through grating under my feet. This placed me within eight feet of the *Vincennes*'s bridge. Before, I had always stood on the pier to wave my goodbyes; standing up here in the eagle's nest gave me one last chance to be at eye level with Will.

On my way to the pilothouse I stopped by the sea cabin to grab a jacket and on impulse picked up a silly cardboard rabbit that Bill had sent me for Easter. I stuck it in the front band of my hat so that the ears stood up. It looked pretty stupid but it was time for a light moment. When I stepped on the bridge my new set of ears had the desired effect on the watch team and the cluster of wives alongside in the *Valley Forge*. I was talking with the young officer whose turn it was to get the ship under way when the chief signalman waved to get my attention.

"Skipper," he said, "can we break the house flag when the last line comes in?"

"Absolutely, Sigs, have it made up and ready!"

The flag was the result of a lively contest among Team 49 crew members to come up with a logo and a nickname for the ship. A number of entries had been evaluated by a panel of chief petty officers, and the popular choice was Checkmate Cruiser, a black chess knight superimposed over a white missile. Someone had done his homework with this winning submission. The black knight had been the personal symbol of King Charlemagne's bravest warrior, Paladin, whom the king had often used to checkmate his enemies. In any case, the signalmen had put their sewing talents to use and made an enormous flag with the paladin in the center. They loved to fly it, and now seemed like an appropriate moment.

I was talking with Ted when a wave of laughter broke out. I looked around and saw Will leaning over the *Vincennes's* bridge rail with those ridiculous rabbit ears stuck in his hat. This is typical of him; he has a knack for making the best of a bad situation. For a second the ears lightened my mood, until the sailors hauled in their last lines. Then there was the long, familiar blast from the helmsman's whistle signaling that the ship was under way and underscoring the sad certainty of departure. The loudspeakers were playing the ship's theme song, "The Runner," from the movie *Chariots of Fire.*

God! The panic you feel along with the realization that once again it will be a long, lonely walk down the concrete pier. The separation begins once more. . .

We were ready for sea, it was time. The lines securing us to our sister cruiser snaked aboard, engine and rudder orders were given, and the *Vincennes* backed slowly into the channel.

No matter what the circumstances or how many times the process had been repeated, getting the ship under way was a thrill. The power, grace, and purpose of a ship always seems to come alive as her bonds to the shore are released. This time was no exception. As we headed fair down the channel the signal lights on ship after ship moored at the naval station began to blink messages of farewell: "Good luck, God speed," "Wish we were with you," "Fair winds, Vinnie." These continued until we faded from the various senders' lines of sight.

Sharon and I had agreed that after we left she would drive to Seaport Village and stand by the seawall where we could exchange one more wave. Unfortunately, traffic was heavy and by the time she arrived we were well down the channel.

As we cleared the outer harbor sea buoy, the ship rolled gently in the ground swell as though sensing her natural element. I've always felt that a ship is more than steel and cables; when infused with a crew it seems to take on a life of its own.

Our plate was full for the westward dash, but this first underway day would be spent just settling in. Many of the items taken on over the weekend still required inventory and proper storage, equipment and systems needed to be checked out and exercised—our house put in order. As soon as sea detail secured, I got on the 1MC (general announcing system), congratulated the crew on their effort, and briefed them on what I still assumed was our future tasking.

The navigator had plotted our westward track along the great circle route, and his calculations showed that we were going to need a 23-knot speed to make our scheduled arrival in the Philippines. At that speed we were going to gulp fuel. I hoped the predicted good weather would hold and that the floating Texaco stations were on time and in place. The first rendezvous of two small dots on a big pond was six days away, about six hundred miles north of the Hawaiian islands.

A series of important exercises had been hastily laid on for us in the Philippine operating areas. Critical in bringing us up to par for Persian Gulf operations, they would involve a lot of expensive assets. We would have only one shot to get it right, and a lot of advance planning was necessary.

As soon as things began to settle into the familiar at-sea routine I scheduled a series of meetings with the department heads and principal players to develop extensive training plans. One area of importance was repeated drills on the current rules of engagement applicable to Gulf operations. Complex, with lots of fine nuances, these couldn't be simply read and filed. We would spend numerous hours reviewing the rules and projecting their application to every conceivable scenario.

We had been under way about two days when the clear blue skies of our departure were replaced by a low, scudding overcast and a chilly north wind. I was on the fantail talking to the after lookout and watching the wake when a magnificent sea bird appeared, diving at the churning water behind the ship.

"What's that, Skipper?" the lookout asked. "He's a long way from anywhere."

I borrowed his binoculars and after a close look said, "It's an albatross. His home is where he flies. I hope he stays with us, they're good luck."

The young sailor turned to me and said, "I hope so, too, Skipper. I'm kind of scared." I patted him on the shoulder. I hoped nothing would happen to that bird; I didn't want any ancient mariner revisited. The albatross stayed with us until we reached the Philippines and then disappeared.

As the first refueling point approached we had not recorded a single surface contact in about three days, so the telltale radar blip and ensuing voice call on the radio were welcome reminders of a world outside our own lifelines. The engineer had hovered over the fuel curves as our onboard stores shrunk to feed those four main turbines. Once alongside the oiler and hooked up, we took on almost 300,000 gallons of distillate marine fuel, approximately half of our capacity. Seven days later the process would be repeated.

On 10 May we transited Bashi Channel, which separates Luzon and the southern Ryukyu islands of Japan, and entered the Philippine operating area. Vice Admiral Paul David Miller and his Seventh Fleet staff had gone all out for our arrival. Vic Guillory remarked that he had never seen so much arranged in so short a time. The scheduled exercises ran the whole nine yards of the ship's capability: live surface and air gunnery; small-boat attacks; high- and low-altitude missile shoots; visit, board, and search drills; damage-control exercises; and even merchant-ship compartment familiarization. Air force assets from Okinawa flew several simulated air raids from both low and high altitude, and the explosive-ordnance-disposal team from Subic Bay developed a realistic mine detonation and avoidance drill.

The performance of ship and crew was summed up in a message from commander, Seventh Fleet, to commander, Middle East Force: "USS *Vincennes* was provided an intense and extensive Middle East Force–oriented package. The performance of the ship's systems and the crew was in all respects superb."

Our original sailing directive had provided for only a "gas and go" stop at Subic. Just prior to our arrival this was expanded to a thirty-six-hour stay. The brief extension was welcome news. We needed to shut down for some minor equipment repairs, and there were a number of things to procure, such as sandbags for the exposed deck cannons, flash hoods, and body armor that we had not been able to get in San Diego. Of equal importance, the crew needed a break. This extra time allowed them to call home, hit the exchange, and grab a short liberty.

As it turned out we were able to get the sandbags, but with the exception of some additional small-arms ammunition the other items on our list weren't available. Regardless, we took maximum advantage of the time.

SAN DIEGO

Picking up the receiver and hearing the overseas operator, I realized the ship had made it to Subic. It was great to hear Will's voice. It had been two weeks since the departure and because the *Vincennes* had sailed directly to the Philippines we missed our usual call from Pearl. He was pleased with the ship and crew's performance, but for the most part was anxious to hear news from home and the latest from Bill. I began updating him. Bill was studying for finals and would soon be home. We wives had already enjoyed a pot luck dinner, and Ted Atwood had miraculously solved hundreds of niggling problems caused by the quick departure.

"Will, remember to look for that replacement TV if you have time. I don't think Bill's going to enjoy the set's rolling picture and I'm darn sure tired of it."

"If I don't get over to the exchange in a hurry," he replied, "there won't be anything left. The crew's buying everything that's not nailed down. Sharon, there are only ten phones in this exchange and half the crew's waiting to use them. I'll call back as soon as possible."

"I love you, Will! Take care of yourself."

Compressing two weeks into two minutes is frustrating, to say the least. I had long ago started keeping a running list of important "don't forget to mentions" by the telephone. Nothing was worse than to hang up and remember I'd forgotten to tell him something important. Now I could begin a new list.

Sensing that this might be their only opportunity at a foreign exchange, the crew had made a severe dent in the store's inventory. They looked like chains of ants swarming aboard with their purchases. We were already loaded to the overhead and I had no clue where they were going to stow all the stereos, furniture, bicycles, and "monkey pod" woodcraft. Somehow space was found; the executive officer was a real tiger at seeing that everything was out of the way and secure.

Sudden Departure   81

Our track moved us through the South China Sea toward Singapore and the Strait of Mallaca. As we steamed south we were all anticipating an "unscheduled training opportunity" with the Soviets. Since the close of the Vietnam war they had maintained aircraft assets in the former U.S. complex of Cam Ranh Bay. Occasionally they would come out to play, generally with mock air raids and reconnaissance and intelligence-collection flights. We felt with the media coverage given our deployment that the Soviets might take an interest. We weren't disappointed.

I decided to run initially with our radar and radios silent to see if we could penetrate their normal operating areas unseen. This seemed to work, but it was no fun, and a training opportunity was going by the boards. So I told the operations officer to change the game plan and light off the SPY-1A radar. Very shortly the CIC passed the word, "Bear in the air!"

The Soviets must have been bored and had fuel to spare, as we picked up two distinctive Bear tracks plus a two-aircraft section of Soviet Badger bombers headed our way. The rules of this game dictated no fire-control-radar illumination of the opposite side and no hostile display. In a hot situation, though, these big lumbering characters would have been "grapes." As they closed, we passed the word so that the photo bugs on board would have a chance to record the flyby. The aircraft really put on a show, making multiple close-formation passes at low altitude. Shiny silver with the Red stars clearly visible, they broke up an otherwise dull afternoon.

Early on 15 May we passed into the Strait of Mallaca. Singapore, the Lion City, shimmered in the morning sun off the starboard side. As we proceeded past the commercial anchorage, a sobering sight presented itself. Row after row of huge petroleum carriers swung on rusty chains, their hulls and superstructures punctured and fire blackened. It dawned on us like a cartoon light bulb that this was the debris of the Gulf tanker war. These once-proud goliaths were rusting at the hook awaiting repair or scrapping. The last in line was obviously a recent arrival, her bridge and upperworks open like a bean can from rocket strikes, the hull blackened and streaked from fires. It wasn't difficult to maintain the crew's interest in damage control after seeing this.

The transit north along the coast of India was uneventful. The days were filled with training evolutions and reviews of operating procedure. We had intended to interact briefly with the USS *Enterprise* battle group as it steamed south, but our transit speeds ruled this out. The best I could do was exchange flashing light greetings with my old friend Rear Admiral Guy Zeller. He had performed beautifully in support of Operation Praying Mantis, and I was glad at least to get off a "Well done" to him.

We arrived in the north Arabian Sea on schedule, out of breath, and in need of fuel on the twenty-second. I fully expected to chop directly to Admiral Less and transit into the Gulf that evening. A piece of incoming traffic modified that thought. The Iranians were preparing to conduct a naval exercise, the Sword of Allah, in the strait, and Less wanted us to position ourselves to observe but not interfere with this evolution. He was planning to send his briefing team to the Fujairah anchorage off the coast of Oman to give us a Gulf information package. The last paragraph of his message welcomed us and indicated that in view of the interest generated by the addition of an Aegis cruiser to the Middle East Force, we would carry the Department of Defense media pool with us on our initial inbound transit. The date had not yet been determined, but it would probably be no earlier than 26 May.

The period at Fujairah was the first time the ship had been at rest since our departure from Subic. The air was still, and it was our first real exposure to the intense heat of the region. Exposed thermometers registered 125°F.

We spent several days milling around monitoring the Iranian navy on our radar and reporting what we saw, then we were directed to return to the anchorage, embark the media pool, and transit to Bahrain on 27 May. We decided to make the passage at night at high speed. The journalists grumbled because they wouldn't be able to see much. Nonetheless, just before midnight we set general quarters and headed through.

Two days before, IRG craft had attacked and set fire to a small Dutch tanker. This vessel had drifted aground on the Omani coast and the flames were visible for miles, a sure reminder that the situation was volatile. But the transit proceeded without incident, and although the media pool was disappointed, we were damned glad for the boredom.

After arrival at the Sitrah anchorage at Bahrain on 29 May I put the media ashore and a short time later followed them. I wanted to touch base personally with the man who would be my boss for the next several months. When I arrived on board the *Coronado*, Admiral Less's aide escorted me to the flag offices. I had brought Vic Guillory and several of his people with me. They scattered throughout the staff spaces to make contact with their counterparts. We had a lot of questions, and this was an opportunity to get some answers.

I knew Admiral Less only by reputation, but I was immediately taken by his ready smile and quick sense of humor. He was a popular and admired naval officer with a reputation for having an excellent grasp of complex problems. I sat on the couch facing his desk with a welcome glass of iced tea. He came right to the point. "Will, I'm glad to have the *Vincennes*'s capability here. I'm looking to you to help with a couple of problems. I'll come back to the Silkworm issue. My immediate concern is the poor tactical picture I'm getting from the pond."

He described at length the limitations of the flagship and his need for a clear and rapid turnaround of information from the ships operating throughout the Gulf. "My biggest problem is the rotten link picture I'm getting. Procedures aren't being followed and it's unacceptable to have important info delayed. I need a tough manager. You aren't going to make a lot of friends but someone has to get a handle on this. The *Vincennes* is it."

The forte of any AAW cruiser is managing the electronic tactical net. This sounded like a solvable problem. I promised to review the procedures in place and give him my recommendations within a day or two.

Less continued, "I'm sure you realize that yanking you folks over here on the fly was not a low-level decision. The Silkworm issue is real, but it's only a possibility. The Iranians haven't done much other than move some dirt around possible launch sites. For starts, I'm going to put you in the western patrol area. See what you can do to fix the picture."

I stood up to leave. He shook my hand and said, "Welcome to the sandbox."

As I left the flagship I walked over to the commercial AT&T phone trailer on the pier. It was not air-conditioned and hot as hell.

SAN DIEGO

"This is AT&T. I have an international collect call from Will Rogers in Bahrain. Will you accept the charges?"

"Of course!" I answered. We hadn't talked since the ship's brief stop in Subic and I was anxious to hear his voice.

"Texas summers can't hold a candle to this. I'm going to last about two minutes, so if you hear a thump, I've just collapsed."

"In that case, I'm sure you don't want a description of the San Diego weather."

"No thanks, if I can't touch it or feel it, I don't want to hear about it. How are Bill's transfer plans shaping up and when do you leave for Texas to pick him up?"

There was an irritating hum on the line. The toll charges were going to be expensive. We were both trying to talk at once, getting little said.

"I'll call again as soon as I can. In the meantime send me a couple of pairs of khaki shorts. This weather is really the pits."

We said our goodbyes and I spent the next few minutes replaying our conversation in my mind. The end-of-year report cards could wait.

THE PERSIAN GULF

The capability of the Aegis system promised a change in the surveillance picture of the Middle East Force. An important part of this equation was the U.S. and Saudi AWACS aircraft that operated out of Riyadh, Saudi Arabia. We asked the staff to arrange a meeting with the air force so we could brief them on our capability and limitations. We had operated with AWACS extensively, but this was a new ball game with lots of political ramifications.

The long range of the AWACS was an integral part of the big picture. The northern Gulf was covered by RAINBOW, a U.S. aircraft with Saudi observers. Its prime tasking was early warning in support of Saudi air space, but on the side, as available, it provided information downlink of the air picture to surface units in the north. SCANNER was a Saudi aircraft with U.S. observers that in support of the Earnest Will convoys covered the southern Gulf. A good understanding of procedures and a solid working relationship with these people were imperative.

Shortly after dawn on 1 June we got under way for our first patrol. As Admiral Less had indicated, we were assigned SOHWPA (Strait of Hormuz, Western Patrol Area). This large body of water stretching from the northern entrance of Hormuz west along the northern coast of Oman was considered a hot area. The majority of shipping attacks and regularly scheduled airline flights were concentrated within its boundaries. SOHWPA was certainly no sea of fire, but it wasn't Lake Michigan, either. It would be foolish and impossible to keep the crew in a constant state of full battle readiness, so like everyone else we operated for the most part in condition III. This status ensured that 50 percent of our combat capability was instantly ready, while the rest of the crew continued normal routine.

We moved randomly through our station. There was no urgency. Our speed was great for fuel consumption, but it magnified the impact of the ever-present heat and dust.

Iranian military activity was limited to regular maritime patrols of one P-3 and occasional brief forays by F-4s from Bandar Abbas and by small craft from Abu Musa Island. All of these were represented by sterile images on the LSDs. We saw nothing visually.

The USS Vincennes, foreground, keeps watch on an Iranian LST, center, and a liquid petroleum gas (LPG) carrier in the southern Persian Gulf in June 1988. (Photograph by Lieutenant Roger Huff, USN)

Admiral Less had been right with his concern for "the picture." For the most part everyone seemed to be acting without regard for protocol and procedure. Units were joining and dropping the link incorrectly, making multiple and confusing reports of previously identified contacts, and unnecessarily challenging the numerous air contacts. Dick Watkins had described it as a "fur ball." He was right. The problem was underscored on 8 June. One of our frigates operating in the southern Gulf challenged and then directed a radical course change to a commercial 747 inbound to Dubai. The aircraft had been clearly identified and the frigate informed of its identity. Had the aircraft not been in contact with the Dubai tower and not altered its flight path, it would have been on a collision course with outbound traffic. The tragic potential of this incident made waves all the way up to the State Department.

A series of direct messages from the *Vincennes* to other ships in the link and more aggressive management of the players began to pay off. Things were getting better, but we still had a way to go before the boss was going to be satisfied. I had no idea how far!

Much of our time was spent in the shipping lanes running parallel to the Omani coast. Steady offshore winds had deposited a fine layer of brown grit over the ship. We were scheduled to return to Sitrah on 10 June, and en route we were subjected to a sand storm at sea. The Shamal desert wind picked up and visibility dropped to virtually zero. When we emerged we could have passed for a sand dune. The water barge was a welcome site.

We had been at anchor for a couple of days when the staff public affairs officer sent us an example of creative news writing. A wire service reporter had sent out a message, "Super cruiser radar fails, *Vincennes* forced to return to port for repairs." If we were broke, it was certainly news to us.

Prior to our arrival, the Iraqis had launched a long-range air strike at the Bandar Abbas port facility. The Iranian retaliatory options were limited, but intelligence rumblings indicated a possible increase in the frequency of IRG craft ship attacks and high-seas seizure of ships suspected of carrying war materiel to Iraq. A notice to mariners, published by the United States, said in essence that protection would be provided to non–U.S. flag shipping if requested.

As we prepared to get under way for our second patrol, the staff intelligence officer briefed us on escalating tensions and the detailed procedures to be followed in the event that assistance was requested.

We were again assigned to SOHWPA. It became quickly obvious that the frequency of military air sorties from Bandar Abbas had increased. Forays of small craft in the vicinity of Abu Musa also seemed to be somewhat coordinated with the passage of tankers in the commercial channel.

We had not seen an Iranian naval vessel since our earlier observation of the Sword of Allah exercise, but on 14 June intelligence indicated that the guided-missile frigate *Alborz* was under way. About midmorning the surface-search radar picked up a ship transiting close to the Omani coast and heading in our general direction. At about the same time a large bulk cargo carrier identified as the *Vevey* passed heading westward. Almost immediately, the small, unidentified contact changed course and increased speed in the merchant ship's direction.

I radioed commander, Joint Task Force, Middle East, and recapped what appeared to be occurring, the first Iranian search and seizure. Both ships were well within Omani territorial waters, and without a call for assistance we could only stand by. We were directed to remain within visual range and keep the reports coming.

Sure enough, the Iranians boarded the *Vevey* and shortly both ships were moving east toward the strait. One of our helicopters was airborne, and the air crew was directed to remain well clear of the frigate and her prize. Sensitive ground was being broken; no one wanted to escalate the problem.

In response to this incident, bridge-to-bridge chatter among vessels in the area was heavy. The talk was easily monitored, and soon a charter helicopter with an NBC news crew showed up. The officer of the deck made contact with the news bird: "Civilian helicopter, off our starboard bow. This is USNWS request you remain clear of this area." At which point the helicopter made a close pass over the bow of the Iranian frigate. The Iranians, nervous with all the attention, fired two long machine-gun bursts in the vicinity of the news team. I wondered how it was going to play on the eleven o'clock news if we had to drag these people out of the water.

The situation was compounded by our aircraft's low fuel. To land it, we would have to move out of our directed surveillance position astern of the *Vevey*. A solution to this impasse presented itself as the USS *Sides* approached en route for convoy escort duties. We requested permission to land and fuel our bird on the *Sides*. It was granted, and we were able to remain in trail most of the day until the Iranians entered their territorial waters.

After those tense hours we were glad to turn away. The *Vevey* was released the following day when it turned out that her suspected war materiel consisted of crates of bathroom tile.

The next evening the IRG craft raised the stakes again. About nine-thirty the bridge VHF erupted with yells and curses from a Liberian tanker exiting the strait. Several small craft had closed and fired at the Liberian. They missed and for some reason did not press the attack. Later that evening as the big vessel passed we escorted her to the western boundary of the patrol area. Her only comment over the radio was, "Damn, where you guys?"

In mid-June, as we were on patrol, several Iranian surface units closed on an inbound Panamanian container vessel. But when the *Vincennes* emerged from the surface haze and came into view, the Iranian craft turned and fled.

Admiral Less directed us to maintain a position in the throat of the strait for the remainder of the underway period and monitor the increasing air activity out of Bandar Abbas. The rationale for this assignment was made clear in a message on 18 June: "All units are cautioned to be on the alert for more aggressive behavior. Reports of Iranian plans to reconvert . . . F-4s for air/ground roles using iron bombs, Mavericks, Iranian-produced 440-pound bombs, or unguided Eagle missiles would all point toward an offensive, vice defensive, capacity." This was followed two days later with another advisory: "Iran is clearly working hard to develop an antishipping capability . . . and innovative techniques for adapting air defense weapons systems for ASM [antiship missile] purposes are continuing."

We had been scheduled for a badly needed five-day upkeep. The ship was covered with dust and grit, and we had a backlog of maintenance matters that required attention. Besides, we had not had an opportunity to see Bahrain, a little jewel of an island kingdom. The crew was looking forward to long hotel showers and visiting the famous gold and perfume souks. This hook was no sooner set than we were informed that the USS *Halsey*, another San Diego cruiser patrolling the northern Gulf, had to come in for urgent repairs. Her station was active, as most of the Iraqi attack profiles against the Iranian facilities on Farsi

Island came right over her head. The boss didn't want the spot vacant so we drew the black bean.

We fueled, got our mail, and were under way at first light on 19 June. This was our first opportunity to monitor Iraqi attack profiles. Following the *Stark* attack, well-defined procedures had been set in place to prevent a recurrence. In essence, the drill consisted of radar monitoring of Iraqi aircraft. If they began to close a U.S. unit, very positive directions were transmitted. The bottom line was this: If the pilot fails to respond, don't take the first shot, blow him out of the air.

The Iranians were taking a hammering from the Iraqis, but they appeared to just hunker down and bear it. Occasionally, a section of F-14s would launch from the airfield at Bushehr, fly around aimlessly, and land. Any aggressive response on their part seemed to be reserved for the southern Gulf. On 26 June we were advised of the "unprecedented deployment of F-14s to Bandar Abbas" and the increased threat that posed for the entire Persian Gulf area.

We continued to operate in the northern Persian Gulf and central

The USS *Vincennes* escorts the merchant vessel *Mighty Servant*, carrying the mine-damaged destroyer *Samuel B. Roberts* out of the Persian Gulf, 2 July 1988. (Photograph by Lieutenant Roger Huff, USN)

Persian Gulf patrol stations until the twenty-eighth. I expected to return to Sitrah for our previously scheduled upkeep, but Admiral Less received a high-level tasking from the Joint Chiefs of Staff: "Position *Vincennes* in the Gulf of Oman in support of *Forrestal* battle group and AAW surveillance."

So much for liberty.

En route we were told that the *Samuel Roberts* and the *Mighty Servant* would shortly be ready to depart and that we would be tasked as escort. We had just arrived in the Gulf of Oman when a directive to return came in: "Proceed to arrive no later than 2000 hours, 1 July, off Dubai approaches for escort duties involving USS *Samuel Roberts*."

The IRG craft was really in a stew as we returned. At least three groups were roaming around the strait poking and shoving at passing traffic. The escort commenced on the morning of 2 July. It was tense but, except for the aluminum cloud of news aircraft, uneventful. Our return was quick but quiet, but the *Elmer Montgomery* had her hands full with a brazen IRG craft attack on the Norwegian tanker *Karama Maersk*.

At last we were going to have a breather. It had been a long few days. Little did I know that the next would be the longest.

7

———◇◇◇———

AN UNEASY
ANCHORAGE

Between the idea and the reality
Between the motion and the act
Falls the Shadow.
—T.S. Eliot, *The Hollow Men*, 1925

BAHRAIN

The bridge watch phoned to tell me the wind had risen to 30 knots with blowing sand. The weather matched my mood. Dick Watkins radioed that Rear Admiral William Fogarty and most of his investigating team had arrived and wanted to come aboard about four o'clock that afternoon. Frankly, I wasn't looking forward to the visit. The preliminaries to the formal board of inquiry had almost begun. I felt as if I were on a train that had left the station with no idea of its destination.

The day seemed to creep by. On the one hand I wanted to get on with it, on the other I wanted the problem simply to disappear. Any hope I attached to that flight of fancy was buried shortly before four as the boat with the visitors approached.

As soon as Admiral Fogarty stepped on board he motioned me aside and asked to speak to me privately. Leaving my executive officer, Rick Foster, to deal with the rest of the board, we stepped into the in-port cabin. As the door closed the admiral faced me and said, "I know this has been a rough time. Have you had enough? If so, I can get you off here."

I could tell his comment was purely one of personal concern, but nevertheless it rocked me back. It was a long moment before I could respond. "No, sir, I'm fine. This is my ship and my crew and I want to stay with both."

"Okay, Will, enough said. Just know the offer is there."

I thought to myself, If I leave, turn my back on these people, it will destroy the ship. I'm sure as hell going to ride this one out.

The issue was put to rest for the moment. Admiral Fogarty commented that most of his people were unfamiliar with the Aegis platform. Could we provide a thorough indoctrination tour for them? Rick had assembled the board in the wardroom and I called him. "Rick, break them into two groups," I said, "tie them up with our best people, and show them anything they want."

It occurred to me that Vic Guillory and Scott Lustig should not be involved, so I directed Rick to use Lieutenant Bill Johnson, the navigator, and Lieutenant (j.g.) Mike McClellan, the assistant CIC officer, to show them around. These were two of my best. Subsequently they played a major supportive role as the investigation unfolded.

As the familiarization tours were going to take time, I extended an invitation for the team to join the wardroom for supper. This turned out to be a mistake. At the mess table the ship's officers were ill at ease because the board members began posing questions about the events of 3 July. The queries were not adversarial, but none of us felt free to respond fully. I glanced at the admiral seated across from me. It was apparent from his expression that he didn't care for the thrust of the conversation. I was relieved when he directed that discussions be kept to topics not related to potential areas of inquiry.

Shortly after the meal, as the board prepared to depart, he motioned me aside. "Will, I apologize for the direction taken during chow. Thank you for your cooperation, but in the future if we need anything I'll make a formal request."

There would be dozens of these in the course of the next few days as our actions and decisions were examined in minute detail. The investigative procedure was an unknown maze to me, and I was anxious to see my counsel, Captain Dennis McCoy, who was scheduled to arrive the next day. Dennis had participated in many inquiries; I had never even been a witness in one.

Soon after Fogarty and his people left, I rode over to the *Coronado* to see Watkins about setting up a three-section liberty for the crew. With our high visibility, pulling liberty in Manama was out of the question, but a trip to the administrative support unit (ASU) for a cold beer and a swim beat watching jellyfish swarm around the ship's hull.

Then I telephoned Sharon, who was just beginning her Thursday.

SAN DIEGO

Although his voice was calm, I knew how upset Will was when he told me about Fogarty's offer to relieve him. But his response didn't surprise me at all. It would have been the easy way out, and Will wasn't going to take that route. The *Vincennes* was his ship, his responsibility. He'd see this nightmare through to the close.

It was reassuring to hear his voice, but I remained measured in my responses. Even with the groundswell of public support, the only thoughts swirling around my head were the negative ones: Why couldn't the Aegis discern the difference between an F-14 and a wide-bodied Airbus? Had the plane been descending? What about the air corridor—was the Airbus in it or not?

"Will, the papers say you should have been able to tell the difference between an Airbus and an F-14. What can Aegis do?"

"Remember," he said, "these displays are not like a TV picture. What you see are electronically generated symbols, not the radar target itself. Besides, even if raw video were being shown it would be hard to tell its size. Depending on what aspect is being presented to the radar beams, the apparent size of the target would vary. What I'm telling you is that the way it's shown, you can't tell a 747 from an ultralite. The press is running out the closet experts—forget it!"

The newspaper articles generated most of my questions, but Will hadn't read them and couldn't address the theories being proposed. The questions were driving me crazy. To hide my growing depression, I was becoming very controlled with everyone except for poor Bill. We were still relying on fast food and takeout, and dirty dishes stacked up in the sink or were simply left on the table. Newspapers lay everywhere, the house was a mess, and so was I. Lost in thought, I was unable to hold a decent conversation with Bill. Somehow, I managed to hide this anger from Will and everyone else who contacted me.

I had to pull myself together. The dependents' meeting was in a few hours. It was time to go before I knew it. I hurriedly threw on a blouse and skirt, picked up Admiral Trost's message and the one from Will, and headed downstairs.

I bumped into Bill. "Are you sure you don't want to go?" I asked him.

"No, Mom, I'll be here when you get back."

Bill was becoming more stoic with me, too. Both of us were afraid to share our true feelings for fear of the emotions they'd unleash. It would be painful for him to sit through the meeting hearing God knew what and listening to the worry and anger shared by others. "I'm sure it'll be over by ten," I said. "See you then."

The meeting was held at the fleet training center at the 32nd Street Naval Station. I entered the big auditorium, where Matt Dillon greeted me and directed me to a table positioned just below the stage. I said hello to the admirals' wives, Jean Davis and Hope Kihune, and sat down. Jan Stanard, the fleet ombudsman, also was at the table.

By seven o'clock close to one hundred dependents had arrived. Ted Atwood opened the meeting with a brief prayer, followed by Admiral Zeller, who had just returned from the Gulf. He painted a graphic picture for us of the many problems our ships faced in that region. The psychologist then spoke, warning us of the stress our men might be experiencing. Commander Dillon explained our right to privacy if we were sought out by the press.

As the commanding officer's wife I spoke briefly. "Good evening, my friends. These last few days have been alarming and tragic. When I first heard the news I immediately sent word to Will via another ship. Just knowing that he had a message from me helped to ease my mind. If there is anyone here who hasn't had the opportunity to reach a husband or son, please see Chaplain Atwood. He'll take your message tonight and transmit it to the ship."

Then I read a message from Admiral Trost that commended the men and underscored the correctness of their actions. Finally came Will's message:

Dearest members of the *Vincennes* family:

The events of the past few days are for all of us a nightmare of almost inconceivable proportions. However, the circumstances, information flow, and decision time available during the course of the incident dictated then and dictate now the precise choice of action that I undertook. All of us deeply regret the end result, but defense of Team 49 and *Vincennes* has been and always will be my first priority.

All of you are aware I'm sure of the ongoing investigation into the circumstances. Please do not be concerned, as it is right and proper for this to take place and all of us fully support this necessity. Please understand that the time-honored precepts of command at sea are responsibility and accountability. I fully accept both.

The performance of every member of the team was magnificent. During the course of a highly compressed and complex situation, all did exactly as they were trained to do, perfectly and without hesitation. I know you are proud of them and you should be. I am! All are safe, spirits are high, and I promise the safe return of all. God bless.

Chaplain Atwood then opened the meeting to questions. And there were many. The wives were angry about the situation. They thought Iran had pulled a propaganda stunt, that all those lives were not lost, that it was not a commercial aircraft that had been shot down. From what they had seen on television they questioned the number of bodies. They just couldn't believe that it had happened.

Of course, most of the questions were unanswerable. One woman asked, "How could the bodies we've seen floating in the water be in one piece and have no clothes on?"

The doctor responded, "When there's a blast the magnitude of a missile the explosion's force would disintegrate the clothing but some bodies would remain intact."

We sat there in stunned silence. Then people began to voice worries as well as questions.

"Will the ship be returning home by itself? If so, won't it be an easy target?"

"Shouldn't it come directly back to San Diego? I understand it may go to Bahrain. How can the men safely leave ship and go on liberty?"

"What precautions have been taken for homecoming? Will there be protection from retaliation?"

Almost everyone was talking now. They didn't want the ship to go into any port. There was no doubt in their minds that some kind of retaliation would be unleashed.

The meeting began to break up around nine-thirty. At its conclusion I wasn't any happier. The wives had raised questions about the safety of the ship that I hadn't even considered, and that added to my anxiety. The meeting did have one important result, though. About ten of the wives who had been unable to contact their husbands wrote messages and gave them to Ted, who sent them to Will for distribution.

And one thing happened that night that dismayed me. As people began to leave, an officer approached and took me aside. "Sharon, we have intelligence that says there weren't 290, the count was 225."

I just stared at him, not quick enough to ask for his source of information. I didn't even ask when this new data would be released to the public. Two hundred twenty-five remained an unspeakable tragedy. I was more than curious as to why Iran would inflate the number.

BAHRAIN

I was pretty agitated after my opening conversation with Fogarty the previous afternoon, and when I heard that Dennis McCoy had arrived and was en route to the ship, it was a relief. Lieutenant Commander Mike Lohr and Commander Ron Swanson, the lawyers for Vic Guillory and Scott Lustig, were due the next day. Their guidance was going to be a big plus.

When McCoy was deposited on the quarterdeck he showed every mile of the rapid trip from Annapolis to the Mideast. I was anxious to unload on him but realized if he didn't get a shower and a decent meal, I'd be talking to a zombie.

Dennis was a friend of longstanding, and Sharon and I had known his wife since our days in Japan. I had a lot of respect for his professional approach and quick mind. Slim and graying with the steady demeanor of a surgeon, he was anything but colorful. Color I didn't need, just thoughtful advice and a thorough understanding of the complexity of the scenario. I felt very confident with him.

"For starters I have to understand Aegis," he said. "I need to think like a line officer. When I've got that base, then I'll want you to talk to me in detail ... and we'll see where we go from there. Right now I need a shower."

I could see the sense of his approach and would just have to bottle myself up awhile longer. I hoped he was a quick study.

Dennis needed room to spread out so I put him in the in-port cabin. As soon as he looked as though he was on the road to recovery, I had Lieutenant McClellan give him a complete tour of the ship. When Mike brought him back to the cabin Dennis shook his head and with a sort of stunned look on his face said, "Will, this is the most complex pile of equipment I've ever seen. Can I have a couple of sharp guys to answer the questions I know I'm going to have?"

I readily agreed.

A combination of several messages, including ten from dependents to their husbands in the crew, had arrived. Among them was a note from Atwood: "You are featured as person of the week in the Peter Jennings report, 'ABC News Tonight.' I did seize the opportunity to tell the American people how grateful you and the crew are for the outpouring of support. One never knows how it will play in Peoria. Will just have to wait and see."

This information was a topper for the day. The last thing I wanted was more visibility.

SAN DIEGO

Reading and rereading news clippings, tuning into morning news shows for last-minute updates, going out to buy the *Los Angeles Times*, clipping stories, driving to get them copied, starting to fold the laundry, getting sidetracked by a phone call—each day was beginning the same way and melding into the next. I tried to accomplish a number of things but never finished anything.

I answered the phone once again and it was Matt Dillon: "I just wanted you to know that tonight Will's to be featured as ABC's person of the week. We'll be taping it if you can't tune in."

"Thanks, Matt. We'll be home. I'll let the family in Texas know."

Shortly before six I tuned to ABC and called Bill to the family room. I perched on the arm of the couch and Bill rested on one of the cushions. We steeled ourselves for the report. Peter Jennings's opening statement poured salt on an open wound: "Tonight we focus on a man who is having the most difficult week of his life. Very soon after he realized he was responsible for having killed 290 people on Iran Air Flight 655. . . ."

I was dissecting each word, every phrase, the tone of his voice, his body language. And what he was saying seemed outrageous. What did he mean, "he's responsible for killing."?

"Today the captain is at the center of a naval investigation which will eventually pass judgment on his judgment."

One week before I would never in my wildest dreams have figured that my husband would be at the center of an investigation—and now here it was, for all the world to hear. His decision would be studied, reviewed, scrutinized, judged. But I appreciated Senator Sam Nunn's comment: "And I see nothing that would indicate to me that the captain of the ship made an erroneous conclusion. He obviously has profound regrets at what happened. It was a real tragedy. But he had a very tough call in a very compressed time frame."

The featured spot lasted only a few minutes, but as Mr. Jennings wound down, his next statement was the one that neither Bill nor I could fathom: "Captain Rogers's career has been steady, not spectacular."

Both of us were stunned. "Where did he get that information?" I asked aloud. "Why would he say that? Two early selections for promotion, three commands, and his career has not been spectacular!"

I sat forward listening to his final remarks: "Even if Captain Rogers is completely vindicated his naval record may well be affected by the tragedy, and it is clear from his record that the navy is his life, a man who had no doubt he is doing the nation's duty in the Persian Gulf."

I sat there in disbelief. I wanted the same opportunity Jennings had just had—five minutes to refute, defend, praise, to plead my husband's case before millions of viewers. The phone rang.

"Hi, Gran," I answered. "Yes, we've just finished watching it." As always, Gran was thinking of my feelings when she began, "We thought it was a nice profile." But I interrupted her. "I thought it was awful. It made Will look run-of-the-mill when we all know the success he's earned. I don't know what he'll think about it."

Later, I telephoned Matt Dillon to vent my anger. He shared my reaction and later wrote Jennings a professional letter in which he said, in part, that describing Will's career as "steady, not spectacular," had upset him and a number of other navy people. "I don't know what your criteria are, but, by any navy standard, Captain Rogers has an outstanding track record. . . . Your interpretation of Captain Rogers's career may lead people to view him as a slow, steady plodder. That would be unfortunate. He's what we call a 'hot runner.' Your otherwise perceptive, well-written, and well-delivered piece denigrated him with a skewed frame of reference."

Mr. Jennings telephoned Matt after receiving the letter and said there was no malice in his report. For two days prior to the newscast, he explained, he had tried to get anyone at the Pentagon to provide some background information on Captain Rogers; all he ended up with was a dry biography. Matt said he understood; he guessed that in the week after 3 July there were not many people around the Pentagon who wanted to even acknowledge that a Captain Rogers existed.

BAHRAIN

I had assumed that the investigation would commence as soon as all the players had assembled in Bahrain. Dennis quickly dispelled that notion when he pointed out that gearing up the administrative support that Fogarty would need, allowing the individual counsels time with the "parties to the investigation," and moving the mass of logs, data, tapes, publications, and statements to the board site would take time. I also thought the proceedings would take place on the flagship, but to avoid disruption in the event the *Coronado* had to get under way, the library in the ASU compound was chosen. Fogarty and the board had been so hounded by the media in the lobby of the Gulf Hotel that he had everyone move to the BOQ at the ASU, which had the added advantage of being close to the site of the inquiry proceedings.

The enormous quantity of information recorded on the Aegis computer tapes promised to be a key part of the fact-finding. These had been sealed, verified as original, and delivered to a courier on our arrival in port, then flown to the Naval Weapons Center in Dahlgren, Virginia, so that the data could be extracted and analyzed. Extraordinary effort was being expended by the laboratory to protect the tapes and retrieve every scrap of information—a time-consuming and exacting process.

Fogarty badly wanted the results on hand prior to the investigation, but it was obvious the analysis would take several days to complete. After numerous discussions, consultations, and messages back and forth to Dahlgren, 13 July was established as the starting date. I'm sure the admiral was under a lot of pressure to get things moving, but it was clear he intended to conduct the investigation at his own pace.

In a telephone call to Sharon over the weekend I learned the gist of the Peter Jennings commentary, and we both tried to make a joke out of the selection. Neither of us saw much humor in it, though. Sharon hid her agitation well, and I didn't want to dwell on it.

Our attorneys were using every available minute to learn the ship and review all the information we had. The three attorneys spent hours interviewing Guillory, Lustig, and me as well as members of the crew. I was impressed with their speed in picking up Aegis jargon and the complexities of general shipboard operations. They weren't spending a lot of time in the sack.

It was well after midnight on Sunday, 10 July, before I climbed into my bunk. I had fallen into a deep sleep when a persistent knocking on my door awakened me. The bulkhead clock read 2:30. I opened the door to a vestibule filled with computer technicians led by Senior Chief Tim Cox and Chief Mike Adams.

"Skipper, can we come in? We have some stuff we'd like to show you, it's really screwy and we can't make a lot of sense out of it. We've been working with the system printouts and want to show you something."

I thought to myself this probably could have waited until at least the crack of dawn, but these guys had been doing their best to interpret the data and I wasn't about to dampen their efforts. As they spread publications and computer paper over my table, Cox said, "Captain, remember our original track number on the Airbus was 4474, then shifted to 4131?"

I remembered, but this was not unusual. Often a unit in the data link dropped reporting responsibility for a particular track in favor of another participant. Or else, with the Aegis system's enormous target-tracking capability, another unit's number would be automatically adopted if the system made a track correlation. This automatic feature allowed Aegis to "save" its own assigned track numbers, which in a dense radar environment would be used rapidly. Also, every unit working the link was assigned a participating unit number, for example, PU

21, so that each input of that ship or aircraft could be identified.

"Okay, Chief, so what? You aren't up here at this hour to tell me that!"

He grinned. "The weird thing we can't figure is that 4474 was deleted as an active number and taken back by us, but it didn't go away, it keeps reappearing over and over and dropping in and out. We can't tell for sure because we don't have everything we need, but it looks like another PU was in the link using our track number assignment."

This was interesting, but still I didn't see much to get excited about.

Cox continued, "We'd like your permission to work this with the Dahlgren guys when they get here—any problem with that?"

I agreed. Anything that shed any light was welcome. But this looked like a dead end to me. They took the time to walk me through the complicated streams of computer data. They were right, 4474 kept popping up, though still I couldn't see the thread they were pulling. As I closed the door behind them, I was struck by the thought that the navy was lucky to have people of this caliber.

We were being inundated with a steady flow of requests for publications, instructions, logs, and the like from the board. The demand became so heavy that I designated Lieutenant (j.g.) McClellan as liaison officer to field the requests and deliver the material. He must have made fifty trips from the ship to the ASU.

By Tuesday, 12 July, Dennis felt that we were as ready as we were going to be, but he could see I was on unfamiliar ground.

"Okay, Will, let me explain what this is and how it works," he said. "First, this is a fact-finding mission, not a court-martial. You aren't charged with or suspected of anything. The whole idea is to explore to the maximum extent possible what happened."

He paused. My mind was turning over a number of possibilities, none of them pleasant.

"Now, having said that, let me underscore a couple of things. One, this is a formal proceeding, and all parties including the board are sworn. Two, if at any time evidence or testimony being presented suggests there is a chargeable offense under the Uniform Code of Military Justice, Fogarty has to stop the proceedings and inform you that you are suspected of a chargeable offense. He will read you your rights. The same holds true for Less, Guillory, and Lustig."

I mulled this over for a moment, then reluctantly said, "Dennis, you've seen the whole ball of wax. Anything that might lead to that?"

He waited longer than I liked before replying. "No, not at the moment, but there is still a lot none of us know and I'll be frank—anything can happen."

For the first time since the morning of 3 July I felt a sense of complete resignation. He went over a number of details concerning the procedures that would be followed, but I was lost in my thoughts and nothing registered. He got my full attention again when he advised me not to make an opening statement. I said I didn't feel comfortable with silence. I had nothing to hide and I wanted to talk.

"Goddammit, Will, we'll provide the facts through me, but don't lay yourself open to avenues which may have no bearing and screw up the issue at hand! Any statement you make becomes part of the record and you can be questioned on your remarks. If you say nothing, they can't ask, and we won't end up having to go back and defend against something we shouldn't. You hired me to look out for your interests and that's my recommendation. Maybe we will want to make a closing statement to sum up or refute. I don't know yet."

I agreed, but still I was uneasy. I didn't want Fogarty to feel I was sitting on something or "taking the Fifth." Apparently the attorneys for Less, Guillory, and Lustig made the same recommendation, for none of us made an opening statement.

Endlessly Dennis and I rehashed the events of the entire deployment. Later, lying in the sea cabin, I kept going over it all. Sleep wasn't in the cards. I was pretty sure the same scene was being repeated in a couple of other staterooms.

Dennis wanted to see the setup at the ASU, and we had agreed to leave the ship at about six-thirty the next morning to accommodate the hour's worth of boat and bus rides it would take to get there. As we gathered on the quarterdeck, most of the crew filtered out to the weatherdeck waving and displaying the thumbs-up sign. Their support was an upbeat way to start what otherwise promised to be a tough day.

When we arrived at the ASU it was clear that security, always tight, had been beefed up. Armed sentries were evident throughout the compound and the entrance to the library was tightly guarded. The library was part of a larger building that contained a game room and two large lounge areas. Even at that early hour the electronic games in the lounges were pinging away. We presented our identification, the sentry unlocked the door, and we filed into the space that would be the focus of so much attention. At that moment I was struck by a bit of gallows humor. Traditionally during courts-martial, the tables at which the court and "interested parties" sit are covered with green felt. The library tables were draped in blue. I remarked to Dennis, "If those covers change to green, we're in trouble." He didn't find my comment amusing.

The room was constructed in the shape of a large L, and as expected, the walls around it were covered with bookshelves. The base of the L had been rearranged with head tables for the board and side tables forming a U for the interested parties and counsel. Tape decks covered one library desk. The board recorder would sit there. A witness chair faced the head table, which was flanked by the flags of the United States and the Navy Department. Microphone and recorder wires snaked along the walls, and several easels with charts of the Gulf and blank sketch paper were arranged next to the witness position.

We were in the room only a few minutes when the senior counsel for the board arrived and pulled Dennis and me aside. He briefed us on what he expected to occur during the day. His feeling was that by the time all parties had been sworn in, the precept to the board and the scope of the investigation read into the record, and numerous other administrative procedures covered, the day would be pretty much shot. The folks from Dahlgren were due in late that afternoon, and Fogarty wanted to talk with them. He didn't expect any formal testimony to begin until the next day.

Shortly before nine, the armored staff cars assigned to the Middle East Force arrived with Fogarty and the board, quickly followed by Less and the group from the flagship. Fogarty wasted no time, quickly shaking hands around the room and holding a brief private discussion with the board. Then he banged the gavel. His opening comment set the tone for the proceedings.

"Gentlemen, these proceedings are closed, and this inquiry will be conducted strictly in accord with the Uniform Code of Military Justice. What is presented will not be publicly discussed until such time as the findings of the board are finalized and approved by the reviewing authorities."

With that comment, the proceedings on which worldwide attention was focused began.

The first day went as predicted, and the proceedings recessed about four o'clock. With the scheduled arrival of the Dahlgren analysts that evening, most of the next day promised to be taken up with briefs of computer data. I didn't anticipate any surprises, a notion that was to be rudely shattered.

Senior Chief Cox, Chief Adams, and Fire Controlman First Class Smith were anxious to see the Dahlgren people. Their painstaking work with the mass of printouts had produced that handful of mysterious bits.

Before returning to the ship, I called Sharon from the AT&T trailer on the pier. She questioned me about the day.

"It went okay, but it's too early to tell anything. There's been no testimony or exhibits, only a lot of legal jargon."

"Tell me about Fogarty. What's he like?"

"He seems fair and I think he'll keep tight control over the proceedings."

"How are Vic and Scott holding up?"

"Vic's okay, but I'm worried about Scott. He's really running ragged."

"Are you okay?"

"Well, honey, under the circumstances I'm doing all right. But I have to go now, the boat's ready to leave. I'll call tomorrow. Give Bill a hug."

For the first and only time, she lost her temper. "Dammit, Will, I feel like I'm in a dark cave. I can't do this. You've got to talk to me. Everything is filtered. I've got to know what's going on. I don't know what to believe."

I insisted that I couldn't tell her much, but promised to fill her in daily with any information available. She didn't feel any better, and neither did I.

When we returned to the ship the senior yeoman approached me on the quarterdeck. "Captain, we have a bunch of mail for you and the crew. What do you want me to do with it?"

"Post it on the bulletin boards. I'll stop by later and have a look."

"Skipper, you don't understand. I mean a bunch of mail. Ten bags full!"

The flow of mail, steadily increasing, had now turned into an avalanche, ultimately reaching more than sixty thousand pieces. Letters, white socks for every man in the crew from a church in South Carolina, boxes of chocolate cupcakes sent air express, art works, quilts, quotes from the Bible—you name it. Without doubt, it was an outpouring of love and support beyond the wildest imagination.

We personally answered every piece. The effort was more than worth it.

SAN DIEGO

The days were dragging by. I couldn't absorb the hurt and grief. My husband was going through the roughest period of his career and I didn't have the wherewithal to help or comfort him. It would have been a help if we were able to talk to one another without sensing that the whole world was listening. The phone was our only means of communication.

I was still sending him news articles, but I withheld the hate stories coming out of Iran. They were something he shouldn't have to read. Some of them made me shudder. One report quoted Tehran Radio stating, "We will not leave the crimes of America unanswered. We will resist the plots of the Great Satan and avenge the blood of our martyrs from criminal mercenaries." Another report the same day, 6 July, said that members and supporters of the Iranian Hezbollah faction had marched through Beirut, Lebanon, vowing to avenge the Airbus victims. Some hours earlier, there had been a threat to kill an American hostage in retaliation. The fact that the police, who had received this call, thought it was a hoax did little to soothe my nerves.

I tried to imagine what the inquiry was like. All I could think of was the court-room scenario written by Herman Wouk in *The Caine Mutiny*. It never crossed my mind that Will would be court-martialed, but it did seem possible that he would end up relieved of duty. I kept these dreaded thoughts to myself. I couldn't bear to voice such fears to him or anyone else.

We were both thankful that Dennis was representing him. Will did agonize more than once over Dennis's advice not to make an opening statement. Agitated or not, however, he was aware that he should take that advice.

8

——✕✕✕——

THE INVESTIGATION

Nothing is sure in a sea fight. . . .
—Horatio Nelson, *Memorandum to the Fleet*, 1805

BAHRAIN

When we arrived the next morning the Dahlgren team was already in the library laying out and taping numerous large sheets of graph paper in front of the bookshelves. Each sheet contained diagrams of a variety of data streams that had been extracted from the system tapes. We were more than curious to see them.

Most of the graphs reflected the overall performance of the Aegis system, broken down in some cases to thousandths of a second. None of the graphs was remarkable; they merely demonstrated that things had worked as advertised. I was moving from chart to chart when I came to one that displayed the tracks of the Airbus and the missile intercepts. Something didn't look right. The aircraft flight path, with the exception of some small dips, showed a steady rise in altitude until missile intercept at about 13,500 feet. I expected to see a decrease in altitude about twenty miles from the *Vincennes*.

It wasn't there.

I grabbed McCoy. "Dennis, this sheet of paper may cause us some trouble, and I don't have an explanation."

I walked him through what the graph seemed to show. "Unless the character had shown a clear commercial profile, which he did not,

I wasn't concerned about his altitude. It looked to me like he was looking for a shot, but I guarantee the board's going to sink their teeth into the descent report."

He absorbed my comment and pulled me into the lobby. "Will, I agree this is going to be an issue," he said, "but it must be taken into context. We know and they know, or if they don't they soon will, this is a complex issue with a lot of sidebars. If it becomes central, we'll work on it."

I nodded, indicating that he had better talk to the other counsels, particularly since I had seen Vic Guillory and Scott Lustig heading for the chart. This piece of news might unwire Scott.

I wanted another look at the data displays before the day got started. My attention had been diverted by the altitude issue. Now something else on that sheet caught my eye. There seemed to be a second track that almost overlaid the path of the Airbus until about 6,000 feet, when it, the second track, turned north along the Iranian coast. I grabbed one of the Dahlgren analysts and asked him what he made of this second trace.

"Oh, yeah," he said, "that's a valid track we can correlate to a link track number over here," and he pointed to another sheet. "Pretty interesting, in that the track is almost an overlay until he turns."

Then it dawned on me this must be TN 4133, which the *Sides* had been concerned with and had called a "birds affirm" on. My attention returned to the altitude question. By this point I should have known not to dismiss anything, no matter how small a grain of sand it seemed. This black trace would turn out to be a big piece of the puzzle.

At 9:00 A.M. Admiral Fogarty reconvened the board with the reminder that all parties were still under oath. He was anxious to hear from the analysts and get the results of their effort entered into the record. Reuben Pitts, the team leader, was sworn in and, emphasizing that the data was still being developed, provided a lengthy explanation of how the information from the tapes had been safeguarded and pro-duced. It was important to get this background into the record, as the findings of the inquiry would be reviewed by numbers of people, many not familiar with the capabilities and limitations of the Aegis system.

It had been a long night and I was having trouble staying awake. I wasn't alone in that regard; when the admiral recessed for a coffee break, the room emptied quickly. I walked outside to stretch my legs and was met at the door by one of the yeomen. "Skipper," he said, "we had an early mail run today. The chief sent me in with your personal mail."

I thanked him for the effort and asked how much mail had been received. "I don't know for sure," he answered, "but you can't get to the post office. The passageway is buried in bags!"

A few yards from the rec center door was a bench under a couple of scraggly, dust-covered palms. As I walked to the seat I was glad to see Sharon's familiar hand on the first envelope. Our phone conversations were important to both of us, but never satisfactory. We both felt that much was left unsaid. Letters, on the other hand, were an emotional vent for both of us. The heat and dust faded as I immersed myself in her supportive words.

I was glad Bill was home from school to provide support. I could picture her propped up in our four-poster bed writing me or poring over those damn newspapers line by line. I thought, Maybe the best move is to take Fogarty's offer, wade through this investigation, take what comes, and get relieved. The shocker with the flight-path graph had turned the day black.

I sat for a moment wishing I was a long way away, then turned to the next letter in the stack. The envelope, marked personal, had been sent by a Major Robin Higgins, USMC. Not knowing anyone by that name, I was about to set it aside when Dennis yelled out the door that Fogarty was talking to the Dahlgren team and the break was extended ten minutes. I opened the letter. As soon as I began to read, it struck me who Robin Higgins was.

In the wake of the terrible tragedy that occurred on the third and the aftermath of questions, suppositions, skepticism and finger-pointing, I felt a need to drop you a line. My husband is Lt. Col. William R. Higgins, the marine officer taken hostage in Lebanon while pursuing his duties as an unarmed observer of the UN truce.

Being a military wife and a uniformed officer myself, I know the devotion to duty, honor and country that brought you to the place you are. As a victim of those who are hostile to us, I know the pain of having to defend our freedoms at great personal risk and suffering. I also have suffered immense disillusionment and the onslaught of faceless accusers and nameless skeptics who come out of the closet when faced with an opportunity for attention and attack those who are on the battlefield. My husband always told me, "When you are out front, people will shoot at you."

I have three quotes on yellow notes over my desk at the Pentagon. Maybe they will help you, as they help me:

"The only guide to a man is his conscience; the only shield to his memory is the rectitude and sincerity of his actions. It is very imprudent to walk through life without this shield, because we are so often rocked by the failure of our hopes and the upsetting of our calculations; but with this shield, however the fates may play, we march always in the ranks of honor."—Winston Churchill.

"True courage swims against the tide. True courage begins when everyone else has either given in or stopped fighting. True courage is never being swept along by what everyone else is doing. True courage is often lonely. On our journey I pray that we will have as our companions Faith to light the road ahead, for dark is the path of the nation that walks without faith; Enthusiasm that has made us great and will keep us a force for good in the world; and finally Courage, greatest of all human virtues since it guarantees all of the others."—Vernon A. Walters.

"Never give in, never, never, never in nothing great or small, large or petty—never give in except to convictions of honor and good sense."—Winston Churchill.

God bless you and keep you during this time of personal trial. Thank you for keeping us safe and free.

I got up from the bench and walked to the edge of the seawall. As I stared at the Gulf, I thought, This is a person who represents everything that courage and empathy stand for. My actions probably have placed her husband at even greater risk, but she took the time to reach out to me.

With this courageous woman's letter in my hand I felt I could face anything the board might come up with, and I couldn't wait to share her words with Sharon.

During the lunch break Dennis and I continued to discuss the altitude issue. The afternoon session was to be devoted to detailed examination of the system data. Dennis kept telling me that there were so many pieces to the puzzle that the board had to take the altitude question in context. I could see he was not too concerned about it. I still thought there was potential for the issue to be blown out of proportion. And I could see that Scott thought so too. He was taking it hard. Over the course of the afternoon his mood changed. When we recessed for coffee he would stand by himself instead of coming over and rehashing the scenario with Vic and me, as he'd been doing earlier.

When the inquiry resumed, it became obvious that Admiral Fogarty wanted to get the overall analysis and not let side issues divert us. Except for questions designed to clarify the various findings, he appeared to want to wait for the testimony from the Vincennes, Montgomery and Sides CIC teams before revisiting any issue in detail. Dennis was right.

As things were winding down for the day, Reuben Pitts indicated that his team needed to ride out to the ship to verify a number of things with the Vincennes technicians. Fogarty asked if I had any objections; I certainly did not. Chiefs Cox and Adams and Petty Officer Smith, one of the technicians, had been jumping from one foot to the other to talk with these people. This would be a perfect opportunity. Admiral Less asked if I would stop by the flagship on the way back, as he had something he needed to discuss with me. When the bus arrived at Mina Sulman pier I told Vic to load the Dahlgren people and our group in the boat, take them to the ship, and send the gig back for me.

When I reached his flag cabin, Less looked as hot and beat up as I did. He offered me a welcome glass of iced tea. "Will, I know you're anxious to get back to the ship, but I need your comments. CinCCent [commander in chief, Central Command] is concerned about the safety of the Vincennes at anchorage and wants to get her under way. How would you feel about your guys moving over to the ASU and your exec taking her to sea?"

My reaction was immediate. "Boss, that's bullshit! First, she is as safe at anchor as she would be boring holes in the water off the entrance channel. The Bahrainis and your people are patrolling the anchorage twenty-four hours a day, the small-arms stations are manned, and one of the chain-gun crews is on standby. Second, she's our data base, all of us need access to everything from the computers to the people. Fogarty and his people are constantly requesting stuff. If we do this I guarantee this mess is going to drag on forever. I can't say it any stronger, but that idea is really screwy."

Less has a great smile, and it was a welcome sight.

"I would've been surprised if you'd said anything else. I agree with you. Forget it, I'll put this one to bed."

I finished my tea and stood to leave. "Admiral," I said, "pardon the outburst, but it's been a long day and there are a hell of a lot of oars in my boat."

He laughed, we shook hands, and I made my way off the ship.

It was past seven when I made it back to the ship. Dennis wanted to go over what he saw developing, but I kept falling asleep. Finally I said, "I've had it. If I don't hit the rack you'll be on your own tomorrow. I can't make an intelligent response to anything at this point."

I made my way up to the sea cabin, bypassed the pile of mail on my desk, and fell asleep as soon as my head hit the pillow.

I had been asleep for three hours when I became conscious of a steady knocking at the door. When I responded, Scott was standing in the entrance. In a barely audible voice, he said, "Captain, I'm sorry. God, I'm sorry. I let you down, the ship down, everybody. I'm sorry." As he spoke, huge tears welled up in his eyes and his head dropped.

Spontaneously, I reached out and hugged him. "Scott, get hold of yourself. Quit trying to shoulder loads that aren't yours. What happened happened. It was my call, not yours. Now get hold of yourself!"

After a moment he straightened up. "I'll be okay. I just want you to know I'm sorry."

"Scott, damn it, I mean it! I know you're sorry, we're all sorry, but we have to go on. We fought as a team and we'll face this as a team." I told him he had to get some rest and if he wanted I'd have the corpsman get him a sleeping pill.

He seemed to come together. "I'm okay, Captain. Thanks, thanks for helping. We'll get 'em tomorrow, right?"

I didn't know about that, but whatever happened had to be better than the day we'd just spent.

I had completely forgotten that Chief Cox and the Dahlgren analysts were involved with data comparison and system checking. They told me later that they spent most of that night on the computer deck surrounded by printouts, diagrams, and publications. The analysts had shown considerable interest in what the ship's techs discovered but had no ready explanation for the anomaly. They had agreed to get together at the ASU and comb the data files for a possible solution.

Will was moved by the letter from Robin Higgins. His voice was the most animated it had been in a long time when he shared its contents with me. I'd read articles in the newspapers noting that the shooting down of the Airbus would probably have an impact on the hostage situation in Lebanon. Both Will and I had agonized over that. So her letter bolstered our morale.

I didn't realize that within a year I'd have the opportunity to meet Robin. The following June Will and I were in Washington, D.C., on business and we dropped by her Pentagon office. As we entered she was standing by her desk in her marine uniform, a petite woman.

I expressed my great appreciation for her letter, then asked if she had heard any word from her husband. She hadn't. Her only hope was to presume he was still alive. I couldn't imagine the strain she had been living under. We told her that if she was ever in southern California and felt the need to get away for a few days, our home was her home.

A few weeks after this meeting we were devastated to hear the State Departments' announcement about the execution of her husband.

BAHRAIN

One of the issues central to the investigation was Flight 655's position in the commercial airway when it was destroyed. The corridor designated Amber 59 extended on a southerly radial from Bandar Abbas to a junction with the airway that funneled traffic in and out of Dubai, in the United Arab Emirates. The intersection of these paths was designated Darax. Slightly less than halfway between Bandar Abbas and the Darax junction was an inflight checkpoint, Mobet.

We had been very conscious of the numerous commercial flight paths crisscrossing the Gulf, as well as the extremely high volume of traffic constantly in these lanes. Prior to our arrival in the Gulf, the CIC officer had extracted from the applicable air navigation charts these corridors and transferred them to the LSDs.

The glowing video spiderwebs were a useful tool in helping to sort out who was who in the Gulf skies. It had been our experience that civilian aircraft conscious of the heavy traffic flew the centerline of the airways. In fact, the radar often showed numerous aircraft spaced along these radials like water bugs on a string.

Flight 655 had not adhered to the centerline. In fact, its path had been one of the factors that alerted us as it approached our position. Shortly after takeoff the aircraft had flown a circular course to the southeast, crossing Amber 59, then turned to a southwesterly heading. At about thirty miles from the *Vincennes* the flight path diverged from centerline and placed its heading "down the throat" in relation to the *Vincennes/Montgomery* formation. I estimated at missile intercept that the aircraft was three to five miles west of center and several miles south-west of Mobet.

Since we now had the radar trace from extracted data, Admiral Fogarty had asked me to have the course of the aircraft superimposed on a navigational chart. He wanted every bit of detail we could pro-vide—the airway, ship positions, navigational reference points, missile intercept, the works. I had instructed the navigator, Lieutenant Bill Johnson, to get with the ship's navigation team and produce this infor-mation on the smallest-scale, most detailed chart we had. They had worked most of the night on the project, and the result was graphic and accurate within yards.

The board counsel indicated that this chart would be the first item of discussion. When the proceedings convened it was displayed on one of the easels. There was not as much discussion as I had anticipated, and it was easy to understand why. The exhibit clearly pulled together numerous scraps of information and verified our memories. The air-craft had never assumed centerline, it was diverging at shootdown, and its position at missile intercept was approximately 3.9 miles right of center.

Dennis scribbled a note and slid it in front of me: "No issues here, straightforward, Johnson did a good job." I wrote back, "Agree, that's one we can put to bed."

Next on the agenda was testimony pertinent to the multiple IFF signals received by the ship. The presentation promised to take some time, and Admiral Fogarty called for a brief recess. When I stepped outside, one of the Dahlgren analysts approached me. "Captain, I'd like to show you something interesting." He handed me a sheet of the familiar graph paper. Entwined on the sheet were a series of fat traces that looked like an earthworm convention.

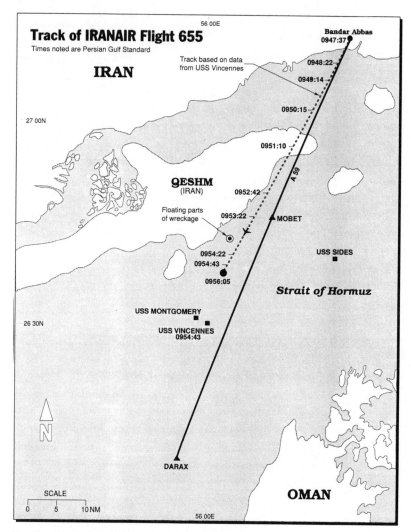

Track of Iran Air Flight 655 (Map by James Burnett)

He pointed at the lines and said, "It doesn't look like much, but these are the radar tracks from the SPG-9 reduction [the SPG-9 is the fire-control radar that directs the fall of shot from the 5-inch deck guns]. These are the small-boat tracks. You can see when they are acquired and when the track ends. Looks like you sank five of the seven. Your people did a hell of a job of staying on target."

I thanked him, asking if I could have a copy of the graph for the gunners. They had done a good job and I felt they ought to see the proof.

As we resumed I whispered to Dennis, "These IFF comments are going to be important. I hope they have some answers that make sense." He nodded. We both knew the direction the explanation took would influence the board's perception.

The individual scheduled to address the issue was an employee of RCA serving as a member of the Dahlgren team. I had never dealt directly with him, but I knew of his reputation as an expert on the complexities of IFF. Using the drawing easel, he spent considerable time explaining the workings of the system, expected ranges, and how IFF was integrated into the SPY-1 radar. With the extracted data he pointed out that the Vincennes equipment had been working properly on 3 July. Based on atmospheric data for the day, however, interrogation ranges would have been greatly extended.

Then he began to explain why he felt the ship would have seen both mode II and III codes ostensibly from the same aircraft. Everyone was leaning forward, trying not to miss a word. This was the gist of his argument:

Flight 655 starts rolling down the runway for takeoff, a military aircraft taxis onto the departure apron and lights off his IFF preparatory to departure. Flight 655 lifts off and is immediately acquired on the Vincennes radar. Moments later the other aircraft is rolling down the runway and the Vincennes interrogates 655's transponder. As both the planes are within the ship's interrogation window, or "box," both aircraft transponders reply. The ship's consoles display only one radar contact because one is not yet airborne, but they receive two IFF responses, mode II for military and mode III for commercial.

Happenstance dictated that the mode II code of the following aircraft was the same as that assigned to an Iranian F-14 two weeks earlier. It immediately dawned on me that this was the second radar trace on the Airbus flight-path graph.

I grabbed Dennis's arm and whispered, "What timing! A few seconds more and we would have had separated radar returns." He simply shook his head.

This explanation made sense and was the only logical reason anyone had come up with as to why the codes broke the way they did.

Those identifiers had helped to drive my decision toward "hostile."

The board had numerous questions. They asked that the scenario be explained again. The gentleman from NavSea was firm in his belief that this was the probable answer. I couldn't speak for the board, but I was convinced!

The inquiry recessed for lunch. This testimony was the hot topic as we made our way to the now-infamous ASU cafeteria. Just as we reached the dining area, Chief Tim Cox came running toward us. He was drenched with sweat and obviously excited.

"Skipper, I think we understand what we've got. There's more work to do but I wanted to let you know this." I motioned Dennis to join us. Cox immediately launched into what his sailors and the Dahlgren analysts had been able to pull together.

"Okay, let's start simple," he said. "As you know, each PU [participating unit] is assigned a block of numbers for its use. Once this authorized track block is entered into the unit's combat system, contacts reported by the unit are automatically assigned track numbers from that block.

"Okay, on 3 July we were assigned the block 4400 to 4576, and we were link manager. The *Sides* was assigned 3400 to 3576 but for some reason was reporting contacts using 4100 series numbers."

This was no news. It was hot, and I was a bit impatient. "Right, Chief, I know how the link works. Where are you going?"

"Okay, Skipper, I just wanted to make sure you recalled the numbers. Anyway, the USS *Spruance* was operating about 180 miles southeast of us in the Arabian Sea and reported a contact using TN 4474, the same number we originally assigned to the Airbus. They pegged this to a low-flying A-6 from the *Forrestal* and apparently didn't update it and let it coast." He paused.

"Now, get this: HMS *Manchester*, which was entering the southern link with us, picked up the *Spruance* contact, updated it, and reported it over the link. They entered this track at almost the same time the Airbus was about twenty miles from us."

I needed to think this one through, so I sat down under one of the palms. I recalled that when the unidentified aircraft was at about that range, I had asked, "What is 4474 doing?" I was unaware at that moment that the *Sides*'s TN 4131 had been adopted automatically by the system and 4474 retrieved by the *Vincennes*.

The answer I'd received over the internal communications net was "descending altitude, speed 450 knots." We now apparently knew that the information referred not to the Airbus but to the A-6 Intruder. Given time, the tactical information coordinator (TIC), Petty Officer Leach, would undoubtedly have discovered the track number conflict and resolved it with HMS Manchester. This sequence was bizarre! I asked Cox what he thought the chances were of this sequence of events being repeated. "Infinitesimal," he replied.

Cox said that Reuben Pitts, the senior analyst who had been working with him, was going to brief Admiral Fogarty. I asked Dennis what he made of this. He wasn't sure he understood completely but felt Fogarty would certainly have to consider the issue. I asked if we should raise the point for entry into the proceedings. Dennis said, "Let's let Fogarty draw his own conclusions after he discusses this stuff with his own expert witness; he can't ignore it."

It seemed to me we ought to press it, but so far McCoy had been right so I didn't persist. I thanked Chief Cox and told him to stay with it. Regardless of the end result, his effort and that of the others had involved scrutiny of hundreds of lines of information and thousands of individual bits of data, and I was proud of them.

The remainder of the day was anticlimactic considering the testimony of the morning and Cox's lunchtime revelations. Captain John Kiely, the Pacific Fleet command's representative on the board, read into the record a detailed summary of the Vincennes's predeployment training. There were no surprises there: The ship had done exceptionally well throughout the workup cycle and during the accelerated conditions of deployment.

The statements of operational readiness from Rear Admiral Kihune, our cruiser-destroyer group commander, and Vice Admirals Hernandez and Miller, the Third and Seventh Fleet commanders, underscored the Vincennes's thoroughness of preparation and her ability to undertake any assignment she might be given. In support of this, Admiral Fogarty had been provided with copies of all our equipment-casualty reports for the previous six months, quarterly maintenance-system documentation, and any files pertaining to on-board training programs.

Everything up to this point painted a detailed backdrop, but the verbal testimony of the CIC teams and Admiral Less's staff was critical if we were to have a complete picture. With the number of people scheduled to testify, and the certainty that their statements would be subject to detailed examination, the inquiry was hardly over.

As we wound down for the day, Fogarty announced his desire to start promptly at 8:00 A.M. the next day with the first witness and remain in session until all testimony was complete. The board counsel then established the order of testimony: first Less's staff, followed by witnesses from the *Montgomery, Sides,* and *Vincennes.* We had previously been provided a list of those individuals who would be called, and it was extensive. Presently the board counsel approached Dennis and remarked that Admiral Fogarty was concerned about not hearing direct testimony from me. Dennis relayed this to me and said he felt I should probably make a statement.

I agreed. As the days passed I had become convinced that I could not remain silent. If the admiral was concerned, I sure as hell was! Dennis relayed my agreement to enter a statement for the record and to testify. It was understood, however, that this would not occur until all testimony was complete.

SAN DIEGO

Congressman Bill Lowery of the Forty-ninth District telephoned me on Friday, 15 July, and expressed support for Will and the *Vincennes* and told me how much he had enjoyed meeting him and members of the crew during the exercises off the coast in early spring. His office was putting together a letter of support, and he asked what I thought about the idea of it being signed by San Diegans and sent to the ship. I told him I thought it was a wonderful idea; the men would appreciate it. He invited me to attend a public session and news announcement at the Broadway pier the next morning at ten o'clock. Unwilling to face the media, I made some apology.

The next morning, however, Bill and I decided to drive down and watch the proceedings. We parked across the street and walked a short way onto the pier where we could see the tables, the long sheets of butcher paper people were signing, the bunting and flags. Members of the Veterans of Foreign Wars and the Navy League were there, but the only person I recognized was Congressman Lowery.

Because the men of the *Vincennes* were so isolated and at the same time hearing confusing news reports, I was impressed with Congressman Lowery's sensitivity to their needs. The letter's message was simple and sincere: "To Captain Will Rogers III and the crew of the USS *Vincennes*, the citizens of your home port of San Diego show our strong support to you as you strive to do your duty to God and country in troubled waters far from home. You have our best wishes during a difficult time and we pray for fair winds and following seas in the future. Good luck and Godspeed."

The news reporters and television cameramen began to drift off, and we left before anyone could spot us. The letter was being signed at various locations around the county, and at one of our dependents' meetings we had the opportunity to write special notes. The letter wound up being a thousand feet long with about ten thousand San Diegans penning supportive notes and adding their signature.

The ship's officers' wives, about ten of us, met every two weeks when possible. Someone would arrange a potluck dinner or an evening out at a restaurant. We tried to talk about things other than the ship, but with that being our major bond it was difficult to stay away from the subject. They were feeling down about the investigation. I routinely gave them a spiel about it being only a fact-finding inquiry, but I don't think they believed me. And I didn't believe it, either. We still had a lot of unanswered questions. The tension seemed to intensify when we got together. Some wives felt awkward with one another. The bottom line was that there had been no preparation for a situation like ours, and there were no hints about how to handle it in the infamous officers' wives book of etiquette.

The wives were worried about their husbands being recognized in port, and they feared sabotage of the ship. In fact, everything worried them. What worried me, and I never told anyone, was that the ship would be ordered back into the Persian Gulf and a similar incident would occur. Obviously, I was not the only person with that idea: The ship never went back into the Gulf.

Will kept telling me to find the book *Fate Is the Hunter* by Ernest Gann, that it might help to explain how this all happened. I looked and finally found a copy. I read it but couldn't figure out what Will was talking about—it didn't help clear up any questions.

As we were returning to the ship, I recalled part of a phone conversation with Sharon the previous day. She and the other wardroom wives were becoming increasingly concerned about Scott's wife, Lana. She had not heard from Scott in a number of days and seemed to be withdrawing from the support network the wives had set up. I had agreed to push Scott to call Lana, and as he and I were standing together on the afterdeck of the gig it seemed like a good opportunity. I felt a little uneasy, as I did not want to appear to be intruding into his personal affairs. On the other hand I was genuinely concerned about both his and Lana's well-being.

I asked if he had any news from home, if he had talked with Lana in the last few days. He stared at the wake for a few moments and responded that he had been too caught up in the investigation to worry her.

"Scott, when we get back to the boat," I said, "I want you to get the cellular, go to the sea cabin, and dial that thing until you get her. You'll feel better, she needs to hear your voice, and I'll feel better. It's not helping her to have the other wives sharing at least the little we can tell and hear zip from you."

He grinned and agreed to make the call. That was the first smile I had seen on his face in a long time. Sharon told me later that his call seemed to be a tonic for Lana, and firsthand I could see that it was a boost for Scott.

On board, Dennis wanted to talk about how best to approach my testimony. He thought I would be called in the next day or so. My options were a written statement for the record, a combination of a written statement and verbal testimony, or strictly verbal comments. He took pains to be sure I understood the ramifications of each choice.

"If you go written only, you can only be questioned on the content of the statement. If you make a verbal statement the board can question you on your comments. If you want to ensure a complete line of thought is included in the record, I recommend a written statement. The rest is up to you. Your call."

I had been worrying about Admiral Fogarty's concern with my silence. I felt bottled up. "Dennis, I'm going with the big combo. I've got some thoughts I want to put on paper, but I also want to respond to any question they've got. On top of that I've got my own tutorial I want to give these people on a couple of points. I'd like to try to tie this whole thing together so they see it as a tactical package. Everything to date chops the whole mess into little pieces. I think it needs to be put together into one sack."

"Will, I told you this one is your call. I tend to agree with you, but I want to go over anything you plan to say. In other words, keep the emotion out of it."

As I went out the door I said to him, "Good luck on me keeping my comments unemotional. Unemotional ain't me!"

I walked to the forepeak of the ship and stared down at the anchor chain, turning over these comments in my mind. I knew what I wanted to say, and regardless of what came in the next few days of testimony I intended to say it. Sitting mute while my every action was scrutinized under a microscope had left me frustrated. I felt a lot better knowing I would have my turn at the rudder.

When we arrived at the ASU the next morning, Commander John Kierley, the commanding officer of the Elmer Montgomery, was standing with his CIC team in the foyer. I pulled him aside, told him that the Monty had done a great job, and recapped the surface-gunnery trace for him. In that hectic melee of rapidly maneuvering and closing contacts, the Montgomery had fired forty-seven rounds from her single deck gun. I was positive the effort had been effective in disrupting whatever the IRG boats were trying.

He thanked me and said, "We were awful glad to see you guys show up that morning. It looked like we had our hands full." He said he didn't think the people from the Montgomery could add much to the testimony. They had not had radar contact on the Airbus until it was practically on top of them, and with the haze his bridge people hadn't seen anything but a flash and smoke trails from the missiles.

I shrugged and shook his hand. "Tell 'em what you saw and call it as you saw it. Every grain helps put the picture together."

The principal players on watch in the Coronado's flag plot on the morning of the third were scheduled to testify first. As the inquiry resumed, Dick Watkins, who was to go first, had to return to the flagship, so staff intelligence officer Captain Dave Houghton led off. Since our arrival in the Gulf Captain Houghton had been our prime point of contact for intelligence matters. I had a lot of respect for him. Tall and quiet, he had always struck me as a pro, unflappable and straightforward. His assessments and the steady stream of information he had provided in the last months had been accurate and helpful.

When he took the stand he made a detailed statement concerning the various indicators and assessments the staff had received regarding the intensity of IRG small-craft activity on 2 and 3 July. He recapped the activities of his people as they monitored the IRG harassment of the transiting merchant ship and the attack on Oceanlord. In his opinion, the Iranians had their backs to the wall politically and economically. The increase in hostility was probably an attempt to shift the focus of the population away from the reverses of the long conflict with Iraq.

Fogarty asked if Admiral Less's staff had received indicators of increased Iranian military air activity on the morning of the third. Houghton replied that none had been received, but he didn't find it unusual that the on-scene unit might notice something before his people had a "heads-up." He clarified this by pointing out that moving airplanes was a lot faster than moving a division of troops, and that real-time notice of air activity was often fed back by units in the area. He had questioned, however, what "the Vincennes was basing their F-14 call on." He "asked the chief of staff who was on the radio to the ship what F-14 indicators were being reported and was told that Vincennes had held a contact squawking mode II, 1100, and mode III, 6675, on the inbound course, descending from 7,800 feet at an airspeed of 425–75 knots. They did not hold any electronic emissions from an AWG-9 [a radar type carried by the F-14], and commair schedules did not show a flight scheduled for that time of day from Bandar Abbas."

He was asked if he felt the lack of radar-signal intercept was significant and confirmed what we had noticed numerous times: Iranian military aircraft often flew with radars silent. A check by his people of commercial schedules had shown no correlation.

Houghton had been tasked previously by Admiral Fogarty to determine the number of radio challenges made by Gulf units over the last several months to aircraft and what the ratio of civilian to military had been. His findings, I thought, were pretty significant. Since late April, approximately 180 challenges had been made, and of these only two had been identified as commercial. Several erroneous comments had appeared in the press that Gulf forces had been threatening everything in the air.

Houghton was asked his opinion regarding the general performance of the *Vincennes* intelligence team. He replied, "They are as good as any I've worked with, as a matter of fact the feedback from the *Vincennes* electronic warfare and intelligence people has been a big help in improving the picture."

As he was excused, I wrote a note to Dennis, "Up or down?" He scribbled back, "Good background. Fogarty knows the picture from the flagship is limited as hell!"

The next individual called was Lieutenant Commander Jim Ward, an A-7 and F/A-18 attack pilot who was the staff strike-operations officer. He stated that on 3 July he had been late relieving the flag watch officer, as the chief of staff did not want turnover occurring in the middle of military activity. The OTCIXS (officer in tactical command, information-exchange system) was not operating for the first thirty minutes of his watch, and watch team confidence in the flag plot JOTS (joint operational tactical system) display of the tactical picture was poor.

> The small boats demonstrated aggressive behavior, and the situation developed until Oceanlord reported being fired upon by a group of small boats at 0910. This led to engagement of the boats by the *Vincennes* and *Montgomery* at 0940. At 0943 Admiral Less ordered CAP [combat air patrol] and SUCAP [surface combat air patrol] to be established. I passed this to Charlie Bravo [the *Forrestal* carrier battle group commander, Rear Admiral Smith]. They informed us that the *Vincennes* had requested Fury Fez, and that two F-14s, an A-6, and an A-7 were en route and an E-2 was being launched.

Commander Ward then recapped the track and engagement sequence of TN 4131.

> Throughout . . . my perception was that USS *Vincennes* had good reason to assume identification as an F-14, either through previous ID, ESM, squawk, or other means.
>
> Having just visited *Vincennes* on 23 June, and personally discussing deconfliction of commercial air with the commanding officer, I was confident track 4131 was indeed a hostile, and probably an F-14. Another thing, no one knows what weapons the Iranians may have on

their F-14s and allowing an Iranian to close to visual identification range is tactically a poor decision.

Fogarty then asked what the watch's evaluation of TN 4133 had been. "We discussed its slow speed and constant climb," replied Ward, "and thought it might be a P-3 or commair, and Captain Watkins called 'weapons tight' and told the *Vincennes* to ensure the tight call was passed to the *Sides*. I believe it turned away."

He recalled that after the missile engagement the watch was involved in trying to reconstruct information, getting an air force KC-10 tanker launched to support the CAP and ensuring that the *Forrestal* kept the CAP/SUCAP up until further notice.

Admiral Less's deputy commander, air force Brigadier General Walter Worthington, was scheduled next but had been delayed along with Watkins on the flagship. Fogarty decided to recess until he arrived.

After the room cleared, I told Dennis that the size and composition of the *Forrestal*'s launch package and the request for air force tanker support was news to me. "I thought they had only put a section of F-14s up," I said. "The SUCAP and tanker were a good call." The *Forrestal* had reacted quickly, but the geometry of the problem was simply too hard. Time and distance wiped out any chance the aircraft might have had of arriving before the whole event was over.

General Worthington arrived shortly and the hearing was called to order. He didn't have much to add, as he had not been in flag plot during most of the action. When he arrived the watch seemed to have things in hand. "I was given a short situation brief," he said. "Admiral Less asked me to coordinate getting one of our KC-10s airborne to support the aircraft carrier CAP/SUCAP package. I returned to my cabin to make the necessary phone calls. When I returned . . . the public affairs officer told me that an Iranian commercial airliner, Flight 655, was overdue at Dubai. . . ."

Captain Watkins still couldn't get away, and with a lot of ground to cover and a lobby full of people waiting to testify, Admiral Fogarty decided to proceed. Commander Earl Shaut, the air operations officer for the staff, was next to take the stand. On the morning of 3 July he had been preparing to assume the watch as staff command duty officer, but the rapidly unfolding events had also delayed his turnover. All he added to the testimony was that when the *Vincennes* had reported the aircraft at twenty-eight miles "and intended to take it under fire at twenty miles, they had less than one minute to solve the problem. Our picture was pretty dependent on what *Vincennes* could provide and her reports of the plane's profile, the IFF code received . . . [N]o response to her warnings were what we had to go on."

The thread clearly emerging from these various comments showed that the flagship depended on information being relayed to it. The staff simply was not equipped to deal effectively with fast-breaking situations.

I scribbled a note to Dennis, "*Everything* we provided is an *issue!*" He read the note and wadded it up.

The testimony of the next two individuals, Ron Winfrey, the staff lawyer, and Lieutenant Commander Chris Nichols, staff duty officer, recapped events as they had seen them and continued to underscore how the staff response to the situation was almost completely determined by the information the *Vincennes* provided.

Fogarty then called for a recess and a conference with the lawyers. There were a number of staff watchstanders yet to be heard. As they had not been in decision-making positions, Fogarty felt little would be gained from their formal testimony. It was apparent from their written statements that we were going to hear the same information endlessly repeated. He asked counsel if anyone objected to simply having the sworn statements of the watch team entered into the record. These people could be called any time one of the parties thought it necessary. Everyone readily agreed.

In other words Fogarty, as well as the rest of us, wanted to hear from the major players as soon as possible. Watkins was still not available, which put Commander John Kierley and his *Montgomery* people next.

I anticipated that this portion of the testimony would go quickly and have little bearing. I was pretty sure Kierley had been correct when he commented that except for the surface action, they hadn't seen much. Insight into the shootdown would have to come from the *Vincennes* and the *Sides*. I was wrong.

Kierley did not confine his statement to air activity. Instead he provided a detailed account of the *Montgomery*'s involvement commencing about two in the morning. Assigned to patrol the merchant lanes to the south and west of the Strait of Hormuz, they had noticed increasing numbers of small craft departing the waters around the

Iranian-controlled island of Abu Musa. As the number grew to thirteen, and the craft began to move in the direction of inbound merchant traffic, "it began to feel pretty lonely." The small boats then closed and began challenging the Norwegian tanker *Karama Maersk*. After radio discussions with the *Maersk* and Admiral Less's staff, the *Montgomery* was directed to fire a warning shot in the general direction of, but on a safe bearing away from, the small boats.

"We did it," Kierley said, "and I was relieved to see them appear to break off and head toward Omani waters. Then, about five-thirty, they returned and started harassing two other merchants. I was glad Golf Sierra [commander, Destroyer Squadron 25] decided to send the *Vincennes* to our position."

Following questioning pertinent to small-craft activity, Kierley commented, "The *Vincennes* was closing when I received a report from the bridge that several explosions had been heard in the direction of her helo. After that things moved pretty quickly, and when the small boats began to close, we engaged as directed by *Vincennes*."

The *Montgomery* was moving at high speed, responding to course orders being passed by the *Vincennes* and "trying to stay on the closest targets. We didn't have a radar contact on the aircraft until it was about nine miles away.

"When the *Vincennes* fired we could see smoke trails and a flash. The bridge seemed to think the plane hit was gray, but we couldn't make out much. In any case, we were busy with the surface engagement."

That comment, "busy with the surface engagement," exploded in my mind. I didn't even hear the rest of Kierley's testimony. The shootdown, necessarily the central issue of this whole mess, was nonetheless part and parcel of our running gun battle with those boats. That scenario had really driven the issue.

Taken alone, the aircraft departing Bandar Abbas and acting in its oddball way might very well have been sorted out differently if it hadn't fit so neatly into the ongoing problem. I couldn't wait for a recess. I wanted to explore this point with Dennis.

As Kierley completed his testimony, Dick Watkins arrived. After a brief whispered conversation with Admiral Less, the latter requested that Watkins's testimony be heard immediately, as he was needed back aboard the *Coronado*. This request was granted.

Watkins had been on the circuit with us on 3 July and was the direct relay for Less's orders. He was an important link in the picture; his comments would help to put things in perspective.

Watkins has a phenomenal capacity for recalling details, and his statement seemed to hit all the points. He indicated he had been called to flag plot about six-thirty when the Montgomery engaged with Iranian gunboats apparently preparing to attack merchant traffic. "When additional traffic entered the area," he said, "Golf Sierra ordered the Vincennes operating to the southwest to proceed to the Montgomery's vicinity. The Montgomery was not link-capable and I told Golf Sierra to have the Vincennes position her helo in the vicinity so we could get a better picture. About an hour or so later the situation looked like it was defusing. I was satisfied with the situation and left plot."

He recalled that about an hour later, the watch called him and told him Oceanlord had been fired on. "I arrived in plot about the same time as the admiral and we assessed the situation. After ascertaining that the small boats were not breaking off, were maneuvering erratically and closing the Vincennes, I relayed from the admiral his permission for the contacts to be engaged with guns.

"The admiral wanted things tightened up and directed the Vincennes to take tactical command of both the Montgomery and the Sides.

"There was a lot of chatter on the execution net and we wanted a single relay point. While we were trying to sort out the surface engagement, the Vincennes reported a closing Iranian F-14 and their intent to engage if it did not heed warnings. As directed by Admiral Less, I told the Vincennes to first warn the aircraft and then fire. I repeated this and she acknowledged."

The staff considered the aircraft a probable threat, Watkins commented, but had no indication themselves of Iranian air activity.

Following this statement Admiral Fogarty asked Watkins if he had confidence in the Vincennes. At this point I was full of self-doubt, and Watkins's reply was a boost. "She's a squared-away ship. Her response to any tasking has always been professional. We've given her some tough assignments and we could count on things being done right—the first time."

It had been a long morning. Everyone was visibly relieved when we recessed for lunch. Dennis and I went to the cafeteria to talk. The first thing I wanted was his gut reaction to the testimony that morning.

"First, Will, I think it provided a good feel for the flagship's isolation. Second, they aren't any better at crystal-balling a situation than you are and obviously had questions for which real-time answers weren't available. The meat of this will come from the *Vincennes* and possibly the *Sides*, but it's my guess that the *Sides* had only a piece of the picture."

I felt as if someone had been working on my nerves with a wood file all morning. My reply reflected my mood. "We didn't have the whole picture, either. If we had I wouldn't be standing up to my ass in this sandpile living my worst nightmare. The questions they had on the flagship are a bit after the fact, but every damn question in the cold light of day makes it look like we didn't have it together!"

McCoy exploded. "Damn it! I'm telling you one last time. You, me, them . . . no one can afford to take little bits of this and stand it alone. I don't have a sense that this is happening . . . so get the hell off it!"

Wisely, we decided to walk our emotion off before the afternoon show started. We proceeded along the seawall without saying much. After a half hour we had cooled off, and as we reconvened there was a sense of anticipation in the room that I hadn't felt before.

9

—◇◇◇—

FRONT AND CENTER

In adversity remember to keep an even mind.

—Horace, *Odes*, 23 B.C.

BAHRAIN

The background was on the table. Now it was time for testimony from the front line.

Commander David Carlson, skipper of the *Sides*, was called first. Most of the people on the stand had seemed uncomfortable, which was not surprising. This was not the set of circumstances any of them would normally encounter. Carlson, however, looked more angry than nervous. His opening statement was clipped and straightforward.

He indicated that on 3 July the *Sides*, returning to the Gulf from an escort mission, had monitored radio communications between the *Montgomery*, the *Vincennes*, and Golf Sierra concerning Boghammer activity and the "sound of explosions." The *Sides* had been directed to close and had gone to general quarters with all topside small-arms stations manned.

> I proceeded to CIC to monitor developments. A radio conversation had been heard between *Vincennes* and Golf Sierra reporting that *Vincennes*'s helo believed it had been fired at by one of the boats being investigated. Shortly . . . we monitored a conversation . . . during which *Vincennes* requested permission to take the small-boat tracks with guns.

At that point I directed the executive officer to come up on the 1MC and inform the crew of a potential for action.

By this time *Vincennes* had been directed to take tactical control of *Sides*. Shortly thereafter, the TAO brought track 4131 to my attention, informed me that *Vincennes* had designated it as an Iranian F-14, and we had a solid . . . radar contact which corresponded.

The TAO assigned fire-control radar to the track and locked on. While he was doing this I noticed the altitude readout . . . was approximately 7,000 feet and climbing, speed 350 knots, course two-one-zero degrees true. The TAO directed the use of CWI [continuous-wave illumination] from the fire-control radar.

I inquired twice . . . if any electronic emitters had been noted. Twice he answered in the negative. I inquired if *Sides* had tried to warn off the aircraft. The TAO answered that unsuccessful attempts had been made to communicate and [attempts] . . . were continuing. I further noted that the use of CWI did not cause the aircraft to change course. I further noted that it was a crossing target which appeared to have a CPA [closest point of approach] of several miles.

At this point, based on the information I had available, I evaluated track 4131 as a nonthreat to *Sides*. This evaluation was based on CPA, F-14 . . . weapons capability, lack of emissions, and precedent. At this point I noted the altitude had increased to 11,000 feet. I shifted my attention to other contacts including an Iranian P-3. Shortly . . . the TAO announced *Vincennes*'s intent to fire on track 4131 at twenty miles.

As he completed these remarks Admiral Fogarty asked, "Did you pass your evaluation of the track to the *Vincennes*?" Carlson replied in the negative, stating in effect that he felt the *Vincennes* had the same picture of the situation as the *Sides*.

Fogarty held a brief whispered conversation with the board, then continued with a number of questions relating to the *Sides*'s experiences with commercial air operating procedures in the Gulf, and Carlson's opinion of the general situation in the area. A portion of his reply caused an audible stir in the room when he commented that although he had had command less than a month, he didn't find operating in the Persian Gulf much different from operating in the southern California exercise area.

Fogarty wryly asked if he had ever encountered any mines off Long Beach. Carlson appeared angry and answered with a clipped "no." Fogarty stopped the questioning, remarking, "Captain, this is a fact-finding procedure. Neither you nor anyone else in the room is on trial. Would you like to take a break before continuing?" Carlson declined, but his replies continued in the same vein until he was excused.

As Carlson left the room, Dennis looked at me, shook his head, and grimaced. To my right I noticed Ron Swanson and Scott Lustig sliding notes back and forth. I wondered why Carlson was so defensive. The only portion of his testimony that had raised eyebrows was his failure to pass on his evaluation of the air track.

Next up was the *Sides*'s TAO, Lieutenant Richard Thomas, USNR, who summarized the picture as he had seen it.

> I noted the track coming out of Bandar Abbas.... [I]t continued inbound toward *Vincennes*. During this time I directed the WCO [weapons control officer] to lock on ... the aircraft with the fire-control radar and illuminate it. At this time the aircraft was on a southwesterly course at approximately 400 knots at about 10,000 feet. I directed the track supervisor to attempt to establish comms with the aircraft on military air distress ... but was told *Vincennes* was attempting to establish comms.
>
> The entire sequence of events from detection to splash took ... eight to ten minutes. During the engagement in question at no time was I informed of the possibility that the aircraft was anything but an Iranian F-14. We locked up on track 4133, but after we called birds affirm, Golf Bravo and Golf Whiskey evaluated it as a nonthreat and gave us weapons tight on the track.
>
> I do recall that *Sides*'s electronic warfare module had no emissions. However, with the reports provided by *Vincennes* I did not have any reason to doubt their evaluation. I recall *Vincennes* made several attempts to contact the aircraft.
>
> Bottom line is I relied upon *Vincennes*'s evaluation, and since my own sensors and console operators reported nothing to counter ... I felt that given the current tactical situation—that is, *Vincennes* and Montgomery under fire after *Vincennes*'s helo had been fired on, and events in the Arabian gulf since *Sides*'s arrival—in fact, this was an Iranian F-14 demonstrating hostile intent.

Lieutenant Thomas was questioned several times as to whether he had passed any information on TN 4131 to the *Vincennes*. Finally he replied, "We called her Robocruiser [since] she always seemed to have a picture, so I don't recall passing anything."

Fogarty asked him if the term Robocruiser was used in a positive or negative sense.

"Well, negative. She always seemed to be telling everybody to get on or off the link as though her picture was better."

There was another audible stir in the room. I was twisting a pencil in my hands and without thinking snapped it in half.

The testimony of these two individuals had taken some time, and I thought we might recess briefly. But Fogarty appeared to want to move ahead without delay. The view of the commanding officer and his TAO were important, but the comments of the sailors at the *Sides*'s air-tracking consoles would fill gaps and provide valuable background.

The picture of a developing tactical situation is supplied by the watch team; it is their input that builds the base for decisions. Exploring this link was obviously the direction Fogarty wanted to pursue, and certainly the reason that my entire CIC team was milling around in the recreation room lobby.

The first *Sides* watch team member called was the air-tracker/detector supervisor who had overseen the activities of the people on the scopes. "I was assisting the air tracker," he began,

> and breaking IFF . . . when I observed [that] an assumed enemy track . . . reported by Golf Whiskey was on a southwest heading. We challenged the contact, and its IFF broke at 7,000 feet with a mode III of 6707, which I interpreted as an Iranian HAJ flight.
>
> I remember reporting to the weapons-control officer and the commanding officer that the contact was climbing 200 feet for every sweep of the radar. We had designated the contact as commair and tried unsuccessfully to establish comms on international air distress.
>
> I yelled out that this looked like a commair flight. I think someone acknowledged, but I was told to shut up as I was making too much noise. To me, the contact was profiled as a recently airborne HAJ flight and was identified in our CIC as such. . . . I was totally surprised when it was actually engaged.

The board seemed to want confirmation of the air supervisor's comments. After questioning him briefly, they called one of the *Sides* officers who had been standing in the vicinity of the trackers. TN 4131, he commented, "was identified as . . . Iranian F-14. Noise level in combat started to get louder as this was repeated. . . . The TAO yelled out, 'Everyone quiet down' and 'Remain calm.' . . . I . . . recall the track supervisor yelling, 'Contact is rising 100 feet per sweep.' I verified this. . . . As I completed this, the noise level was . . . again rising and I went over and ordered personnel in the vicinity of the air trackers to shut up, . . . trying to reduce excess noise."

The remainder of the *Sides* testimony repeated much of this. Scott's lawyer slid a note over to mine: "At break, we need to talk recall. It's time to rack these guys up!" Dennis had no sooner wadded up the slip than Fogarty declared a thirty-minute recess, indicating that when we resumed the *Vincennes* general-quarters watch would be called. As the room cleared Dennis motioned to Lohr, Guillory, Swanson, and Lustig to remain behind. A discussion of the *Sides* testimony kicked off at once.

"Here's how I see it," Swanson said. "The *Sides* assumed away her responsibility to share information with the guy in charge. Whether that information was accepted by the *Vincennes* or not, she should have passed it on."

No one disagreed with this, but what could we do about it? There were two options: recall selected witnesses and beat the obvious to death, or simply let the testimony speak for itself. After considerable debate we arrived at a consensus to let it go rather than engage in finger pointing. We all realized by this time that no one point could unravel our case. Any attempt to challenge the *Sides* testimony would be wrong.

Since the three principals, Guillory, Lustig, and myself, would not testify until later, the *Vincennes* commentary would start with Rick Foster and work through the bridge and CIC watch teams. When Rick was sworn in, he appeared nervous. Normally self-assured and anything but shy, he acted withdrawn and uncomfortable. As exec, his general-quarters station was on the bridge, where he was responsible for overseeing the safe navigation of the ship and ensuring that all battle stations were properly manned. He had not been in the CIC during the action on 3 July, and his observations were restricted to what he had seen on the surface.

Other than the single small craft that had passed between the *Vincennes* and the *Montgomery* with her occupants lying in the bilge, and the incoming shell splashes, his view consisted of shadowy forms maneuvering through the gauzelike air. His comments, nervously delivered, were nevertheless detailed and dramatic. I slid a note to Dennis as Rick spoke: "Rick's description is right on. We were like a blindfolded bear fighting off rats!"

As exec, Rick wore the hat of shipboard training officer. This required him to plan and oversee all on- and off-ship training and have it properly documented. Admiral Fogarty questioned him at length about every detail of our program. For some reason this line of questioning seemed to further unnerve Rick, and his responses were incomplete. The ship had a solid program—Captain John Kieley, as well as message traffic from commander, Navy Suface Forces, Pacific, and commander in chief, Pacific Fleet, had underscored this—and Rick had been its principal author.

I scribbled another in the growing stream of notes to Dennis. "Damn it! *Foster ran the program.* Now it sounds like he never heard of it!" Dennis slid one back: "Better comments from outsiders."

Following Rick's lengthy testimony, we began hearing from a parade of people whose stations had been on the bridge and topside. None of the statements took much time, as what these men had seen and heard was limited. From Lieutenant Bill Johnson, who had been general-quarters officer of the deck, down to the lookouts, all painted a picture of professionalism, each man having concentrated on his particular job. There was a light moment when the signal-bridge recorder was asked what he had seen. "Not a thing," he replied. "When I saw those shell splashes I hit the deck!" The whole room erupted in laughter.

Following a short break, the CIC team began their testimony. Of all the comments made so far theirs would be the most critical. Seated at consoles and passing information through the various communications nets, they had been at the core of the action. It was their skill at operating the complex Aegis system and interpreting information that had formed the base for numerous decisions.

The air engagement was the portion of the scenario under greatest scrutiny. The important air information had come from two positions, the identification supervisor (IDS), Petty Officer Richard Anderson, and the tactical information coordinator (TIC), Petty Officer John Leach. There were many others who contributed to our understanding of the situation and ultimately to actions taken as events unfolded, but Anderson and Leach were focal points.

Anderson was a "plankowner," a member of the original commissioning crew, and the most experienced IDS on board. As he took the stand, his opening statement reflected the poise and confidence I had come to expect of him: "TN 4474 was initially assigned to an aircraft departing Bandar Abbas. I interrogated it and picked up a mode III, code 6675 IFF. I hit it again and received a mode II, code 1100, and the same mode III 6675. I checked, and the mode II had been used previously by an F-14 out of Bandar."

How had he known the mode II code had been used before? "Sir, I kept a list at the console of ones we had seen and IFF breaks reported by other ships."

He was asked if he had taken any other action and how he had relayed his information. "I passed over the net, 'Possible F-14.' The net was busy so I called over to the TAO off the net to make sure he heard me. I think the intelligence guys also said it was a possible F-14. I checked the commercial flight information in the Fleet Intell Center message and it showed no match. I couldn't find anything which looked close enough to fit."

Anderson was asked to describe the Airbus flight profile. "When I first interrogated, it was climbing and just crossing the commair route center off Bandar. When we engaged, it was doing about 400 to 450 knots at an altitude of 7,000 feet and descending. It never followed the commair route."

Admiral Fogarty asked him if he was sure of the engagement altitude and speed, as the system data did not agree. "Sir, that's what I saw at my console and that's what I reported."

Anderson was asked numerous questions regarding the position of his IFF interrogation box.

"Was it positioned off Bandar Abbas?"

"Yes, sir!"

"Did you reorient the box?"

"I don't remember, but I don't think so."

"How long did it take to check the commercial flight info message?"

"Not long."

"Could you have made a mistake?"

"I don't think so; it's broken into time blocks, not hard to interpret."

These were followed by repeated questions pertaining to the aircraft flight path. He was sure of what he had seen.

Next up was Petty Officer Leach, who as TIC had a hand-in-glove relationship with IDS. As Leach spoke, the combined picture as seen by him and Anderson clearly emerged:

> The 5-inch mounts had opened fire on the group of patrol boats. Approximately three minutes later we detected an aircraft launch from Bandar Abbas. At the same time the P-3 to the west, at seventy-five miles, turned inbound. After launch from Bandar Abbas, the aircraft was designated as assumed enemy per our standing orders. He turned directly inbound toward *Vincennes*. He was about forty-four miles away.
>
> I passed the identification "Possible Padre" [Iranian F-4] on TN 4474 over the AAW coordination and reporting net due to the launch time closely coinciding with our engagement with the patrol boats.
>
> After we got the mode II break, I passed a new identification, "Astro" [Iranian F-14], on the track, which at this time, due to auto-correlation, had changed to 4131.
>
> I called Astro based on intell space on the net saying, "That track is possibly an F-14," and my IDS saying, "I have a mode II, 1100 on that track, which also correlates to an F-14."

As the board questioned Leach about his comments, I slid another note to Dennis. "I don't remember any calls from the intell space, but unless the spook supervisor called me on the secure phone, I probably would have missed it."

Dennis scribbled back, "Those intell relay comments are in the written statements. The super says he didn't pass anything but somebody did—lots of stations heard it."

Meanwhile Leach continued: "At twenty-eight miles we had no response to MAD or IAD warnings, and these stations were ordered to continue warnings. I remember each station reporting back, 'No response.' The aircraft maintained a heading directly toward us and was never above 11,000 feet.

"His speed was between 360 and 450 knots. At fourteen miles an illumination order was sent but the aircraft maintained course."

Leach paused for a moment, then with a note of finality in his voice said, "At eleven nautical miles the aircraft started descending at a rate of a thousand feet per mile. [When it was] at nine miles and 9,000 feet, the missiles left the rail. . . . They . . . intercepted at about seven miles and 8,000 feet."

Leach's voice was steady as he finished, but from across the room I could see tears in his eyes.

Though it was approaching midafternoon, Admiral Fogarty was intent on taking as much testimony as possible before closing the day. Following a brief recess, the now-familiar process resumed. A witness would be summoned and sworn in; he would tender his statement and respond to a variety of questions. Then Fogarty would admonish him to remain silent outside the inquiry about the content of his statement and dismiss him—always with a polite thank you for his cooperation.

As my people came and went, the threads of their statements began to weave a single picture. I could almost shut my eyes and see the morning of 3 July unfolding in slow motion.

—Our aircraft was in a port turn when [the crew] called and said they were being shot at. The pilot said he saw about ten or twelve bursts and sparks coming from the boats.

—We fired one round forward, but the small boats kept closing and the bridge reported shell splashes. We were steering evasively and splitting our fires on the tracks. We had a casualty on mount 51 and had to complete the engagement with the after mount.

—We were engaged in a firefight when this aircraft started heading right for us. I hooked him and his altitude was 10,000 feet, 300 knots. About two minutes later I hooked him again; this time he was 8,000 feet and up to 400 knots.

—To determine the size of an aircraft by analyzing the . . . scope display is impossible, but . . . the target dropped in altitude to 5,000 or 6,000 feet at twelve miles and directly inbound. I feel we responded properly.

—I was asked if we had emissions on the contact at least four times; each time I replied negative. We sure as hell had some from the F-4s that came out, but we broke their lock.

—When the aircraft lifted off I tried to report the contact to the

SUCAP, but no joy. The aircraft did not respond to warnings. We splashed the contact at six to seven miles; he was north-northeast inbound, altitude low, mode II and mode III. Afterward there was another launch from Bandar Abbas. Electronic warfare supervisor reported he tried to lock us up several times, but we broke his scan.

—We started to try to communicate with this guy at approximately forty miles and tried to illuminate at about twenty miles. I don't know if we were successful. Things were moving fast. At impact, the target was six to seven miles away at about 7,000 feet, something over 400 knots.

—When I took first look at the contact over Bandar Abbas, he was tracking northeast in a starboard turn between 250 and 300 knots. I took five looks. I noted between third and fourth looks target was descending and increasing in speed according to my display. At missile intercept he was tracking toward the *Montgomery* at 400 to 450 knots, about 8,000 feet.

—I heard a direction to initiate illumination, but I didn't get the alert. I kept hitting "Request radiation assign" but getting "Alert ineligible." I think we finally assigned about twenty miles, but I don't remember for sure.

—After I saw my fire-authorization flash, I asked AAW coordinator if I had a take order, just to make sure. He said, "Take." After launch I didn't monitor the range, just the speed. It was 437 knots, then at intercept it went to 0 pretty quick. From the first time I hooked the track I never saw much course change, just a drop in altitude. I recall it dropping at twenty miles when we were trying to illuminate.

—I only saw a mode III. I jumped up and said "Possible commair, possible commair" to Mr. Lustig and the commanding officer. Both seemed to acknowledge.

—I kept challenging over international air distress, which was my job, but nothing was heard.

—The last altitude I observed was 9,000 feet. I remember feeling the engagement had to be made due to the closure profile and the ongoing surface engagement.

—The small boats were keeping us busy on the surface side. I didn't pay any attention to anything else. I was busy coordinating firing bearings with the *Montgomery*. Then I heard the missiles go off.

—The P-3 responded to my challenge, but I never got anything from the inbound. TAO told me to keep challenging as he got closer. I was adding as much information as I could.

It was after six-thirty when the final *Vincennes* witness was excused. I felt physically and emotionally drained, as I'm sure everyone else did.

Admiral Fogarty stood and announced that the proceedings were closed for the day and would remain in recess through the following day, reconvening Monday morning. He asked the counsels if their clients would be prepared to testify at that point. Each indicated that his would be ready.

10

—◆◇◆—

UNSHACKLED

Go forth to meet the Shadowy Future, without fear. . . .
—Longfellow, Hyperion, 1839

Monday morning was long in coming. I spent most of the time reviewing with Dennis the course of the inquiry so far and arranging and rearranging my statement. This was my shot, and it had to be right on. I wanted my comments to capture events as I had seen them and reflect what I felt the ground truth of the investigation now showed.

After the latest recess there was almost no interaction between Scott Lustig, Vic Guillory, and myself. I had insisted on this approach, and they agreed. I wanted to make sure the board heard three viewpoints. A lockstep, united front would serve no one well.

As we took our places, the atmosphere in the ASU library was electric. This was it.

Admiral Less led off and elected to have his counsel, Ron Winfrey, read his remarks into the record. These recapped the events as he had seen them unfold from the flagship. His description of the feverish activity in flag plot as the watch there tried to sort out incoming information and provide command direction was crisp and graphic. He recalled the situation in the Gulf in late June and early July and underscored Dick Watkins's earlier comments.

Less's statement was brief and to the point. A general discussion followed that dealt with the flagship's tactical display capability. This was acknowledged to be pretty slim.

Vic Guillory apparently wanted to review his statement with his attorney, Commander Lohr, and a recess was requested. Hypersensitive to every comment, I took the opportunity to huddle with Dennis. Then Vic was sworn in. His statement concentrated on the surface firefight. He felt that his direct involvement with the air scenario had been limited, but that the picture he had seen and the track data warranted taking on the aircraft. As he covered these points, his emotions seemed to bubble to the surface. He was having a tough time even reading his statement.

Should he have recommended a "No engage" to Lustig and me? He paused and in a barely audible voice said, "Hindsight is clear, but I thought we had the picture and at the moment it seemed right."

The emotional impact on Vic had been dramatic. Now I was concerned about Scott Lustig's reaction. He had been on a mental roller coaster for days, and I was worried that he might stray from a purely factual account and go off on a mea culpa tangent.

My fears didn't materialize. Scott bootstrapped his way through. Although his voice had a forced, determined inflection, he described the developing situation concisely. He regretted not taking TN 4131 under close control at his console, but commented, "Even if I had, I'm not sure I wouldn't have made the same recommendation to the skipper."

Admiral Fogarty asked him how many times he recalled hooking the track. He replied, "About three, but I don't remember hooking inside twenty miles. Things were moving fast. I was talking to commander, Middle East Forces, and trying to make sure we had illuminated."

Scott was asked if he queried electronic warfare to see if they had anything. "I remember asking at least three times. The commanding officer kept pushing me to ask. It was negative each time, but I didn't think that was unusual."

In the case of Admiral Less, Vic, and Scott, the board simply accepted their statements, asked a few questions, and appeared satisfied. I whispered to Dennis as we rose for a break, "I think they're saving all their questions for me."

He grinned. "Don't get paranoid on me."

During the recess I took my now regular seawall stroll. I wanted to get a grip on my emotions and mull over what I thought I might have to respond to. This was going to be the bottom line.

After the recess, Dennis made a brief comment to the effect that I would read a statement for the record and then respond to questions. The first portion of my statement consisted of a detailed rehash of our predeployment training. I explained the modifications we had made to the watch structure to accommodate the unique operating environment of the Gulf. All of these points had been visited in previous testimony. However, Dennis and I had agreed it wouldn't hurt to emphasize the intensive preparatory effort. I wanted the board to see the *Vincennes* as a pro outfit, not a loose cannon.

As I reached the end of these preliminary comments I was in danger of losing my composure. Fogarty asked if I wanted a brief recess. But I shook my head and continued, aware of Dennis gently squeezing my arm under the table.

From the instant of rail departure until this moment, numbers of people, ranging from those eminently qualified professionally and technically to those considerably less so, have dissected a four-minute time frame in the life of a ship and her crew. In many cases, ... this is subdivided into a thousandth of a second. This is certainly a tribute to the ability of our navy to develop a technological warfighting masterpiece—able to fight and win in almost any conceivable war-at-sea scenario.

However, I urge the board, as we sit surrounded by the masses of extracted data, to remember that although *Vincennes* is a marvelous machine, she is only that—a machine. She is maintained, sailed, and if need be, fought by men, and these same men must process and communicate rapidly developing, time-critical information so that one man, the commanding officer, can exercise his judgment in order to fight and defend his ship. This latter process is no different aboard an Aegis cruiser than [aboard] yesterday's sailing ship of the line; certainly the implements are different, but the process remains the same.

The critical difference, of course, is the time factor. Instead of hours to sail to the weather gauge, this decision process is now, at best, measured in minutes. Accordingly, we have developed a technological masterpiece to manage this compression of time. However, as I think we have demonstrated during the course of this hearing, if small, unnoticed, but critical elements fail to perform as expected, the information flow to the commanding officer can be faulted.

Regardless, the decision must be made and, as commanding officer, I am fully responsible and accountable for the decision. I deeply regret the outcome, but not the decision.

Vincennes's role in the Gulf has been air surveillance, link management, Silkworm defense of high Earnest Will transits, and in view of Aegis capabilities, surveillance of the Strait of Hormuz. Since our arrival the ship has operated extensively in the SOHWPA [Strait of Hormuz, western patrol area]. I consider that *Vincennes* was exceptionally well prepared for these tasks.

Until approximately two weeks prior to the engagement in question, F-14s had not been active in the Strait of Hormuz area. Following their appearance, *Vincennes* had been monitoring these as well as other flights of interest for their intelligence value in close concert with CJTFME [commander, Joint Task Force, Middle East].

During the period preceding the 1 July *Vincennes* escort of USS *Samuel B. Roberts*, Iranian surface and air activity in the Strait of Hormuz and SOHWPA had increased, including operations by one of the SAAM [Iranian] FFGs in the vicinity of Dubai. Additionally, IRG navy small craft in the vicinity of Abu Musa and the Strait of Hormuz were quite active. Although intelligence information had been received which indicated the possibility of heightened activity during the Fourth of July period, no extraordinary modification to the ship's readiness posture was made.

Early on the morning of the third, *Vincennes* was notified by GS [Golf Sierra] that USS *Elmer Montgomery* was in contact with a number of small craft thought to be Iranian Boghammers and armed patrol craft. At the time of this notification, the small craft in the vicinity of *Montgomery* were in the process of closing a merchant vessel of German registry. Their intent was unknown.

Vincennes's embarked Lamps [helicopter], Oceanlord 25 [OL 25], was recovered and refueled. Shortly after Lamps was recovered, *Vincennes* was directed by GS to proceed north in order to close the position of *Montgomery*.

The ship proceeded at best speed and launched OL 25 when within approximately fifty miles of *Montgomery*'s position. The purpose of the aircraft launch at this time was to establish link tracks on the contacts of interest for further relay by *Vincennes* into the southern Persian Gulf link 11 net, as *Montgomery* was not link capable.

On arrival in the vicinity of *Montgomery*, the small craft were maneuvering in various directions, closing and apparently interrogating merchant vessels. No hostile intent or action on the part of the small craft was noted, either by OL 25, *Montgomery*, or *Vincennes*. The German merchant in question, to the best of my knowledge, did not request assistance.

In view of the fact that the small craft were not exhibiting hostile intent toward any USN units or merchant vessels in the area, and it appeared as though USN presence had acted as a deterrent to any attack, board, or search activity, GS directed both *Vincennes* and *Montgomery* to clear to the south and resume duties assigned. OL 25 was directed to remain temporarily in the vicinity of the small craft in order to monitor their activities.

Montgomery and *Vincennes* commenced clearing to the south as directed. Very shortly after a southerly course was executed, OL 25 reported taking antiair fire from the northernmost group of Iranian small craft (the small craft at this point had split into two groups, hereafter referred to as the northern/southern groups).

I personally verified with the aircrew that they had been engaged, informed GS and GB [Golf Brand] of this fact, and turned to close OL's position at best speed. This direct engagement of a USN helo . . . was an unusual move on the part of the IRG navy, particularly in view of the fact that two U.S. naval warships were operating in the . . . vicinity.

As directed by GS, *Vincennes* took tactical control of *Montgomery*, and both units were formed into a loose line abreast. OL 25 was directed to vector toward *Vincennes*'s unengaged side at approximately eight miles.

The southern group continued to operate on various courses and speeds but did not threaten either USN unit. A single craft which had broken off from the southern group and configured with what appeared to be a bow-mounted recoilless rifle closed within 1,000 yards but displayed no overtly hostile intent. His approach was covered by the starboard 25-millimeter-gun crew.

During this period, an Omani patrol boat in the immediate vicinity engaged in a one-way bridge-to-bridge conversation directing the southern group to clear Omani territorial waters. No response was noted. The northern group appeared initially to be disbursing on a northeasterly course in the direction of Iranian territorial waters.

As is *Vincennes*'s standard operating procedure whenever the potential for hostile surface action is present, a gun solution for the 5-inch batteries was developed on this group and GS/GB so informed. The guns were centerlined, as is also standard procedure, so as to display no threatening posture. Just as I was about to clear the area, three of the northerly group reversed course and commenced closing *Vincennes*/*Montgomery* at approximately 17 knots.

Since this group had already committed a hostile act against *Vincennes*'s aircraft and was now closing, I requested permission from GB/GS to effect gun engagement.

We were queried by GB as to whether the contacts were disbursing or closing. We replied that they were closing, and permission was immediately given by GB to engage with guns. Almost simultaneously, the bridge reported that the small craft were firing at us.

Range was approximately four miles from *Vincennes* at this point, and *Montgomery* was directed to engage. Batteries were released and 5-inch-gun fire commenced. *Vincennes* and *Montgomery* maneuvered on various courses and speeds to maintain unmasked batteries, while attempting to present the smallest possible target profile. Instead of breaking off and retiring after our first salvo, which I expected they might do, the boats continued to fire.

My concern at this point was that the closing small craft might be attempting to execute a "swarm" attack technique previously briefed to us by the Gulf MAGTF [Marine Air-Ground Task Force] representative.

Shortly after initiation of the surface action, an air contact to the northeast [was] displayed on the LSDs at a range of slightly over forty miles. I was notified by Lieutenant Commander Lustig, and I directed him to watch and inform me if the contact closed. Almost immediately, I was informed that the contact was on a closing course, and appeared to be climbing. [In accordance with] the standard operating practice for an unidentified aircraft closing from the Iranian coastline, the contact was designated "assumed hostile" and a series of warnings was initiated in compliance with standing procedures on both IAD and MAD circuits. I was informed shortly that no response was being received. At this point, although I was more than concerned about the closing air contact, it appeared to be composition 1, and I was confident that if the circumstances should dictate, I could execute a timely and successful engagement. However, the aggressiveness of the small craft was of extreme concern, as I gauge small, high-speed boats attempting to press home an attack to be very difficult to deal with.

Their ability to sink *Vincennes* was not a question, but high-volume fire into the superstructure would certainly result in personnel casualties and damage.

As the air contact continued to close, we had indications from several consoles, including the IDS operator, that the contact's IFF readout showed a mode III squawk but, more significantly to me, a mode II squawk which the operator indicated had been previously identified with Iranian F-14s. I also received reports via the air alley operators that indicated decreasing altitude. Warnings were issued on regular and rapid basis. No responses were received.

The contact continued to close on what appeared to be a CBDR [constant bearing, decreasing range] course. At this point, I considered that the aircraft was displaying hostile intentions, as it appeared to be maneuvering into an attack position. I directed Scott to request from GB permission to engage this contact, if the contact penetrated within twenty miles of *Vincennes* and did not respond to warnings. Permission to do this was granted by GB, and I was directed to ensure the contact was again warned.

In view of the fact I had no electronic correlation associated with an F-14, . . . I negated Lustig's query if I desired to engage at twenty miles and directed that warnings continue. Given the reaction time of the Aegis missile battery, I felt I could hold bird release while continuing to watch.

However, the flow of information being provided to GW over the interior comm net reflecting CBDR, which was confirmed by the LSDs, descending altitude, and speed increases, plus my confidence in Lieutenant Commander Lustig, convinced me that the aircraft was, in fact, a threat.

I requested that [Lustig] verify again that IFF modes and codes indicated Iranian military aircraft and was told that they did. At nine miles, I felt I could no longer delay defensive action and granted firing permission. Intercept took place approximately six nautical miles from *Vincennes* at an estimated altitude of 7,500 feet or less.

Gunfire directed at the small boats continued for about five minutes. Ceasefire [by] both *Vincennes* and *Montgomery* was directed when it was apparent that the remaining two surface craft were disbursing. *Vincennes* and *Montgomery*'s speed was reduced, while [they attempted] to make a battle-damage assessment; however, both surface and air visibility was extremely restricted . . . and no surface- or air-target damage assessment was possible.

. . . Both myself and the condition I and III watch teams were intimately familiar with Arabian Gulf commercial air routes, which were constructed on the LSDs prior to inchop in order to ensure watch team familiarity.

These routes are continually displayed on at least one of the CIC tactical LSDs. It has been my experience to date that commercial air operations in the Gulf maintain guard on the IAD frequency and strictly adhere to centerline routes of established commercial air lanes.

I have no explanation as to why this particular aircraft failed to heed or respond to multiple warnings. The mood in CIC throughout this period was tense but professional. Information flow to me was clear and every action taken was deliberate. Communications on the Middle East Force execution net with GB and GS . . . were quickly responded to, and I felt at all times that my communication link with higher authority was both effective and timely.

Given all the information available to me at that time and in view of the situation, I was convinced beyond any doubt that the aircraft was in support of the surface engagement in progress. I had already been surprised by the sudden turn of the small boats to close and attack, and I considered that the track displayed by the aircraft presented a real and imminent danger to my ship and crew and took action accordingly. . . .

No one is more anxious than I to extract from this incident information which will enable us to reduce to near zero the chance of repetition. In today's environment, we must have the technology inherent to the Aegis system in order to deal with the threat to own ship as well as those we must protect. However, at the same time, we must accept that no system, electronic, mechanical, or man, is perfect, [and not] delude ourselves into believing that [any system is] or can be.

As I finished, Admiral Fogarty asked if I had anything to add. The whole of these events, I said after a pause, reminded me of Ernest Gann's book, *Fate Is the Hunter*, throughout which numerous, seemingly unrelated events come together to spark a larger event. In both cases, had any of the preliminary events not taken place, the outcome would probably have been different.

Fogarty posed a few general questions and, after a brief conversation with his senior JAG (judge advocate general) officer, announced that the proceedings would recess until the following morning. I was surprised, having expected an in-depth interrogation from the board. Instead Fogarty had restricted the questioning to himself, and his approach was anything but adversarial.

The recess was a relief, but I couldn't help feeling the day had been anticlimactic.

I wanted to share the events of the day with Sharon, but my several attempts to contact her from the AT&T booth were in vain. For the first time in several days I was not able to raise her. It did nothing for my mood.

Later, as the boat approached the sea ladder, the crew had as usual assembled on the weatherdeck, aware, I'm sure, that the day had been a big one. Though I was feeling uncertain I gave them a thumbs-up. Satisfied, they filtered away. Small gestures such as this daily show of concern meant a great deal to me, and to Vic and Scott as well. I felt a lot better as I climbed aboard.

The next morning we discussed a number of side issues, one of which was Admiral Fogarty's request early in the proceedings for State Department assistance in gaining access to Flight 655's flight recorder information, the black box. The Iranian government claimed they were having difficulty locating and recovering the recorder. This raised a number of eyebrows. The splashdown point was well marked, in shallow water with fairly low prevailing currents. Fogarty directed that a follow-on request be sent.

We had discovered that the voice quality of the internal CIC communication net tended to deteriorate when the circuit was heavily loaded. The admiral was interested, and from the flow of the discussion it was apparent he intended to forward a recommendation to correct this problem.

He asked me to explain my view of the tactics employed by the small boats during their attack. I pointed out that they appeared to utilize their high speed and fast turns to present a difficult target, meanwhile closing and attempting to concentrate as much firepower as possible. There was no way to be sure, but one craft might have stood off, acting as a control platform.

This sort of interaction continued until the lunch break and into early afternoon. At about three o'clock Admiral Fogarty declared a recess but asked that the board remain behind in the library. When we returned, the admiral stood and thanked everyone for their effort and support in providing an enormous quantity of information to the board. Then he proclaimed, "The formal inquiry proceedings into the circumstances regarding the downing of Iranian Air Flight 655 by the USS *Vincennes* on 3 July, 1988, are closed."

He turned to Admiral Less and remarked, "Admiral, I am returning operational control of the USS *Vincennes* to you."

I felt a flood of relief as I turned these words over in my mind. However, the process was anything but complete. I asked Dennis what we could expect to happen.

"First," he said, "during the formal portion of the inquiry the board found no grounds for disciplinary or punitive action. But . . . that doesn't mean that cause cannot surface during the review process."

He picked up some of his notes and glanced at them before continuing.

"The board will have to compile everything that has been presented for the record. A report of the inquiry will be prepared, and Fogarty will include his findings and recommendations. Needless to say, that's not going to happen overnight."

Although I was familiar with the procedural chain, I asked Dennis to lay the whole thing out step by step. I wanted Sharon to know what to expect.

He continued: "Okay, at each level in the review chain the report will get a close look, and forwarding endorsements with or without recommendation will be attached. It's the guy who started the whole ball rolling, the convening authority, who will make the final decision to accept, reject, or modify the original. In this case that's going to be the secretary of defense. However, you can bet he'll pay attention to what comes up the chain, particularly from the chairman of the Joint Chiefs."

As we moved toward the ASU library doors for the last time, I said I was surprised that the proceedings seemed to finish so abruptly. Continuing much longer, he commented, would just be to "plow the same ground." He grinned and remarked, "If you'd like to continue, I can ask the admiral to reconvene."

"No thanks!"

When we reached the lobby, Dick Watkins was standing with Admiral Less. Less smiled and said, "I already know the answer, but can you be under way at first light tomorrow?"

He was right, the answer was obvious. Within the hour would have been fine with me.

Less moved away to discuss something with Admiral Fogarty and I collared Dick. "What's the chance of gathering up my people and going out somewhere for dinner? Obviously someplace we won't be noticed. I'd also like to invite you and Admiral Less to join us."

He agreed, though added that Admiral Less had another engagement. Then he went and phoned in reservations to the Bahrain Yacht Club. We were to meet on the pier at eight. After the intensity of the past few weeks, a quiet meal somewhere other than the ship or the ASU cafeteria promised to calm a lot of nerves.

Before shoving off for the run out to the anchorage, I ran to the AT&T booth. Be there, Sharon! I thought as I gave the operator the connection information. After what seemed like a thousand rings, she answered.

"Sharon, it's over. We're going to sea tomorrow."

There was a long silence on the line and I realized she was quietly crying. Finally she asked, "Are you okay? What happens now?"

I explained the steps as Dennis had laid them out.

"God, Will. How long will that take? How long will this go on?"

I tried to assure her that I didn't think the process would drag out. We needed to be positive about where things stood.

"They found no fault with what I did. If they had we'd still be at it. I think that will be the end result."

"I'm relieved, Will, but I just feel numb. I want it all to be over. I want you home."

"That'll come. All we can do is take this thing one day at a time."

She didn't say anything for a moment, then said, "After all this, have they figured out what happened? What do you think happened?"

"It's not simple or clear cut, but I think the reasons lay in the combination of time compression and a convoluted series of events we couldn't control or explain. Not to mention the goddamn environment of the moment in which everything fit."

I couldn't go into the whole complicated mess over the phone. She seemed to sense this and didn't press. She deserved, and at some point would get, the best explanation I could give.

"There've been several articles in the papers," she went on, "saying the Aegis system wasn't properly tested by the navy and doesn't work the way it's supposed to."

"Sharon, somebody is just looking for press time. From the start these things have been tested more rigorously than anything the navy has ever brought on line. All of these ships, including the *Vincennes*, have been put through the hoops over and over."

"So it works perfectly, you didn't have any problems?"

I wanted to reach out to her, because my next comment would be as thin as my earlier reply. "I didn't say that. It looks like the system as a whole worked the way it's supposed to. However, there are problems with the way the consoles are designed, the displays are presented, and the communication nets work. Fogarty saw all of this and I'm sure some changes will be recommended. We made mistakes, but nothing I saw was the central cause."

"I just hope if things need to be changed the navy won't stick its head in the sand." I assured her that I didn't think that would be the case.

As we continued the conversation her mood seemed to brighten. She absorbed the news that by morning we would put Bahrain behind us.

"I'd like to tell the wives," she said as we started to hang up.

"You bet. They deserve some good news."

The evening at the yacht club was a tonic for all of us. It was out of the way and quiet. We discussed the inquiry in general terms, but no one wanted to dwell on it, certainly not me. Most of the conversation revolved around topics as far removed from the Persian Gulf as possible. It was good to be with friends and to eat food other than cellophane-wrapped sandwiches.

The three attorneys hoped to catch a flight back to the States the next day and had moved off the *Vincennes* onto the *Coronado*. When we returned to the Mina Sulman pier, I pulled McCoy aside. "Dennis, it goes without saying that I appreciate more than I can express everything you've done. Every call you made was right on. I know Vic and Scott feel the same: You, Ron and Mike were the team we needed. Thanks."

We shook hands and, as he turned to walk away, he said, "You did the right thing. Sail safe."

11

OUT OF ALADDIN'S LAMP

Passage, immediate passage! Away soul! hoist instantly the
anchor!

—Walt Whitman, *Passage to India*, 1871

The rattle of the chain was like music, each link sounding a note that
brought us closer to breaking our tether to Bahrain. As the anchor
came free the ship shuddered, as if saying, "I'm out of here!" The
whine of the main gas turbines never sounded better as we started
moving down the channel. As we cleared, a pair of dolphins swam up
and took station off the bow, welcoming us back to sea.

I had spent the night rehashing every point of the proceedings,
every word of my conversations with Sharon. Subconsciously I was
afraid that sometime during the night the phone would ring and someone would tell me Admiral Fogarty wanted to reconvene the board of
inquiry. Instead, 20 July dawned bright, one of the few days we'd seen
with no haze and no wind. The sun came up like a big fiery ball. It
was hot but clear.

After we cleared the channel, the senior enlisted adviser
approached me on the bridge and said the crew wanted to have a
"steel beach" barbecue that afternoon. I readily agreed. We all exhibited
signs of relief. It was a pretty day, the seas weren't up, the monotony

of our long period at anchor had been broken. The barbecue turned out to be a good idea.

Two days after leaving Bahrain we exited the Gulf, passing through the Strait of Hormuz that night at high speed. The ship returned to her routine. The crew, stifled by the long hot days at anchorage, seemed to approach even the most mundane task with enthusiasm. The chief boatswain mate said to me, "Captain, it's not going to be long before the guys have her looking like a diamond in a goat's ass," and he was right.

The aviation detachment, grounded during the in-port period, finally got into the air, first flight-testing the birds, then resuming a normal patrol routine.

Petty Officer Terry Jordan, the ship's yeoman, continued to answer the many thousands of letters, telegrams, and messages still being sent to us. I was grateful to each person who had taken the time to express support, and personally signing each letter of reply was a high priority.

Out of cellular phone range, I now had to rely on MARS (military-affiliated radio system) to talk with Sharon, which was just as well since our phone bill had grown beyond our budget. Our MARS equipment had been presented by the Vincennes's commissioning sponsor, Marilyn Quayle, wife of Indiana Senator Dan Quayle, when the ship was commissioned.

We had about six amateur radio–qualified volunteers who would stagger their time on the set. Because of atmospherics and location we came on the air between 1:00 and 4:00 A.M. I haunted the radio shack when I thought conditions would allow a connection. It could be to anywhere—Utica, Pomona, Miami, you never knew. After 3 July there was competition among ham operators to talk to us since they all recognized our call letters. Sometimes we'd have five or six "hams" lined up in rotation working phone patches across the country. In rare instances the atmospherics were so good it sounded as if you were talking to someone in person. But usually there was heavy static or override, and at any moment you could lose the connection or sound as if you were yelling into a tomato can.

We had been on station several days when we got word that Congressman Lowery's letter had arrived on the Forrestal, just as she was being relieved by the carrier Carl Vinson battle group. I sent one of our helicopters for it. We were thrilled when this thousand-foot missive finally reached us. We spread it all over the flight deck so that the crew could read the thousands of notes and signatures. Then it was sectioned and taken to the mess deck, where we hung it from the overhead like paper curtains.

The people at home were eager for the crew's response, so I sent the following message to Congressman Lowery: "Team 49 and the U.S. cruiser *Vincennes* extend our heartfelt appreciation to the wonderful people of San Diego who 'cared enough to send their very best.' *Vincennes* was ready then and is ready now; your prayers and thoughts serve us as a second shield of Aegis. God bless." Included in my message were numerous comments from the crew that underscored the real value of the letter, helping ease their fears about the kind of reception the ship might receive upon our return.

Shortly afterward we received more good news: a port visit sched-

Crew members unfurl portions of the thousand-foot letter from San Diegans on the flight deck of the USS *Vincennes*. (Photograph by Lieutenant Roger Huff, USN)

uled for the Seychelles, an archipelago off the east coast of Africa. A request for liberty for the crew had been approved, a real break for them. Any liberty port would have been appreciated; this plum was beyond all expectation.

On the heels of this I received a message from Admiral Less informing me that a medical team of psychiatrists was coming from the Portsmouth Naval Hospital to spend up to thirty days evaluating the crew for any symptoms of post-event traumatic stress. My immediate reaction was anger. I couldn't see the reason for subjecting us to any more fishbowl stares. I sent Admiral Less a message questioning the need for evaluation.

Promptly he responded, "This is a CNO-directed action; he wants you to have all the help you need in case anyone wants to talk or unburden himself." Additionally, his message stated that the team, Commander John Matecvun, Commander John Aitken, and Lieutenant Commander Robert Bishop, had arrived in Bahrain earlier than expected. They would be sent to the *Carl Vinson* on 2 August for transfer by helo to us.

The visit was a done deal, so I put out the word that these people would be here to assist, not to inspect or investigate, and if anyone wanted to talk to them, the sessions would be private. The next morning, 3 August, we closed the *Vinson* for the pickup. We had some light cargo and mail for transfer, so both helicopters were scheduled for the flight. At the last minute I decided to go along for the ride.

Our aviators, to put it mildly, had an active sense of humor. They had adopted a pink plastic flamingo as their detachment mascot. After the helo touched down on the *Vinson*, the senior medical officer, Commander Matecvun, climbed aboard and was greeted by the air crewman wearing a cheesy grin and cradling this stupid pink flamingo in his arms. Even above the noise of the helicopter's rotors we could hear Matecvun's laugh. From that moment on, our relationship with the medical team was warm.

SAN DIEGO

It was 2 August. For the first time in a month my son Bill was spending the night out with a friend and I was alone. Deep in sleep, I was awakened by the telephone's repeated ringing. Rolling over, I reached toward the old-fashioned phone that sits on the night stand. "Hello."

A voice with a Mideastern accent demanded, "Is this the home of Captain Rogers?"

Trying to collect my thoughts, I asked, "Who do you want?"

Again in that halting speech, "Is this the home of Captain Rogers?"

The clock said 1:00. "This is awfully late to be calling. Who is this?"

"I'm a representative of the International People's League. Are you the wife of the murderer?"

Slamming down the receiver, I was now wide awake. I scribbled down the group's name and the conversation as best I could. And then I moved into Bill's bedroom, which overlooks the street. I sat upright on Bill's bed, leaning against the sill to see out the window. Perhaps I would hear a car; perhaps this person also knew where I lived. My mind was racing, my fears were coming true. Not just someone, but a group was here in the United States. The phone connection hadn't sounded like long distance; they were close, maybe even in San Diego. The hours dragged by and I was relieved to see daybreak.

The next morning I called Ted Atwood and Harry Stovall, special agent in charge of the naval station's Naval Investigative Service (NIS). I recapped the phone conversation with Ted and informed him I was on my way to Mr. Stovall's office. And I asked him not to tell Will about the incident. He had enough on his mind. When I arrived at the NIS building I was surprised to see Admiral Kihune's chief of staff, Captain Jim Perkins, waiting for me in the parking lot.

"Sharon, I'm representing the admiral. He's sorry he couldn't be here himself."

We were escorted directly into Mr. Stovall's office, where I repeated the contents of the phone call in detail.

"We'll investigate this group," Mr. Stovall said. "Also we'd like permission to place a trap on your phone."

I agreed and left his office feeling somewhat better, knowing I was doing something active rather than reactive. It was the first time since 3 July that I'd felt in control of anything. I hoped the caller would phone again. On the drive back to the house I stopped to pick up a copy of the New York Times. A headline blaming the Vincennes for downing the airliner jumped out at me. On top of the threatening call, Will was now being publicly blamed even before the results of the investigation were released. I couldn't believe it!

Later that day my sister phoned and I told her the news. "Pat, I'm really afraid for Will's life! I think he might be a target of an assassin. I don't think he's going to make it home alive."

I was at my lowest point since 3 July. I had begun losing weight, and that night at the dinner table I quietly picked at my food. Finally Bill, looking somber, said, "I'm really worried about you, Mom. I'm really worried."

Offhand remarks people had made kept popping into my mind. "You're a military family and when things like this happen you should be prepared for it. Will is in the navy; it's his job." Or, "When things like this happen you can roll with the punches." It has always amazed me how some people consider a uniform a magic shield capable of deflecting anything.

That night of 3 August, as I sat in front of the television to watch the network news, I was unaware that the *New York Times* article had set the stage for every anchor's lead story. CBS reported that no fault was found with the Aegis system, that human error had caused the shootdown and Will hadn't been given adequate information. While human error had embarrassed the navy, officials were relieved that the billion-dollar Aegis system wasn't a "dud." Switching to ABC, I heard Peter Jennings questioning the complexity of the Aegis system and whether the technology was designed to be user-friendly.

In the last few weeks I had discovered that all three networks usually delivered the same report. I was halfheartedly listening when I decided to check out NBC. If I thought the 8 July Peter Jennings broadcast had been upsetting, I had only to wait a few seconds for worse. I tuned in just in time to hear Tom Brokaw announce that "defense sources say an officer is standing by to relieve Captain Rogers." As I repositioned myself on the couch and sat forward, Mr. Brokaw introduced John Chancellor. His voice and demeanor struck me as aggressive. He began by drawing parallels between the *Vincennes's* downing of Flight 655, the *Stark* incident, and the marine barracks bombing in Beirut. He railed on about how responsible parties in these other cases, in order to avoid political consequences, had not been tried. "This time we should demand a full court-martial," he said. "Too many people have died to brush this case of human error under the rug."

I can't recall who initiated the phone call, but within minutes I was talking to Dick, Will's brother in San Antonio. "Sharon, I'm going to call NBC and lodge a complaint. That commentary was totally irresponsible." I was anxious for him to make the call. Dick telephoned the network in New York City but could only get through to a secretary, who promised she would relay the message to Chancellor.

The *New York Times* article, which had been the basis for the network news stories and commentary, prompted the CNO, Admiral Trost, to issue a directive advising all naval personnel that it would be inappropriate to comment about the incident until the investigation was completed and reviewed.

Later, another leak led to a story about a team of psychologists being sent to the *Vincennes* to work on the problems the crew was having. It was just one more news item that alarmed me until I learned the truth.

ARABIAN SEA

Despite my initial misgivings, the support team of psychologists turned out to be a real asset. Professional and competent, they had a relaxed, easy manner and quickly fit into the ebb and flow of the ship's routine. The in-port cabin was quiet, and I made it available to them for private counseling sessions. We agreed that unless they discovered a problem that might require medical evacuation or affect the ship, the content of any session would be strictly confidential.

A number of the crew were concerned over the reception they would get when we returned to San Diego. The big letter had done a lot to ease this concern, and now the team's private counseling sessions and work-space bull sessions were helping. Regardless, there would be lingering concern until we tied to the pier in San Diego. The whole CIC team and I went through the shootdown scenario with the crew in great detail. We had done this a hundred times before, but it felt good to talk without having every nuance of every move critically examined. This cathartic feeling was shared by all of us.

We kept the team busy virtually around the clock for three days. Late in the evening of the third day, 6 August, they came to the sea cabin to brief me. Commander Matecvun opened the brief: "We have an open schedule to support you and the ship, Captain Rogers, and frankly we are thoroughly enjoying the time onboard with you and the crew, but we feel that we have done all we can do. The *Vincennes* is in great shape, and unless you feel there is more for us, we're ready to wrap up."

He showed me a draft report of the team's findings, which concluded: "There are no identifiable clinical factors which would preclude immediate combatant roles and several which signify potential for highly competent functioning. The team considers the crew of USS *Vincennes* (CG 49) to be psychologically prepared for operations in a hostile environment." There was another statement of great importance to me: "Individuals were reviewed for evidence of overt psychopathology and none was found. No recommendations are made for changes in crew or procedures as no objective clinical data supports it."

I had posed to the team the question of how five people at five separate consoles could have seen something that hard data did not support. Like the rest of us, they didn't have the answer, but their response to the question was interesting:

> The question of perceptual distortion or misinterpretation of data in relation to combat stress was examined. It is well known that an expectant mind-set can lead to misinterpretation of data. . . . Chances of occurrence can be related to combat stress and perceived threat, but other factors such as experience, uniqueness of data, lack of confidence in equipment or leadership and length of time to evaluate data must be considered pertinent. That five or more combatants, some with prior combat experience, most with extensive equipment experience, all viewing separate displays for cognitively significant periods of time would have the same perceptual distortion or misinterpretation of data is highly implausible.

As they left, I thanked them warmly for their help. They had proven to be a real asset to Team 49.

After transferring the intervention team back to the *Vinson* on 7 August, we resumed our patrol station in the Arabian Sea approaches to the strait. At about 2:00 A.M. on 8 August the officer of the deck, Lieutenant Ross Holcomb, blew into the sea-cabin speaking tube.

"Captain, request you come to the bridge. The lookout thinks he sees something."

"Sees what, Ross?"

"He's not sure, but he thinks he saw a small flickering light on the port side."

"I'll be right up."

When I got to the bridge I couldn't see a thing other than the dim outline of people moving on the bridge wing. It would take a while for my night vision to adjust. Lieutenant Holcomb had slowed the ship and begun turning in the direction of the alleged light.

The lookout, a young sailor who must have had the senses of a bat, said, "There it is again."

I said, "Son, I'm not about to override you. My eyes are not adjusted and I've got a few years on you anyway."

"Captain, I see it out there. I've seen it twice."

"I saw it too, that time," Holcomb added.

I told Holcomb to conn the ship in the direction the lookout was pointing. Then I saw it too, a brief pinpoint flare-up. As we closed, I had the signal bridge illuminate the water with lights. We could just make out what looked like a small skiff with five people huddled in the center. The boat was half full of water, and one of the occupants was holding up what turned out to be a butane cigarette lighter. The lookout had seen that flickering dot of light.

The men helped aboard were badly dehydrated and sun blistered. There wasn't enough room in sick bay to set up the IVs required to treat them properly, so cots and blankets were arranged in the crew's lounge. The place was rapidly transformed into a medical ward.

By the next morning they had started to recover. One of them who spoke halting English explained they were Iranian fishermen. Eight days previously their fishing boat had started to take on water. Just before it sank they abandoned it with two thermos bottles of water, a plastic bowl, and the now-treasured Bic lighter. They owed their lives to a sharp lookout. Even if the boat had stayed afloat through the night, which was doubtful, another half day of Arabian sun would have finished them.

The condition of our guests improved rapidly. Our departure for the Seychelles was imminent, and arrangements were made to transfer the Iranians to the cruiser *Texas* while efforts began through State Department channels to return them to Iran.

Before leaving they expressed their gratitude through their English speaker: "God is great and we thank you for our lives. May you be safe." On behalf of the crew I wished them a safe return to their families. It was clear they understood how narrow their escape had been. In recognition of the young sailor's alert performance, I awarded him the Navy Achievement Medal. There was a noticeable feeling of euphoria among the crew for having saved these lives.

So morale was on the rise as we departed for the greatly anticipated visit to the Seychelles. On 11 August, after an eight-day transit marked only by the time-honored ceremony of welcoming King Neptune aboard as we crossed the equator, we sailed into Victoria Harbor on the main island of Male. This picturesque anchorage nestled at the base of imposing granite hills was small, almost too small for the ship. But with the aid of a knowledgeable pilot, we squeezed her in at the commercial wharf. The island's tropical vegetation was the first green we'd seen in three months and it was a welcome sight.

The first U.S. warship to visit the islands in more than a year, the *Vincennes* received a warm welcome. The U.S. ambassador to the Seychelles, James Moran, and his staff were most hospitable, going out of their way to ensure our visit was one we would long remember.

Through the auspices of a U.S. Air Force satellite tracking facility, we were able to make long-distance phone calls to the States. It had been too long since I'd talked with Sharon, and I was anxious to take advantage of a conversation unencumbered by radio procedures.

"Sharon, we just arrived."

She cut me off. "Have you heard?" she asked. "Carlucci and Crowe have released the investigation results, and they said you did the right thing."

"God, that's a relief. Tell me everything they said."

She recapped as much as she could remember. "I just talked to Ted and he's sending you a copy of the entire press conference."

"Sharon, I want to get back to the ship and let the crew know. I'll call you tomorrow."

Hurrying back, I passed this good news over the ship's 1MC system. It didn't take long for the word to spread, even to those already on liberty. The crew had expected these results. They would have been destroyed if the outcome had been different. As far as they were concerned, it was over.

After an hour or so I began to feel restless. I left the ship and walked to a nearby strip of beach. As I walked along the tide-line, the rolling splash of waves was like a metronome encouraging introspection. I kept thinking of the numerous and seemingly unrelated events, the separate pieces of the puzzle that had collided to create the tragic events of 3 July. What if one or two events had altered the sequence, or a piece had been removed from the equation? Would the actions and decisions of those few moments have taken a different course? I didn't have the answer, but I knew with certainty that 3 July would never be completely behind me or my family.

SAN DIEGO

Although unable to put the threatening phone call out of mind, that night I slept more soundly. Will and I had shared the first good news since 3 July. Telling him of the inquiry results made me feel for the first time that part of our nightmare was coming to an end. He still didn't know about the call.

The next morning I was brewing a cup of coffee and waiting for the toast to brown. As I unfolded the morning paper my eyes caught the headline in the *San Diego Union*: "Probe Clears Navy Skipper." Cleared of what? I thought. Negligence? Incompetence? Murder? Why couldn't they simply have written, as the *New York Times* did, "Support for Skipper"? But nothing could dampen my spirits. Another dependents' meeting had been scheduled for the evening. As much as I dreaded the one in July, I now looked forward to this one.

About seven that night some seventy dependents showed up at the meeting. Ted Atwood opened by reading a message from Will:

> All of us are relieved and pleased to see the factual end results of the investigation into the events of 3 July made public by competent and informed authority. It would be nice if we could assume that the release of the information by Secretary Carlucci and Admiral Crowe would bring an end to speculation and dissection. Unfortunately, this will not be the case.
>
> The content of the public report is drawn from a large and very detailed body of information amassed over a period of a month by a group of professional, competent, and unbiased naval officers and civilian experts. Most of this data will and must remain classified.
>
> Suffice it to say, and this is made most clear in the remarks of the secretary of defense and the chairman of the Joint Chiefs, your loved

ones performing as a team in a complex, compressed, and violent situation did precisely what was required of the moment, without hesitation and in a completely professional fashion. Be proud of them, I am! There are no finer.

At the same time be proud of yourselves, for whatever difficulties we have faced, yours have been orders of magnitude greater. You have had to deal with unknowns and uncertainties, inaccurate media reports, and perhaps most difficult—time and distance.

Throughout, you have kept the home fires bright, the bills paid, and the children's tears dried. We have steadily drawn from your courage, strength, and support—for you there are no bits of colored ribbon remotely sufficient.

God bless you, our country, our navy, and the United States cruiser *Vincennes*.

There was silence as Ted read Will's words. I sat there feeling great pride in my husband, his crew, and their families.

Later, as we sat and visited, we watched a sixteen-minute video of the news conference at which Secretary Carlucci and Admiral Crowe had announced the findings of the board of inquiry. Admiral Crowe said that on 3 July there were six significant problems that Will could not control or discount:

Vincennes was engaged on the surface against Iranian boats.

The unidentified, assumed hostile contact had taken off from a military airfield.

The contact was heading directly toward *Vincennes* and its range was relentlessly closing.

The unknown aircraft radiated no definitive electronic emissions.

Vincennes's warnings went unanswered.

The compression of time gave him an extremely short decision window.

Captain Rogers had every right to suspect that the contact was related to his engagement with the IRGC boats—until proved otherwise. The proof never came.

Afterwards, Ted gave me a copy of the fifty-three-page investigation report, and Commander Dillon provided copies of the Department of Defense press release to everybody present. Even though the wives were buoyed by this good news, the same old worries continued to plague us, and during the open discussion many voiced their concern about the crew's safety.

About twenty of us met with Ted after the meeting to discuss our travel plans to Hong Kong to meet our husbands. Hong Kong is a routine port visit for homeward-bound ships, and many of us had been saving our "egg" money for this trip. Will and I had done this before; this reunion, with all that had transpired, would be even more special.

The idea of seeing him again and the resumption of school were giving me incentive to rejoin the human race. Armchair experts and the media would continue searching for a scapegoat, but the results of the investigation gave me reason to believe that better days lay ahead.

ARABIAN SEA

Our time in the Seychelles flew by. There was no one on board who didn't fall in love with this beautiful and isolated spot. As we eased our way out of the harbor, one of the lookouts turned to me and said, "This was great, Captain. There was a big tree in front of my hotel and I took a whole roll of film of it." I could understand how he felt.

We arrived at our now-familiar patch of water in the north Arabian Sea on 24 August, reported for duty, and settled in to count the days until our 12 September departure from the Middle East. The evening of the twenty-seventh I was working on the ever-present pile of paperwork when the radio messenger knocked on my door. "Captain, we just received an immediate personal for you. Some of it came in garbled, but the chief wanted you to see it right away."

I'd had more than enough high-precedence traffic, and my first thought was that I could probably do without this one. But I received a pleasant surprise. The message was from Admiral Less, relaying a request from the emir of Bahrain, Isa Bin Salman Al Khalifa, to meet with him prior to our departure from the Gulf. The invitation was for dinner at the emir's beach house on the evening of the twenty-ninth. The radio gang is trying to pull a fast one on me, I thought, then realized that this sort of invitation was beyond their wildest imagination.

Rear Admiral Dave Rogers, commander of the *Vinson* battle group, was also invited, along with Admiral Less and his family. On the morning of 29 August we cranked up Oceanlord 25 and flew to the *Vinson*. Admiral Rogers and I were then flown into Manama on board the *Vinson*'s cargo aircraft. At 7:30 P.M. Admiral Less and Admiral Rogers picked me up at the Gulf Hotel in Less's Chevrolet. It would have been more appropriate if he had mustered up a magic carpet—the whole evening turned out to be a night inside Aladdin's lamp.

I was completely unfamiliar with the city, and as we drove I was struck by the wide streets lined with desert palms and what appeared to be large residences set back from the street behind high walls. Unwilling to miss a detail, I had my nose pressed to the window as we drove.

The house could not be seen from the road and it was pretty dark, but past the gate, through which we were waved by alert sentries, the driveway seemed to wind through a parklike setting thick with date palms. Admiral Less commented that the estate was set up like a game park. It wouldn't have surprised me to see a brace of lions standing in the road. The driveway ended in a large, open courtyard in front of the "beach house." This didn't have weathered shingles, plumbing that doesn't work, and sand fleas; this was a palace. The Moorish exterior appeared pale pink in the soft bath of exterior lighting.

The emir and a small entourage were waiting in the courtyard. He was dressed in traditional robes trimmed with gold lacework and his *agul*, or headdress, was held in place by gold beads. I felt a little inadequate in blazer and tie. He stepped to the car, greeted us, and escorted us to the front doors, which swung open silently as we approached. Inside, a servant ushered us into a long central hall lined on both sides with original works of art, many of them with a desert theme. We were shown into the reception room, which after the confines of the ship seemed about the size of a small gym. The walls were pale peach and accented in white. The room was beautifully furnished; it was obvious that a lot of thought had gone into putting it together.

Admiral Less's wife and daughter had already arrived. I was introduced to them and to the emir's private secretary, a retired British army major. We sat and chatted for about an hour as servants filed by in a steady stream with champagne, white wine, and orange juice for the emir, who as a Muslim does not drink alcohol. Throughout the conversation, the emir repeatedly made mention of how he and his people appreciated the presence of the *Vincennes* and the U.S. Navy in the Gulf.

We were directly responsible, he believed, for ending a terrible and violent war.

As though on signal, one of the servants entered, the emir spoke briefly to him, and we were escorted into the dining room. This room appeared to seat about fifteen. The decor was as elegant as the reception area's, but being smaller, the room was more intimate. There were various photographs on the walls of the emir with Queen Elizabeth, President Reagan, Prince Charles, and Princess Diana, and of the emir's family.

Although we were a small group, all places at the table were set. The plates were Wedgewood bone china emblazoned with the royal crest, so translucent you could read through it, and set off with Waterford stemware. The flatware looked to be heavy Sheffield silver, executed for the royal family with the Bahraini royal crest on the hilt of the knives and forks.

As the meal proceeded through multiple courses, the conversation was spirited, and the emir continued to express his goodwill and warm wishes to the *Vincennes*. For dessert we were treated to a huge bowl heaped with strawberries about the size of small apples. Admiral Less's wife commented that they were the most magnificent she had ever seen, and Major Greene explained that the emir had sent his Boeing 727 to Cypress to pick them up.

After the final plates were cleared, we stood for toasts. I wished the emir good health, and he responded with best wishes to the ship, the U.S. Navy, and the United States. In the drawing room as we prepared to leave, the emir offered a toast to all, and then turning to me said, "Captain Rogers, you are the lion of the Gulf. Please accept the appreciation of the people of Bahrain." I thanked him and presented him with a plaque of the *Vincennes*, which he said he would hang on his yacht. I couldn't think of a better spot for it.

12

———◇◇◇———

HOMEWARD BOUND

Home is the sailor, home from the sea. . . .
—Robert Louis Stevenson, *Underwoods, Requiem*, 1887

EN ROUTE

On 1 September, two days after I returned from the visit with the emir, Lieutenant Commander Doug McDonald relieved Commander Rick Foster as executive officer of the *Vincennes*. Our scheduled departure for home, 12 September, was getting close. But as the days went by we didn't receive any detaching orders, and I could feel anxiety growing throughout the ship. The reason for the delay was eventually clarified in a message to the effect that several of the Gulf Council states had filed a request with the U.S. State Department for the *Vincennes* to remain in the Gulf area as a politically leveling influence.

I'm sure this played well in diplomatic circles, but it was a bitter pill for us. A message from Admiral Less expressed his understanding of the impact a delay created. He and Vice Admiral Paul David Miller, commander, Seventh Fleet, had gone to bat to protect our schedule, but this was a sensitive political issue.

After two long days, we were told to commence our departure but to radio our position every 200 miles. We did so, and each time we were told to keep moving. We were headed in the right direction; whatever political maneuvering there was seemed to be working in our favor. Until we rounded the tip of India, there were several hundred pairs of crossed fingers aboard.

Enjoying a beautiful sunset and calm seas, the USS *Vincennes* sails through the Strait of Malacca on her homeward-bound voyage in September 1988. (Photograph by Lieutenant Roger Huff, USN)

Our return would generate considerable press interest, and I exchanged several messages with the Pacific Fleet and Seventh Fleet commanders regarding the pros and cons of a news conference when we finally reached San Diego. Admiral David Jeremiah, commander in chief, Pacific Fleet, left the choice to me. I mulled this over for several days. If I don't do it, I thought, they're going to be hounding me. I might as well do it and get it over with—get off center stage and fade away. I sent Admiral Jeremiah a message indicating my decision.

En route to Singapore, we stopped at Phuket, Thailand. The Seventh Fleet public affairs officer, Commander Steve Clawson, joined us there and planned to stay until we reached Subic Bay. He was available to advise me on possible formats for the press conference.

As we departed Singapore on 21 September and entered the South

China Sea, the day was one of those you carry with you always: clear, with a soft feel to the air, and topped with a spectacular sunset that reflected like fire off the surface of the water. The evening was warm and comfortable, with a hint of rising, shifting wind. It felt good to have the waters of the Indian Ocean behind us and to move securely into the hands of the Seventh Fleet commander.

At about two in the morning I was awakened by a call from Ross Holcomb, who as luck would have it again had the deck. "Captain, you'd better come to the bridge. We've got a fire on the horizon."

This time I didn't have any problem seeing, and I directed Ross to steer for the flames. The sea was starting to roll with the steadily rising wind. As we closed we made out a small junk adrift and rolling in the wave troughs. A figure frantically waving a burning rag was braced between what appeared to be a canvas sheet covering the fore and aft sections of the boat.

It could only be a boatload of Vietnamese refugees. With the deteriorating weather, we needed to be quick in determining their status. Was the boat seaworthy and capable of making the nearest landfall? Did they have adequate food and water? Did they need medical attention?

The ship was positioned so that the junk could ride in the lee of our fantail, protected somewhat from the wind and waves. I had one seaman aboard who spoke some Vietnamese, but he was far from fluent. In vain, he tried to make himself understood over the wind and language barrier.

Our floodlights revealed that the boat had a makeshift canopy of plastic bags, canvas bits, raincoats, and tree branches. The mast was shattered, and several large planks had been torn free from the side of the junk. It looked pretty ragged, but nevertheless warranted an inspection. Desperate, the boat people were not beyond intentionally disabling their craft.

I directed the chief engineer, Lieutenant Commander Jonathan James, to rig out with a life jacket and safety line, board the junk, and assess the situation. It took several tries before he was able to bridge the heaving gap between us and the boat. Shortly afterward he yelled up to me, "Captain, this thing is full of people. I'm having trouble even getting to the engine." He disappeared for what seemed like forever. Then he emerged and, cupping his hands around his mouth, yelled,

"The damned engine is a mass of rust. Doesn't look as though it's been run in a long time. They're shipping water, and the people are really beat up."

"All right," I ordered, "bring them on board!"

By now the wind was starting to squall and the waves were boiling around the fantail. Lieutenant Commander James was under the canvas covers with his flashlight. With each breaking wave pieces of the boat were torn free.

"Captain," he yelled again, "they can't make it without help. Most of them are too weak to make the fantail, and there are a bunch of kids in here. Can I stay down?"

I was concerned for John's safety, but nonetheless agreed. I yelled to the sailors tending the safety line, "If the boat starts to go, yank the engineer clear and I mean quick." They nodded, bracing themselves against a mooring chock.

James started passing people out, but it was slow going. Each person had to be put into a life jacket, secured with a safety line, and carefully hauled up and aboard. This procedure was much too risky for the children. A boatswain's mate hit on the idea of using one of the big canvas coaling bags we had on board. The small children fit inside perfectly. James tucked them one after another into a bag that was being raised and lowered in quick succession.

The boat could not have been much longer than twenty feet. I was dumbfounded by the number of people crammed into its small interior. Finally, it looked as if we had them all. John disappeared again to make a final check and under the foredeck found a tiny girl, curled up, silent and forgotten. There were twenty-six in all—ten men, six women, and ten children. It was pitch black and noisy and the sea was beating the boat to pieces. Yet the people were completely stoic. Not one child cried, not one adult said a word. Huddled on the deck they showed no emotion, simply stared into the night.

On top of everything a hard, wind-driven rain began with drops the size of quarters. Lieutenant Commander McDonald asked if I wanted the gunners to sink the junk with small-arms fire, as drifting wrecks are a navigational hazard.

"I don't think we have to do anything," I said. "Just wait a few seconds, it's going under."

About three minutes after James and that last little girl were hauled on board, the junk broke up and sank. One of the older couples was in bad shape. The woman's pulse and blood pressure were dangerously low. Her husband, who could speak a little English, was badly dehydrated and shaking with hypothermia. It looked close for him, too.

The deck of the crew's lounge was covered with mattresses and blankets, and word was passed that dry clothing was needed. Within five minutes there must have been six hundred pounds of clothing gathered and stacked by the crew. We could have outfitted those folks for the rest of their lives.

By first light the children were rapidly recovering from their ordeal, and the corpsman assured me that the couple in sick bay were going to make it. Suddenly toys, Barbie dolls, teddy bears, and games started appearing. It dawned on me that the sailors were emptying their lockers of presents they had bought to take home to their own families.

The children were initially shy and unsure, but it didn't take long for the barriers to drop. More attention was being showered on them than they had probably ever had in their lives. At first we had to keep them in the lounge for medical checks, but shortly the crew was taking them up and down the passageways, to the soft-drink machines, their work spaces, the bridge, and most popular of all, the mess decks. One memorable picture was the back of a boxcar-sized sailor, a child in each arm with another clinging to his neck, heading for the Kool-Aid dispenser.

We were still two days away from the Philippines. By the time we reached Subic Bay the Vincennes had expanded her family by twenty-six. We turned the refugees over to the United Nations relief agency. The farewells were anything but easy.

While we were in port, a telephone hookup was arranged between us and Vincennes, Indiana, for a broadcast conference call with leaders of the community. Mick Birge, news director of WAOV, had originated the request through the Department of the Navy and served as moderator.

We received direct words of support from the mayor of Vincennes, members of the Vincennes crew association, the chairman of fund-raising for the USS Vincennes monument, and the editor and publisher of the Vincennes Sun-Commercial. These people had waded through a lot of red tape to set up the connection. We felt like a floating extension of the community. Although the connection was poor, the call was much appreciated.

Subic was an important stop. The huge naval complex had everything we needed in the way of food, fuel, and support for the trip home. Seventh Fleet Commander Vice Admiral Miller happened to be in port, and I was pleased to have the opportunity to brief him and thank him for his assistance throughout the cruise.

Ted Atwood, who had been such an enormous help to us, was accompanying Vice Admiral Kihune on an inspection tour. He had agreed to meet us in Subic to ride the ship to Hong Kong.

Despite the flurry of activity that surrounded us in Subic, my thoughts concentrated on Hong Kong. The long-awaited reunion with Sharon would allow us to vent some of the anxiety that had covered us like a blanket for the last months. There was no better place for it. We both loved this exotic city. Revisiting our old haunts and favorite places would be exciting, but most important, we could submerge ourselves in the teeming population . . . become invisible.

HONG KONG

What a beautiful sight it is flying into Hong Kong at night, with the thousand lights of the city and floating sampans reflecting off the surface of the harbor. Between San Diego and Hong Kong the only stop is Seattle; after that, it's an eleven-hour nonstop flight. I had arranged to arrive a day early to get a good night's sleep before starting the exciting five-day reunion with Will. Once off the plane and into the busy terminal, I got separated from the other wives when I heard my name being paged. Greeting me was a master chief from the U.S. embassy's naval attaché staff. She helped me with the luggage as we walked out to a staff car, then drove me to the Hilton Hotel.

The Hong Kong Hilton is a special hotel to Will and me. We had stayed there during our other visits, always at special serviceman's rates, and this time Will had worked hard to reserve us a room through the American embassy. Walking into the elegant lobby, I felt once more as if I'd been dropped into a magic, romantic world. The lush, patterned carpet beneath me, I gazed around the lobby where Will and I had so often laughed, hugged, and planned.

"Mrs. Rogers," the master chief said, "I'll pick you up at seven-thirty sharp in the morning. The ship is scheduled to be in at dawn, and I know you're anxious to see Captain Rogers."

"Anxious . . . you're so right! I'll be in the lobby bright and early, and thank you again for the lift."

Pulling my suitcase behind me, I checked in, found my room, and pulled back the covers on the bed. Within hours, I'd be with Will once again. It didn't take long to get ready for bed. I turned off the light and settled back on the pillow. The flight and building excitement had tired me out. I was soon asleep.

The wives converged at the China fleet landing at eight o'clock the next morning to ride the ship's gig out to the *Vincennes*, anchored in the harbor. Some of the ship's crew greeted us with coffee and dough-nuts. The gig is small and can hold about a dozen people. We settled in for the short ride. The water was choppy and it required three approaches to the ship before we could successfully pull alongside. The gangway reared up in sync with the waves. I had to time it just right, moving from the boat to the little landing platform. As I stepped out of the gig it rolled and I was momentarily hanging in midair, over the churning water, before I stumbled backward into the arms of a young sailor. All the while Will was on the deck recording my arrival with his camcorder. I held my footing and climbed the ladder. For the first time since 28 April, we were together.

At last! I wrapped my arms around him and I couldn't seem to let go. Laughing, we stood back, took a good look at each other, and walked past the watch on the quarterdeck, covering the short distance to Will's stateroom. The ship sparkled. Every line was coiled, the brass shone, and the deck was so polished it captured my reflection. Seeing the ship in this condition, observing the proud crew, and watching Will's confident stride as he led me along the passageway convinced me that everything was all right.

There was so much for us to say to one another, so much com-forting to be given, so many unanswered questions to ask, but I knew there'd be time. Most things would have to wait. I was content to sit on the couch, watch, and listen as he conducted last-minute business before we left.

After all, we had five long days ahead of us, and I intended them to be the best ever.

The first evening we ate dinner at Jimmy's Kitchen, a steakhouse and favorite landmark for navy personnel. Gathered at one of the long restaurant tables were all of the nonduty officers, the wives who had flown over, Ted Atwood, and Admiral Kihune. Everyone seemed to have a good time. There was lots of laughter and easy conversation. Will later told me that it was the first night all the officers had been together off the ship since the beginning of deployment.

Later that evening, back at the hotel, the two of us sat in the lobby enjoying a nightcap, catching up on Bill and the rest of the family. We resisted talking about the incident, and as we held hands and rode the elevator up to our room, I realized that neither of us wanted to spoil the moment. Locking the door behind us, we also locked out the events of the recent past. I felt alive for the first time in a long time. I was with my husband. We were together and that was all that mattered. We had the rest of our lives ahead of us.

The next morning over juice and coffee we discussed our plans for the week. Most days belonged to us, but the evenings were filled with official functions that Will was committed to attend. One night we were dinner guests of the American Club, a group of business people assigned to companies in Hong Kong. Their premises downtown take up one entire floor of a highrise offering a breathtaking view of Victoria Harbor.

As we were trying to choose a selection from the extensive menu, a delicious steamship round was wheeled out on a large rotisserie cart. Most of us selected a cut from it. When the night wound down the men were offered their choice of cigars from a cedar-lined mahogany humidor. This was a particular treat for Will. The American Club routinely and generously opens its facilities to all visiting navy officers, and we appreciated their hospitality.

Another evening we were invited to call on the commanding officer of HMS Tamor, the Royal Navy's shore facility. His quarters occupy the penthouse of the base administration building that overlooks the harbor. While talking with his wife I learned about "Egg Alley." On her veranda was a profusion of plants in beautiful glazed brown pots. She explained that the pots, used for shipping eggs from Macao to Hong Kong, were common, cost practically nothing, and could be found in a local farmers' market. I knew where our first stop would be the next morning.

The egg pots, decorated with coiled dragons, led us to our next outing. Will and I had always wanted to see Macao so we took the hydrofoil there. It was scenic cruising among the small islands that lay between Hong Kong and Portuguese Macao. We joined a tour and viewed the city by bus. At a temple we saw a Buddha surrounded by hundreds of burning joss sticks thought to ensure luck and prosperity. Figuring a little luck would be welcome, we purchased two and added ours to the others. In front of the gate that connects Macao with mainland China, tourists were taking pictures of the border guards in their green uniforms and red-starred caps. We were on the doorstep of Red China, within steps of a different world.

On our last day we indulged in high tea at the Peninsula Hotel in Kowloon. The Peninsula is a British colonial landmark reflecting the elegance and grace of an era long past. That evening, walking along the narrow winding streets near our hotel, we settled for dinner in a less posh atmosphere—McDonald's.

On our return to the Hilton the sights, smells, and sounds of Hong Kong seemed more intoxicating than ever. The last five days had been everything we'd wanted and needed them to be.

PEARL HARBOR

Hong Kong had been perfect. Sharon and I made every moment count. All of our favorite spots down to the last shop had been revisited: "Cat Alley," the street of antiques, the stalls of Stanley Market, the Star ferry to Kowloon. Privately we both felt this might be our last visit, and we were determined that it would be the best. Not even Hong Kong's spell, however, could completely erase our concerns for the future.

During Admiral Kihune's brief stop in Hong Kong he had commented, "Will, you're visible, controversial, and caught in the center of a storm, and you and Sharon may be there a long time." We hoped he was wrong, but knew that he wasn't.

The last stop before San Diego was Hawaii. As I expected, the brief stay was busy. Admiral Jeremiah offered me the assistance of two naval reservists, Lisa and Carl Benshneidt, who in civilian life teach business executives to deal effectively with the media. They were temporarily attached to his staff. I accepted the offer and was told to spend two days with them.

They knew their business, subjecting me to every conceivable format—a benign interview, a hostile interview, a one-on-one, a twenty-on-one, a talk show, any and everything they had in their bag of tricks.

Though it was role playing, at the end of each day I was mentally and physically exhausted. Still, it was worth the effort; my previous exposure to the press had been limited, and certainly not controversial.

As we left Pearl Harbor there was a growing sense of anxiety among the crew. What awaited them stateside? To ease these concerns the executive officer initiated activities. The wardroom baked pizza for the crew and provided delivery service. We had a talent show, a game night, and a mock ceremony during which I presented my last can of cream soda to Petty Officer Jordan for typing the responses to our flood of mail.

Even with these diversions, the final leg dragged.

SAN DIEGO

Home from Hong Kong, the wives feverishly began to plan for the return of the *Vincennes* on 24 October. West Coast tradition dictates that the families hand-make an artificial lei to adorn the ship's bow as she transits into port. After many telephone calls, we decided to meet at Admiral Baker Field, a navy recreation park, to work on this project. A small group of wives, children, parents, and good friends gathered around picnic tables. Fortified with snacks and sodas, we lovingly assembled flowers from red, white, and blue plastic paper and strung each flower onto a 100-foot line. We crammed this creation into the back of my van and stored it in my garage between the cars.

Other family members were busy making smaller neck leis to hang around our men's shoulders. It was important to the families that this homecoming be special. Ideas were bandied about, and from them our plans began to crystallize. Out of monies received from the ship's welfare and rec fund, we chartered a small Cessna to fly over the ship with a Welcome Home banner. To entertain the children we hired a clown and Shamu, purchased balloons with the message "Team 49 We Love You" printed on each one, and designed handheld signs carrying various messages.

At the last minute a patriotic individual from San Diego Yacht Club offered to carry a number of dependents aboard his yacht. They would be the first to spot the ship, and we were all envious of their good fortune.

As any navy wife will admit, time stands still during a long deployment of a combatant ship, but just before homecoming you never have enough time. One of the last-minute errands is buying new clothes for the children and something special for yourself. Everyone wants to look his best for Dad. In Hong Kong I'd purchased two dresses from Stanley Market, an open-air discount area that sells everything for a fraction of the cost back home. My new dress was short-sleeved, and the morning of the twenty-fourth was cooler than I'd expected. I threw on a jacket for warmth. As I was leaving I noticed for the first time that I was dressed in a blue and white jacket and white dress. All I needed was something red to complete the color scheme.

With Bill and our Texas family in tow, I headed toward 32nd Street and the homecoming we'd all been longing for. The pier was crowded. Music was playing, families greeted one another, people milled under a great blue and white tent sipping coffee and eating doughnuts. Excitement was in the air. Carmella Lutz and Debbie Pipkin approached and sweetly presented me with a gorgeous bouquet of red roses. One of the officer's wives hurried over and handed me a lei she had carefully made.

"Sharon," she said, "I want you to wrap this around the captain's neck and give him a big hug for me."

We were flying every bit of bunting, every streamer we had, when on the gray overcast morning of 24 October 1988, the Vincennes entered the San Diego channel. The mole area at the entrance to the bay was choked with small boats. A novel touch was a small plane that flew overhead towing a banner reading Welcome Home, Team 49. We responded by playing "Chariots of Fire" and Neil Diamond's "America" over the external speakers.

For the benefit of those not on deck I announced, "If anybody has any concern about our welcome, I'll put someone on the 1MC to describe it until all of you can see for yourselves."

A good-sized yacht appeared with some of the wives. This first glimpse of family created an electric atmosphere aboard. As we passed down channel small boats clustered around us, seeming in some cases to move clear only at the last moment. The centerpiece of this gaggle was two fireboats pumping streams of colored water into the air. A navy tug worked its way through the little fleet surrounding us and delivered a huge lei made by the wives that we draped over the prow of the ship.

Any place along the bay there was a place to gather, there was a crowd. As we closed the Coronado Bridge, the signal lights of ships at the naval station began to transmit a stream of Welcome Home messages, and the end of pier 7 looked like an anthill. I had never seen anything like it.

There was not a person on that ship who did not feel welcome. All of the mental leper bells went into the trash. Surprisingly, one of the newspapers went on to report that "a few hundred people" met the *Vincennes* in a "funereal" atmosphere.

It was thrilling to watch the ship turn toward the pier and then slip alongside it. You could feel the collective pride and love flowing through the crowd. I was anxious for the gangway to be put in place. Finally aboard and in Will's arms, I presented him with the beautiful lei. His first words to me were, "I've never seen such a homecoming. I'm anxious to thank the families for this. But let's go to the in-port

The USS *Vincennes* gets a huge welcome home, 24 October 1988. (Photograph by Marjo Rogers)

cabin for a couple of minutes. I want to get myself in the right frame of mind for this press conference."

"Will, the pier's loaded with media," I said. "When we get down there I want us to both keep smiling. I don't want any doom and gloom pictures for posterity."

Alone in his stateroom, we took a moment to collect ourselves. Then Will broke the silence.

"Okay, let's get this over with. Are you ready?"

As we inched our way along the pier, through a crush of reporters and cameras, I could hear myself reminding Will, "Keep smiling."

Rear Admiral J. F. Smith, Jr., new commander of Cruiser-Destroyer Group 5, was the master of ceremonies for the program. Prior to the press conference there were brief remarks from Horace Still of Holbrook, Massachusetts, president of the USS *Vincennes* Association, Mayor William D. Rose of Vincennes, Indiana, San Diego Councilman Ron Roberts, and Congressman Bill Lowery. I followed, expressing the crew's deep appreciation for the extraordinary welcome and show of support.

After this brief welcoming ceremony, nervous and trying to remember Sharon's admonition, I faced the assembled press. Hoping to keep things factual, I read a brief opening statement that recapped my remarks to the board of investigation. "As you are aware," I concluded, "a formal investigation, headed by Rear Admiral Fogarty, was convened and charged with examining the events of 3 July. Although faced with an enormous quantity of data derived from computer extraction, voice tapes, logs, and records, the board did a thorough and professional job in developing a cohesive time line of the events and the associated decision points. I support the findings of that investigation and hope you have all taken the time to go through the unclassified version released by the Department of Defense."

The question-and-answer session that followed was more orderly and less adversarial than I had expected. The queries were not overly difficult to deal with, and my responses were straightforward. There were only a few abrasive shots, such as "Do you expect the navy to get rid of you?" and "Do you feel you should apologize to the American people?"

Then out of the blue two men spoke up, introducing themselves

The joy of homecoming is reflected in our faces 24 October 1988. (Photograph by the *San Diego Tribune*/Jerry McClard)

as from the Iranian-language radio station in Los Angeles. "Captain Rogers, our listeners would like to know if you hold any animosity . . . toward the Iranian people. Do you hate Iranians?"

I hesitated momentarily. There should be no misunderstanding of my reply. "The loss of innocent life in any combat engagement is regrettable. Regardless of the order of magnitude—one, ten, or hundreds—it's wasted human life, and I regret that. However, my absolute responsibility was and is for the safety of my ship and my crew. This does not mean that I regret the loss of life any less, and I certainly have never considered the Iranian people my enemy." They thanked me, turned, and walked away.

As Sharon and I walked off the pier, a photographer snapped a picture of us that captured the relief and joy we both felt. I was home, and the well-worn saying that today is the first day of the rest of our lives fit perfectly.

13

—◆◆◆—

RETURN TO NORMALCY

There is no better ballast for keeping the mind steady
on its keel . . . than business.
—James Russell Lowell, *Literary Essays*, 1870–90

Sailors have been coming home from the sea for centuries, and I'm
sure that most of them have done so with joy, anticipation, and anxiety.
As the central figure in an episode with worldwide repercussions, I
had more than my share of the last. But returning to a normal life was
our primary goal, and Sharon and I intended to do just that. My mother,
my brother, and his wife remained for a few days. We didn't talk about
the deployment, the events of 3 July, or the investigation. Sharon and
I didn't feel like revisiting it, so it became a nonsubject. I quickly got
into puttering around the house, tending to the cars, working in the yard,
and performing the list of chores that accumulate during any cruise.

Sharon and I continued to receive correspondence and invitations
asking us to speak to various organizations. Some we honored but
most were turned down. We both felt the sooner we became invisible,
the better. One handwritten piece of correspondence to which I didn't
respond had been delivered to the ship. It read, unedited, as follows:

Sunday, July 3, 1988 is a day which I will never forget in my life,
neither you can afford to remove from your mind the most disastrous
human tragedy taken place over the Persian Gulf waters in a most
horrendous and inhuman manner.

Among the crew members of the jet-liner I lost my dear brother, a unique pilot, an extraordinarily dignified and innocent man, late Captain Mohsen Rezaian who was the head pilot of the ill-fated Airbus. He was turned into the powder at the mid-air by your barrage missile attack and perished along with so many other innocent lives aboard, without the slightest sin or guilt whatsoever.

I was at the area of carnage the day after and unfortunately I saw the result of your barbarous crime and its magnitude. I used to be a Navy Commander myself and I had my college education in U.S. as my late brother did, but ever since the incredible downing I really felt ashamed of myself.

I hated your Navy and ours. So that I even quit my job and I ruined my whole career. Because of that calamity, me and my family are left with an everlasting misery and deep sorrow and the empty place of a real close brother who was living at the same building with us has created us a great mental distress and emotional upset. We could some-how bear the pain of tragedy if he had died in an accident but this premeditated act is neither forgivable nor forgettable.

I was always been thinking of the U.S. Navy as the guardian of the human rights and protectors of peace and security of the world, but I am sorry to say that this ugly and scandalous crime against human-ity has put a perpetual stigma on your Navy's face. The reaction of U.S. authorities toward this unmanly massacre also disproved your adherence to human rights because the U.S. government as the culprit in this horrendous incident, showed neither remorse nor compassion for the loss of innocent lives. And even President Reagan called it an understandable accident and your act as a "proper defensive action." It's a pity for a super power this childish attitude. Didn't we really deserve a small gesture of sympathy? Did you have to say a pack of lies and contradictory statements about the incident in a bid to justify the case?

You knew well that your flimsy alibis would [be] worth nothing while there exists undeniable evidence. I hope that at least you wouldn't forget your moral responsibility and please try not to disintegrate the glorious name of America.

I'm wondering why the plane was mistaken for an F-14 which is an interceptor and was not a threat to you anyway, or it was the result of panic and inexperience. I do appreciate your prompt response.

The letter was signed, "Yours sincerely, Hossein Rezaian."

Despite the diatribe, the pain and grief pouring from this letter struck me hard. All of the sorrow and regret that had haunted me since July returned in force. My immediate inclination was to respond and tell him, to the extent I could, that I shared his burden.

I contacted Matt Dillon and relayed the content of the letter. Following a discussion with the hierarchy, Matt said that return correspondence could be used by the Iranian government as some sort of political lever. Accordingly, I elected not to respond, and Matt forwarded the letter to the NIS.

Not long after our return, I flew back to Washington, D.C., with Vic Guillory and Doug McDonald to give a deployment debriefing to Vice Admiral John Nyquist, then deputy chief of naval operations for surface warfare. The presentation was well received, and both Admiral Nyquist and his deputy, Rear Admiral Grant Sharp, spent considerable time with us going over the details of the cruise, start to finish.

While we were rattling around the Pentagon I was able to speak briefly with the CNO, Admiral Trost, and thank him for his support. He had publicly and clearly been in our corner from 3 July on. Not a bad elephant to have backing you up. Following my session with the CNO, the vice chief, Admiral Leon Edney, asked me to stop in and see him. I had never met him, but after forty-five minutes in his office I could see why he wore four stars. Concerned about my well-being and that of my family and crew, he asked several times if there was anything he could do for us. These were not idle, polite requests.

On the other hand, for the first time I experienced the "wounded buffalo" syndrome. Several officers whom I knew well, had served with, and considered close friends were obviously uncomfortable when I contacted them. One individual hurriedly closed our conversation with, "Rogers, I can't believe they didn't hang your ass." I should have expected some reaction of this type. It was tough to take, the realization that in some quarters I "glowed in the dark." Admiral Kihune had been right.

A more positive note was a brief visit with Major Robin Higgins. I was determined to thank her personally for her powerful letter. Doug, Vic, and I found her in the public affairs office of the secretary of defense. We were honored to meet her, a strong, courageous, and dignified woman.

Early in November, back in San Diego, I was visiting Sharon during one of her breaks at school when the headmaster, Dr. Tim Burns, approached and asked me if I would consider delivering the commencement address the next spring. This was an invitation I was happy to accept. We had been members of the La Jolla Country Day School family for fourteen years, and I felt the graduating seniors would be interested in my remarks. The request meant a lot to Sharon, too.

A day or two later, Petty Officer Jordan buzzed me in my in-port cabin and relayed that the White House was on the line. "Jordan, my humor is a bit thin today. I'm not up to any ship's office jokes."

"Skipper, no bull, this really is a call from the White House."

President Reagan's military aide was on the line and explained that Reagan was coming to San Diego for a political rally in support of Vice President George Bush. He wanted to meet with Sharon and me privately on board Air Force 1. We agreed this was purely private and would not be tied to his political appearance. When I called Sharon, I got the same initial reaction Jordan had received from me. We were both excited and looking forward to the encounter. Unfortunately, someone mentioned this plan to the media and it had to be scrapped to avoid possible political ramifications. We were disappointed. I told Sharon if she had purchased a new outfit for the nonevent I would have sent the bill to the White House press pool.

The Christmas holidays were looming and plans for the *Vincennes* party had been made. It was scheduled to be held the second week of December at the Holiday Inn near Montgomery Field. Bob and Hope Kihune were to be our guests of honor. Kihune was now a three-star admiral whose schedule was so tight he didn't have two minutes in a day to sneeze, but he made sure he and Hope would stay the whole evening.

The mood was upbeat at the party. Everyone seemed to radiate warmth and closeness. I don't think I'd ever felt such rapport with a navy group other than our friends who had been stationed with us in Japan. The evening began with Ted Atwood leading us in the invocation. Then there was delicious food, lots of laughter, a few joke awards, and after-dinner dancing.

During dinner I was seated between Bob Kihune and Will. They were discussing the future. "I'd really like to have you take the job as commanding officer of the tactical training group," the admiral was saying. "We need someone with Aegis background, and you really are the right man. I'd feel more comfortable with you and Sharon here rather than overseas."

The admiral knew we'd been considering London. We had often talked about Will doing a European tour as a cap to our time in the navy, a nice way to go out. Will had been negotiating for some months for a job in London. He was told he had the inside track on the assignment. We hadn't decided whether he would retire after being relieved from the *Vincennes* or take one more assignment.

"I think it's unwise for you to go abroad," Bob continued. "You should stay stateside for the next couple of years. I'd feel safer with you and Sharon here in San Diego."

I was relieved that the admiral shared my concern. I, too, felt stateside would be a more risk-free assignment. Earlier when I voiced my concern, Will had simply humored me and said, "I don't think there's a thing to worry about."

Overseas billets and vehicles left outside at night continued to haunt me. I was even insisting that Bill park his car outside the neighborhood after dark and skateboard back to the house. So we continued to discuss Admiral Kihune's offer of the training group command, and just before Christmas Will accepted the position.

The *Vincennes* change of command was still a few months away. We were hoping to have a quiet family Christmas. Bill was home for the holidays, happy with his transfer to Colgate, and Will's parents were here from San Antonio.

On the morning of 22 December, I was in our upstairs office when I heard about the bombing of Pan Am Flight 103 over Lockerbie, Scotland. Two hundred fifty-nine people had been killed on the plane and eleven more on the ground. The news report speculated that the incident was in retaliation for the *Vincennes*'s action. It was mostly conjecture, but later television news shows began showing film of the missiles being fired on 3 July and the wreckage of the Airbus in the Persian Gulf. I felt a knot in my stomach and wondered if it was ever going to stop.

This horrible disaster cast a pall over the holiday. We tried to work around it and get on with things, but it was always there. I could sense a dark undercurrent, particularly between Will and me.

We received a telephone call from a local television station asking for our comment regarding Flight 103. We had none.

After Christmas we followed a quiet routine of working, taking in a movie on Friday, and puttering about. Sharon's sister Pat and her husband Faris came from Fort Worth for a visit, and we got away for a long ski weekend at Big Bear. Faris and I were on the lift when he turned to me and said, "I know how relieved you and Sharon must be to have all this behind you."

"You don't know the half of it."

One afternoon in late February Sharon and a friend, a fellow fourth-grade teacher, were discussing some problems and I overheard Sharon say, "Rest assured, we're going to be together at Country Day forever." How little we knew!

The detailer had called me with the news that I would be nominated as commanding officer of the Tactical Training Group, Pacific, following my relief from the *Vincennes*. In the meantime I was busy with a nev-erending cycle of inspections, conducting local-area operations, and planning for the late-spring change of command. Thrown into this was a scheduled drug-interdiction operation in concert with the Coast Guard. As this involved a southerly transit from San Diego, a stop in Acapulco was included. The Acapulco chapter of the U.S. Navy League and units of the Mexican navy flat out adopted the crew. Everybody went out of the way to make us feel welcome.

A major event was our upcoming OPPE (operational propulsion plant examination). This particular inspection is demanding and dreaded. Every man had been painstakingly preparing for the monster for months, and we were looking forward to getting it over with. It was scheduled to start on 14 March.

On the afternoon of Thursday, 9 March, I was attending a change of command for a friend of long standing, Captain Bill Kelly. Ted Atwood turned to me at one point and said, "Isn't it nice for things to be so quiet, no one bothering us?"

I was beginning to wonder why I continued to insist that our cars be parked in the garage. As the only person who seemed to be concerned, I began to question my anxiety.

As I hurried home from school Thursday afternoon, 9 March, my mind was fixed on preparing a quick meal before the monthly ombuds-man meeting that night. Because of Will's workbench our sedan only fit the length of the garage's righthand side, and I always parked my van on the left. But that day I inadvertently parked it on the righthand side, outside the garage.

Will was rushing that day, too. He hurried into the house and we ate quickly in order to make it to the 32nd Street Naval Station by seven o'clock for the meeting. It broke up about nine-thirty, and by the time we arrived back home we were exhausted. So, instead of backing my van out of the righthand side of the driveway and switching the cars, we left them outside.

This was the first night since 3 July that both cars were parked side by side in our driveway.

The next morning, 10 March, Will woke up early as usual, dressed, and drove the van to a nearby doughnut shop. He was home within twenty minutes with his delivery. This was a daily routine with us. Normally he would have dropped the food on the counter and left for the ship, but this morning was different. We had made an early-morning groomer's appointment for Paddock, our Westy, so that he'd look good for our guests the next night. We were hosting a special dinner party in honor of Admiral and Hope Kihune and Ted Atwood.

So Will was still at home. We were discussing the next evening's dinner plans as I bagged some lettuce and put it into a crystal punch-bowl for a birthday party at school. As I carried the bowl out to the van, Will quipped, "Don't drop it, we need that for tomorrow night."

"Nothing's going to happen to the punchbowl," I said.

We were standing in the driveway when George, our neighbor, came walking across the street carrying a large flat of fresh strawberries. In his warm Greek accent, he said, "I want to give you these. They're organic."

"Thanks, George, they're beautiful. They'll be delicious for dessert tomorrow night."

Will returned to the house with the fruit. I waved goodbye and began driving to school. It was a beautiful, crisp morning. I followed my usual route, turned south on Towne Center Drive to Nobel, west on Nobel to Genesee, then north. I had been gone from the house about four minutes when I stopped for the traffic light at Genesee and La Jolla Village Drive.

There were a couple of cars ahead of me, and I noticed in the rearview mirror that traffic was backed up as far as I could see. It was seven forty-five and I was right on schedule.

14

THE BOMBING

A peculiar kind of fear they call courage.
—Charles Rann Kennedy, *The Terrible Meek*, 1912

I heard a loud explosion and my body was slammed forward. It felt like being rear-ended by a locomotive traveling a hundred miles an hour. I could smell smoke. Something burning! Opening the door, I tried to get out. "Oh, God!" My seatbelt. I fumbled with the latch, but couldn't disconnect it.

"Sharon, if you've ever done anything right, get this damn thing off—get it off!"

Free of the belt, I jumped down from the seat of the van and turned to run to the rear. I was unsteady on my feet and thought I could lean on the car directly behind me. But the cars were all gone.

Stumbling and half running around the back of the van, I could feel the heat from the fire engulfing it. On my way to the curb I felt someone touch my arm. A man was directing me toward a pickup truck parked off the street.

"Are you okay? Let me help you into my truck."

He took off his leather jacket and hung it around my shoulders.

"Is anyone else in the van?"

I was trying hard to listen to what he was asking me. His words sounded as if they were traveling through a tunnel.

"No. No one else is in there." I wasn't completely sure of what I was saying, and I couldn't remember if I was alone or not. Was there anyone else in the van?

He asked again, "Is there anyone else in your van?" His words were steady and calm.

"No. No one's in there."

He nodded. "I'll be right back."

I watched him run toward the burning van. He got as close as he possibly could to see if it was empty.

When he came back, he said, "I've got a cellular phone. Is there someone you want to call?"

"My husband."

"Give me the number."

I recited the numbers and he punched them in. Nothing.

"Give me the number again."

My thoughts seemed to move in slow motion. I could hear my responses, but they sounded as if they were coming from someone else. I was numb, and though I knew it was a bomb I heard myself ask, "Do you think it's a bomb?"

He didn't answer, just continued punching the numbers into the phone.

"I think it's a bomb. Don't you think it's a bomb?" Even as I was asking this question, I realized how bizarre it was that I was saying this to a stranger. I had to get hold of myself.

I could hear him talking to someone and I hoped it was Will.

"I've just spoken to your husband. He'll be right here. Are you okay?"

"Yes, thank you. Thank you very much."

He walked a short distance from his truck to take a picture of the van. And I sat there. Sat there watching my van burn.

I was going from the garage to the house when I heard the telephone. "Hello."

A calm voice said, "Your wife is all right, she's had some trouble with her van but she wants you to come. We're on the corner of Genesee and La Jolla Village Drive."

"What kind of trouble?"

"There's been some trouble with the van. Her van. But she's all right."

"I'm on my way."

Sharon's Toyota van burns after a pipe-bomb explosion, 10 March 1989. (Photograph by John R. Christy)

I stayed in the truck. A policewoman approached. I recognized her as someone I'd met at the house when Bill and I returned after 3 July. "Officer, I don't know if you remember me, but I'm Sharon Rogers. My husband is commanding officer of the *Vincennes*."

With barely a response, she began ordering everyone to stay back from the van and alerted other officers to call in the bomb squad, the FBI, and the Bureau of Alcohol, Tobacco and Firearms. Eventually they came, as well as people from NIS, the San Diego County sheriff's office, the San Diego Police Department, and the San Diego Fire Department.

I screeched out of the driveway. George, who was standing in front of his house, must have thought I had lost my mind. As I came to the intersection of Genesee and Nobel I could see traffic backed up. And as I approached the corner I could see a towering column of black smoke to the north. I drove straight through the red light to the south-bound lanes of Genesee and turned north on the wrong side of the street.

About halfway toward La Jolla Village Drive a police officer waved frantically. Slamming on the brakes, and before he could say anything, I yelled, "That's my wife! And that's my wife's van!" I must have looked like a wild man. He waved me on. I pulled up next to the median, facing the wrong way, and abandoned the car there.

The catalytic converter must have exploded, I thought. I ran across the street toward a horrifying image: The entire back half of the van was enveloped in dark orange flames and billowing oil-black smoke. The left rear tire was a ring of fire and the driver's door was closed.

Oh, Jesus, the thought screamed in my mind, she didn't get out, they didn't get her out! I was running, not conscious of anything except that paralyzing picture. Then I saw her huddled in the cab of a pickup truck. Nothing else mattered. The confusion, rage, and hatred would come later.

I hugged Sharon. "Thank God you're safe!" Her washed-out face and rigid stare told me she was in shock.

"They're going to get us all," she said.

"Now, Sharon, it's not going to happen. Don't worry about it." I was trying to play it down, but it was hard to do that with the van burning in the street.

As they were putting out the fire I walked over toward the van. It looked as if the world's largest shotgun had been fired inside. There were jagged holes the size of tennis balls blown through the roof. The back inside compartment was gutted. The explosion had ruptured the gas tank, and fire had engulfed the back of the van and swept forward.

Sharon's charred purse was lying in the front passenger seat, soggy from the water. The ignition key had melted into a solid mass. The punchbowl and lettuce didn't make it.

No faulty catalytic converter had caused this. If I needed any confirmation, lying in the street was a piece of pipe that looked like part of a clothesline pole, about a foot long and two and a half to three inches in diameter. It was split open from end to end.

I don't know how long I sat there. It seemed like my van just wouldn't stop burning. I caught myself thinking about how we'd just had it

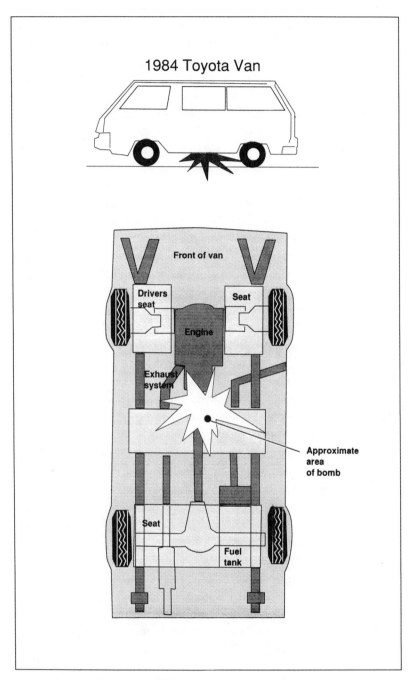

Approximate placement of the bomb underneath Sharon's van. (Drawing by James Burnett)

washed and how clean it had looked. The blackened rear and the untouched white front made an ugly contrast.

The man who was so kind to me was John Christy, a concrete and masonry contractor supervising work on a new sign at the corner of the shopping complex. That's why his truck and others were parked on the embankment off the street. One of his crew, Charles Archer, helped Mr. Christy to look after me. Mr. Christy used the Polaroid camera he had for work to take a picture of the van. He said later that he had never seen a car burn like that.

The Associated Press purchased the shot and agreed to syndicate it. Eventually it was shown worldwide. I appreciated his capturing the horror of the moment—raw terrorism.

Just before we were transferred to the police station, I asked Will to call the lower-school director and tell her I wouldn't be coming in. He used Mr. Christy's cellular phone to tell her I'd been in an accident and would contact her later. Then Will helped me out of the truck and into a police car and we were driven to the North City substation a couple of blocks away. Another officer drove Will's abandoned car to the station.

Now almost immobile with fright, I imagined that someone was after the whole family. I was sure it was a conspiracy and was desperate to contact Bill at Colgate. I wanted him home on the next plane.

As we entered the police station, Captain Dave Crow ushered us into his office and turned it over to us. He was very solicitous. "Anything we can do?" he asked. "Would you like coffee, water, anything? I'll just get out of your way, and if you need anything, let me know."

I had never experienced such fear and confusion. I had to reach Bill. Will picked up the telephone on the captain's desk and called the administration office at Colgate.

Not wanting to frighten Bill, I said, "This is not an emergency, but it's imperative that I talk with my son immediately. Please locate him and have him call his father at this number."

Hanging up the phone, I turned my attention to Sharon. She kept repeating, "We have to get hold of him, we have to know where he is." She was frantic, and I realized that in her mind conspirators were coming out of the woodwork. I wasn't that concerned about a conspiracy—couldn't conceive of it. But, then, I couldn't conceive of anybody blowing up the van, either. So who the hell was I to say she was wrong? We were frantic.

Sharon couldn't sit still. She paced. She went over and stood by the telephone and stared at it, trying to will it to ring. We got her coffee and she couldn't drink it. She put the coffee down and started pacing again. At about that time a parent of one of her students appeared in the foyer. Ironically, Country Day was across the street from the police station. Sharon hurried out to speak with the parent, but their conversation was cut short when reporters poured into the station.

Wearing a yellow oxford-cloth shirt, gray wool slacks, and a hand-knit gray and yellow pullover, she'd looked fresh and pulled together leaving the house. Now she stank of fuel, cordite, and smoke. Her hair was uncombed and her eyes were fixed and vacant.

I ran my fingers through my hair and began pulling out pieces of metal. The FBI agent placed a white sheet of paper on the desk and I shook the jagged shrapnel onto it. When I had gotten nearly all of it, they poured the stuff into an envelope, sealed it, and added it to the evidence they were collecting.

As time dragged by and we had yet to hear from Bill, Sharon grew irrational. I asked the FBI agent to leave the room. "Sharon, you've got to get hold of yourself. Bill will call, it's going to be all right. We've got a long, hard day ahead of us and we need to be strong for each other. Please don't fall apart."

"I want him home now—don't you understand?"

"Listen to me: He's safe where he is and we're going to cover him like a blanket. He'll be home in two weeks after exams. It won't do him any good to come home and miss those. And we don't want to drag him into the middle of this."

"Then he has to have protection, Will."

"I guarantee he'll have it."

At that moment the phone rang. It was a New York operator. In a shaking voice, Bill asked, "Dad, what's up? Why are you at the police station? Is Mom all right? They told me that you were okay."

"We're both fine, we're both okay."

"What's wrong?"

"We think someone tried to blow up Mom's van, but she's okay.

Bill, there will be some people coming to stay with you until this gets sorted out."

As I spoke with him I could see how badly Sharon wanted to hear his voice, but I needed to keep assuring him in case she broke down. "Mom's okay—we're both okay. Here she is."

I knew I had to be as calm as possible. With my heart pounding and my hand shaking, I took the phone from Will. "Bill, honey, are you all right?"

"Mom, I'm okay. What happened?"

The moment I heard his voice I started to relax. Briefly I recounted everything up to the moment, never mentioning that I wanted him to come home. Toward the end of our conversation, I assured him we'd talk to him again that evening. Hanging up, I couldn't begin to imagine the bizarre experiences he was about to encounter.

Will called the FBI agent back into the office and made arrangements for Bill's protection. "Will you please get hold of the senior NIS agent? I want to talk to him."

Within five minutes Harry Stovall was on the line. Will explained to him what we wanted. And he said, "I'll take care of it."

Media reps were all over the station. There was a partition between the foyer and the office area beyond which the press was not permitted. They were hanging around it, thrusting their extended boom mikes in our direction. To get to the restrooms we had to pass by this electronic gauntlet. Out of nervous necessity we both made this trip several times.

In the foyer, returning from one of these trips, I was astonished to see our neighbor, George, hurrying toward me with outstretched arms. This impromptu embrace was captured on news video and ran repeatedly on network news.

Back in the office the phone rang. It was my sister, Pat, in Fort Worth. My niece had seen a report on CNN regarding the bombing and telephoned her. She then called our home, where the screeners and police were working, and one of them had referred her to the police substation.

"Sharon, are you all right?" Her anxiety came through loud and clear. "You can't imagine what they asked me before they'd let me talk to you." Assuring her I was fine, I told her I'd call later in the day when we could talk. It was only at this point that it dawned on us that this was no local news story. As soon as I hung up, Will dialed his folks in San Antonio.

Shortly, Commander Matt Dillon arrived at the police station to deal with the media. He explained that authorities from a number of agencies were working on the problem and that Captain and Mrs. Rogers were all right but had no statement to make.

The NIS people had not decided yet what we were going to do, but returning home was soon ruled out. The authorities were going over the garage and house inch by inch.

Sharon didn't want to leave the police substation and be away from the telephone. Once she had talked to Bill she relaxed a little, but she became nervous again at the thought of him not coming home. Once we got the call that a state trooper was with Bill and NIS agents were en route to take over the security, she agreed to leave.

A decision was made to move us into the BOQ at the naval amphibious base in Coronado, where Sharon and Bill had stayed a couple of days the previous July. We were placed under the protection of the NIS personal-security detachment. The PSD is a highly trained, specialized group similar to the Secret Service. The hand of the vice chief of naval operations, Admiral Leon Edney, was behind the NIS's quick and thorough response.

As we exited the substation, the sheriff's department helicopter was hovering overhead, agents were lined up in two rows on each side of the back entrance, three unmarked cars were waiting, agents with automatic weapons surrounded the vehicles, and no one was allowed to approach. If this operation was supposed to be covert, it failed miserably. In addition to the three NIS vehicles, we had black and white police cars leading and following with flashing lights and sirens.

We hit I-5 going south at close to 80 mph, shooting past other cars. When we arrived at the entrance to the BOQ, Admiral Kihune and his wife Hope were waiting.

Kihune said, "Senator Pete Wilson will be here in a few minutes. He wants to hear firsthand what happened, so let's go up and wait for him."

We rode the elevators to the ninth floor and entered a room looking over a construction project. The NIS agents were nervous about the room's proximity to the construction site and wanted to move us.

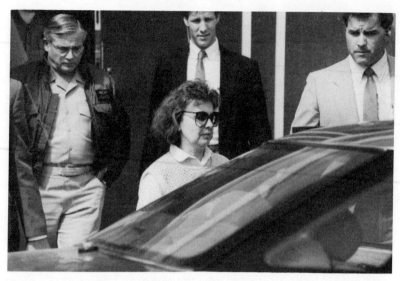

Escorted by NIS agents, we depart the police substation in north San Diego after the bombing. (Photograph by Bob Redding, the *San Diego Union*)

Much to their consternation, the Wilsons arrived and we stayed in the room for about thirty minutes.

Gayle Wilson looked fresh and neat, while Sharon still reeked of smoke and fuel. I was no prize myself. I had been sweating heavily and felt dirty and uncomfortable. Appearances, however, were not the issue with Pete Wilson. "This is something that simply cannot be tolerated," he said. "An overt attack on American soil against American citizens."

After the Wilsons left, Bob and Hope Kihune expressed their wish to help in any way they could. Bob said if a house was available on the amphibious base or at the naval air station on North Island, he would arrange for us to use it. Hope, who rarely loses her composure, was visibly shaken. There were tears in her eyes as she told Sharon she would be available for her, as would the other navy wives.

"We were supposed to come to your home tomorrow night. Now will you come to ours? Tell me who was on the guest list."

After the Kihunes left we moved across the hall to a two-room suite. That made the NIS people breathe easier. There we were, Will in his sweat-stained khakis and me in my foul-smelling outfit. We had nothing else. We sat on the end of the bed, unable to believe what was happening to us. And fears about Bill still nagged me.

We tuned into CNN and began watching the scene that had been recorded earlier. There was the burned-out van with the collapsed rear tires. The authorities swarmed around the hulk, literally vacuuming the street, the sidewalk, and the embankment for every fragment of debris.

As the cameras zoomed in, I could see that the transmission had absorbed part of the blast and that the high headrest on my seat had shielded my head and neck from the fragments. Will put his hand on my shoulder. I had been very, very lucky.

We'd been sitting on the edge of the bed for about an hour when Bill called from the Colgate Inn, a small hotel located near the university campus. He sounded concerned and tired as he related the events of his day. He told us how he had been in a lecture hall with about two hundred other students when the dean stepped in and asked, "Is Will Rogers in the room?"

"I didn't know what I'd done, and as I left the hall I'm sure the other students were pretty curious."

In the dean's office he was told to telephone us. Of course he hadn't recognized the number, and when he asked about it he was told it was a police station. As if that wasn't enough, whoever answered the phone put him through the third degree, grilling him about everything but his shoe size before putting him through to us.

"From the dean's office, Dad, I was taken to a windowless room in the basement of the campus security building. Inside waiting for me was an enormous state trooper who broke out a riot gun, assembled and loaded it, told me to sit in a chair, and took a seat facing the door. He told me, 'If anyone tries that door, Roscoe will take care of them.'

"I stayed in the basement with Roscoe for a couple of hours until the NIS arrived. We went back to my dorm, but I guess they had to check everyone's ID coming and going and it got too hard. So they moved me here to the Colgate Inn. We've got four or five rooms, most of the third floor.

"I'm not sure what to do about getting my books and clothes and things, Dad. How long is this gonna go on?"

Ted Atwood leads the way for Paddock, held on a leash by Police Officer Pam Smith, as the dog is led from our home after the car bombing. (Photograph by Jerry Rife, the *San Diego Union*)

Basement to attic, our son had been surrounded by enough firepower to start a small war. When Bill told his mom that he was literally surrounded by security, it was the first time since morning that Sharon relaxed. She had been able to hide her emotions from everyone except me. After a quarter of a century with her I could tell when her lips were set a certain way or her posture was fixed that she was upset. Until the moment of Bill's call, she looked like a bowstring.

We were blanketed by security. There were NIS agents all over the BOQ. If we so much as stuck our heads out of the room, they came popping into the hall like rabbits. We decided to walk over to the officers' club with Ted for dinner, but it wasn't as simple as that. First the NIS had to make "arrangements." They telephoned and preempted the grill room, then sent an advance team over to scour the place. This level of effort within the fences of a military installation seemed like overkill, but my opinion wasn't asked.

The three of us sat at a corner table discussing a supportive call

Congressman Lowery had made to us at the police station moments after our arrival, and Ted's adventures getting our dog out of the house. The diners nearby all had strange bulges under their coats or flat black briefcases next to their chairs. Living with this protective curtain was going to be tough, but we were grateful for their watchful presence. It was the beginning of a strange, new, and frightening experience.

15

——◆◆◆——

AMID THE FALLOUT

It's a mad world. Mad as Bedlam.

—Charles Dickens, *David Copperfield*, 1849–50

Our lives were turned upside down and inside out, and it seemed as if we were riding a carousel that kept picking up speed. We were surrounded by the NIS, and our every movement was monitored.

The shock had still not worn off on Saturday when NIS agents drove Will to the ship. Although torn and not wanting to leave me, he felt he had to go because the OPPE was scheduled to begin on Tuesday. I sat in the BOQ looking out the window, wondering once again when my life would return to normal.

I telephoned the lower-school director and received the first indication that things were not all right at La Jolla Country Day School. "Sharon, I've been putting off calling you because I haven't known what to say. The parents are upset, really scared. But how are you?"

I could sense she wanted to say more. "I'm doing okay."

She repeated herself. "Sharon, the parents are fearful, really apprehensive."

"Well, I understand their feeling of fear, and I'm the last person who would want to place anyone in danger. I just wanted you to know that I'm ready to come back whenever it's possible. I'll have NIS agents with me, but they've assured me they'll be unobtrusive. They've promised me that the children won't even know they're there."

There was a long silence.

"Sharon, we really have a problem. The parents are hysterical."

"I see. Well, I wanted to give you my number anyway, so you'd know how to contact me."

That was it. The conversation was over. I had just talked with a friend of fourteen years, and she had treated me as if I were a stranger.

The school's fund-raising auction had been held the night before, I later learned, and not surprisingly, the bombing had been the topic of conversation.

On Saturday morning the FBI visited me on the ship and later both of us at the BOQ. We made it clear that we had not seen anything, heard anything, or talked to anyone that might shed light on the bombing.

They were patient but persistent, going over the same ground repeatedly, hoping to spark something we had unwittingly overlooked. "Can you think of anybody you know who might want to do this? Did you notice anything? Any place you might have gone that was unusual? Notice anything in the neighborhood? Have you received any phone calls?"

One of the FBI agents said that "It was a dinosaur of a pipe bomb," the largest they had ever seen. Sharon, who was having a hard time digesting the reality of the attack, said, "Maybe the bomb was intended just to frighten or scare us." The response was, "No, ma'am, this was intended to kill."

No matter how farfetched the idea, the investigators pursued all avenues. "Did you ever see anybody when you were out walking the dog that you didn't recognize? Have you ever seen a black Mercedes in the neighborhood? Have you ever seen a beige-colored BMW with personalized California plates around your house?"

They wanted to recover an accurate timeline for Friday morning. What time had I left for the doughnut shop? Had I let the van warm up before leaving? Had I let it run while in the doughnut shop? How long was I there? How long was the ignition off? When I came back, where did I park the van? Why there? How long was it in the driveway before Sharon got into it? These questions were asked over and over. The men were attempting, of course, to determine how the bombing device had been fused, and if it was mechanical, or heat sensitive, or remote-controlled.

I needed to buy a couple of things, so the NIS entourage took me to a local supermarket. I didn't know the procedure for getting out of the sedan or walking into the store with agents following me. Was I supposed to talk to them or ignore them? As it turned out, I was supposed to act as if they weren't there.

I picked up a loaf of bread, orange juice, and crackers, then at the checkout counter found I was ten cents short. The bag boy said, "I know who you are. Don't worry about the dime." Anyone in the store could look out the front windows and see three cars idling in the no-parking zone, with NIS agents standing by.

On Sunday afternoon Will and I returned home to get some of our clothes and personal items. The place was littered with guns, ammunition boxes, flak jackets, hand-held searchlights, empty pizza boxes, and overflowing ashtrays. Leaning against the refrigerator door was a twelve-gauge riot gun. I stood there wondering how to get past this weapon and into the freezer.

"This is not a cheap flophouse!" Will told the supervisor in charge of the detail. "I want these people to respect this place, it's our home. I don't want them smoking in the house, I don't want them laying their gear all over the place, I don't want them lounging around in their damn flak vests shoveling pizza into their mouths!" Will is normally slow to anger. I realized then how much frustration he had bottled up inside. We did nonetheless appreciate what these young men were doing.

During this period the house next door was burglarized. Had the robber chosen our home instead he might have abandoned his life of crime, if he had any life left at all!

A few days later Will was escorted to our house to pick up a uniform. A reporter standing behind a large tropical plant by our front door stepped out as Will rounded the corner. As the man raised his camera, an NIS agent pushed Will aside and exposed his weapon. The reporter dropped his camera, produced an ID, and left in disappointment.

On our visits home we would listen to the answering machine, collecting messages from TV and radio stations as well as from friends. After returning calls we'd sit around for a couple of hours, reluctant to leave. I don't think I could have tolerated the idea of being away from home for six weeks had I known of it beforehand. Time was crawling by.

Monday morning I received a message to call Tim Burns, the

school's headmaster. "Sharon, I want to talk to you and Will," were his first words.

"Fine. Would you like for us to come over to your house?"

"No," he said, "that wouldn't be wise. Is there anyplace else we could meet?"

"We can have the NIS pick you up and bring you to the BOQ."

"That sounds good. I'll do that."

So we made arrangements for him to be picked up that evening.

The agent assigned to me, Sheri Rostodha, was an attractive woman in her early thirties, a kind, low-key person. She seemed sensitive to my moods and needs. After Will left for the ship Agent Rostodha asked me if I'd like a change of scenery. I suggested we drive to the University Towne Center shopping complex close to my house. I wanted to be close to home and to walk for a while. It was around ten o'clock, and there weren't many people in the mall. We were wandering around, Sheri and I together, the other agents several feet behind, when a neighbor of mine who had a child enrolled at Country Day walked up behind me and asked, "Mrs. Rogers?"

As I turned, the agents formed an instant human shield around me. The parent stared at me with an expression of fear and confusion in her eyes, a look that would become familiar as time went by.

"Do you know this person?" one of the agents asked.

"Yes, I do."

Still, they wouldn't let me get too close to her. She asked me how I was. We exchanged a couple of words, and after telling her I was glad to see her, Sheri and I started walking again. This was my first meeting with someone connected to the school, where I was respected and well liked. Now, it seemed, I was simply cause for bewilderment.

Tim Burns arrived at seven that evening, thrilled with his ride with the NIS agents. His first words were, "Sharon, I knew you were fine when I saw you on television greeting your neighbor at the police station, the way you walked." With little additional preamble, he began to describe and underscore how frightened the parents were. He kept talking about how much better off he would be if the parents wouldn't get involved and if he didn't have to deal with them.

And right in the middle of this he turned to Will. "Oh, by the way, it's going to be impossible for you to be our commencement speaker now. Nothing personal, you understand."

Will just nodded. I was proud of him for maintaining his composure.

Tim was dressed as usual in button-down shirt, bow tie, loafers, and round tortoiseshell glasses. He seemed almost buoyant that night, which struck me as somewhat peculiar, in light of the situation.

"Tim," I said, "we need to handle this situation carefully. It's important that we let the drama of the moment pass. Two weeks of spring vacation is coming. We should all try to step back from it and see how things work out."

"That's exactly what we'll do," Tim answered.

As we walked him to the door I thought to myself, He doesn't understand. He sees this as a local problem, doesn't realize that the country's focus will be on him and his actions. The only good thing to come out of the meeting was that Tim agreed to set up a time for Sharon to telephone her classroom and talk to her students, most of whom she had taught in the first grade as well as fourth.

As we were saying goodnight to Tim, Ted Atwood arrived. When the door closed Sharon turned to both of us. "There's no one who understands the parents' fear better than I do," she said. "I'm a mother. If I thought I'd be a danger to those children I'd never go near the school. The danger will pass, won't it?"

"Of course it will, Sharon," I said. "Whoever was behind this made his point. I can't imagine Tim would go so far as to cut you off permanently." All the time I was thinking his agenda was clear.

"I don't think I'll ever be allowed to teach at Country Day again," she said.

Will went to the ship on Tuesday to commence the OPPE. I spent most of the day in telephone conversation with my fourth-graders. They were concerned about my welfare and interested in what I was doing. We talked about home and school, and I assured them that I was okay and that I missed them. They kept asking me when I was coming back. That was a good question, because on top of everything else a bomb threat had been phoned into the school that day. I was given a copy of a letter Tim Burns subsequently wrote to the parents:

Late in the morning on Tuesday, the school received a recorded bomb threat. After discussion with the investigative authorities of its contents, the decision was made not to evacuate. Search dogs were brought in to sniff for explosives, and nothing was found.

We discussed the idea of sending a note home to parents describing the incident, but in fact, such a note would have been counterproductive. Alerting students with a letter that described the details of a bomb threat would have created more fears on a campus already filled with tension. We also received advice from authorities that since safety had been assured, we would be wise to consider not making an issue of the threat.

. . . Both local and national press continue to attempt to draw our school and its name into issues which I feel are quite separate from us. . . . It is my strongest intent that we remain separated from them.

After catching up on the Thursday morning news, I ran an errand and then returned to the BOQ to find a message asking me to call Tim. I returned the call.

"Sharon, you're going to be furious with what I have to tell you."

"What's that, Tim?"

"I really wish I could tell you this face to face, but it's so hard to get through to you. Logistically it's so difficult."

"Well, then, I'll come over to the school."

"Oh, no, you can't do that."

"What is it you need to tell me?"

"I've been with the executive board all morning. They feel that you can't return to school."

"What do you mean?"

"Sharon, I know this is rough for you. I was talking to my wife over an hour last night and she kept saying 'This will destroy Sharon's career. Can we do that to her?' "

Silence.

"But there's just no way you can return."

It was a moment before I could reply. "I see. Well . . . after this dies down and a few months pass I'd appreciate it if you'd write some letters of recommendation for me."

"Sharon, you're an excellent teacher, but if I can't hire you . . . who could? . . . But I'll do what I can. I want to read to you the press release we've written: 'To ensure the safety of the children, the confidence of the parents, and the integrity of the educational environment of La Jolla Country Day School, Mrs. Rogers will not be returning to the campus.' "

With those words, my career collapsed. After almost getting killed and then having to move out of my home, I needed to hold on to something, and all I had left was my self-respect.

When he finished I said, "Tim, why don't you add that it was by mutual decision."

"That's a wonderful idea! Sharon, you're really a professional." And I heard him adding the words to the statement.

"You're right, Tim, I am a professional."

He reread the news release and asked how it sounded. I told him it was fine. I hung up and walked over to the window. As I looked out over the ocean Tim's words, "You're an excellent teacher. . . . But if I can't hire you, who could?" continued to echo in my mind. Like Alice in *Through the Looking Glass*, I could feel myself spinning and tumbling into a deep, dark unknown.

The *Vincennes*'s return to port was anything but jubilant. We had failed the OPPE. Things had gone well enough during the first portion, but our performance during the critical underway drill fell short of the mark. The snap and sparkle that had been there during our workup was gone; the performance of the engineering watch teams had simply been flat. My mood was black. I should have taken my group commander's advice and asked for a delay. The events of the past few days had affected the crew more than I realized.

When I returned to the BOQ at about seven o'clock, the look on Sharon's face told me the OPPE was not the only issue at hand. As we were trying to cope with our latest troubles, two FBI agents showed up. We moved to an adjoining room and during our conversation one of them said, "Captain Rogers, we'd like for you to take a polygraph test."

"Fine. When would you like to do it?"

"Now."

The timing seemed a bit strange, and with everything the day had brought I wasn't happy about leaving Sharon alone again, but Ted had dropped by, I figured the feds must have a good reason, so I agreed. I looked at my watch. It was approaching nine o'clock. "Okay," I said.

I walked back into our suite and asked Ted if he would stay until I returned. He agreed. On the way to the Federal Building it struck me how bizarre this procedure was, but I figured when we arrived we would simply go in, do what was required, and be out of there. Wrong! The polygraph operator wasn't there. They had put a call out for him. I sat down in the resident agent's office to wait, flipping through magazines. Two hours passed. If the polygraph measures anger, I thought, I'm going to peg the needles.

Finally they were ready.

"Have you ever considered killing your wife?"

"No."

"Have you ever wanted to kill your wife?"

"No."

"Have you ever thought about getting someone to kill your wife?"

"No."

"Have you ever built an explosive device?"

"No."

I kept thinking, I'm willing to do this, but why not tomorrow? I'm not going anywhere. I've got NIS and FBI standing around while I go to the head. Why yank me out of the BOQ, at night, and today of all days?

Up until tonight, like most people, I held G-men in awe. I had closely followed the exploits of Eliot Ness, but this episode did a lot to cool my admiration. And as if it weren't enough, the fact that I had taken the polygraph test was leaked from the FBI office in Washington. When queried by the press, the bureau indicated it was their policy not to divulge results.

What a day! Sharon fired, the ship fails her first inspection ever, and then the circus with the FBI.

16

IN LIMBO

Be not afraid of life. Believe that life is worth living. . . .
—William James, *The Will to Believe*, 1897

The next day I lay in bed watching Will dress. Pinning the insignia to his khaki shirt and adjusting his belt, he turned to me. "Sharon, I won't be gone long, but there's some business I need to attend to on the ship. Can I bring you anything?"

As I watched him going through his normal morning routine, it seemed everyone else was getting on with business as usual. Rage welled up inside of me, and then I exploded. "What's happening? I feel like a prisoner and I don't know what I'm doing here. My profession's been ripped out from under me and no one will ever give me a job again. Our home's an armed camp and someone's out to kill us. What am I going to do?" My voice was getting louder and louder. Will just stood there with a stricken expression on his face. He walked toward me but I turned away—hating him, hating the navy, hating the school, loathing the cowards who tried to kill me, but most of all detesting myself because I could no longer rein in my emotions. Finally I lay back on the bed and began to cry.

Will stayed with me until I'd calmed down, then suggested I get dressed and get out of the BOQ. As soon as I gained my equilibrium I was sorry I'd blown up. After all, we were in this together.

After Will left I dressed and opened the door to the hall where the

NIS agents were stationed. Someone located Agent Rostodha for me, and when she knocked on the door I asked her if she felt like walking. She did. It took a while to contact the drivers and other agents. When you're under protection, spontaneity flies out the window. As we left the BOQ and walked the station grounds, I had NIS agents walking in front of me and behind me and a car slowly trailing.

The walk was a tonic and helped to put things in perspective. As we returned to the BOQ it was close to noon and I was hoping Will would join me for lunch. I wanted to apologize and assure him that I wasn't down for the count. I had a lot more fight left in me.

It was St. Patrick's Day. We'd been invited to two celebrations in Coronado. Congressman Lowery was hosting a large party, but we ruled that out because of the logistics involved with the NIS. We decided on the smaller gathering that he would be attending later. As usual, the NIS advance team screened the property, all the entrances and exits, all the possible routes to and from the place, toured the house, and stationed a team on the premises. When we arrived the Lowerys were already there and the congressman questioned me in depth about the termination of my employment. He was concerned by the turn of events.

Later, in a press conference, he said, "What Americans need to understand is that the way to deal with terrorism is not to isolate the victim but to stand together. The terrorists' weapon is fear. Most Americans realize that, and I hope the parents and administration at La Jolla Country Day realize it."

The next day in conversation with friends, I learned that rumors were flying thick and fast at school. The word was that Will and I were being escorted everywhere in disguise and eventually would have to undergo plastic surgery, that a government agent "double" was filling in for me, that we were to be flown out of state to a safehouse, that the Vincennes was being transferred to the East Coast. When one friend told me how sorry she was that Bill had been asked to leave Colgate because he was a security risk, I said, "Enough is enough." It was time to write a letter to the school administration, the board of trustees, and the parents of my class.

In it I told them that I was ready to resume my full class schedule, that NIS protection did not preclude me from teaching, and that I could meet with the children any time, anywhere. I concluded by saying that Bill was continuing his university studies and that Will and I considered San Diego our home. We had no plans to leave.

An April issue of Time magazine reported that I had written an angry letter. I considered it straightforward.

Emotional and confused by the bombing and Sharon's dismissal, we had avoided any public statement other than the brief one-liner provided to Matt Dillon on 10 March. However, following Lowery's comments to the press and the tangents the rumor mill was taking, we thought it was time for an additional open letter. After considerable discussion regarding content, we agreed on the following, which was sent to the San Diego Union, the Tribune, and the Los Angeles Times:

> The image of a burning van in the middle of a street of our community must not become a symbol of fear and unreasoned reaction. Instead it should represent the resolve and courage of a community and nation to resist and defeat the mindless and cowardly process of terrorism—whatever the source.
>
> If we react either individually or collectively without applying rational thought to our actions, we have surrendered the field to those who would invade and attempt to destroy our way of life.
>
> If on the other hand we press on with our lives, taking appropriate precautions, and assist constituted authority in punishing those responsible, we ensure the safety of the community and send the right signal.
>
> Finally, we would like to extend our appreciation to those who have given us support and to our hometown of San Diego. This support had been a needed bolster in a difficult period.

The editors of the papers gave this letter considerable visibility.

When it appeared, I commented to Sharon, "Country Day has an opportunity to put this to rest. I hope they don't miss the window."

We could see our long and close association with the school being swept away. Not only had Sharon taught in the lower school for twelve years, but Bill had been enrolled there from the second grade. The quiet twenty-six-acre campus and tree-shrouded open classrooms had been a perfect educational environment for him, and certainly worth the financial stretch the tuition had represented. For Sharon it was a classroom dream. To see it all disappear in clouds of misunderstanding, rumor, and emotion was like experiencing a death in the family.

Almost immediately after the bombing I was contacted by the local Crimestoppers organization, which works with all local, state, and federal law-enforcement agencies. It encourages citizens with knowledge of a crime to call a hotline. If the caller wishes to remain anonymous, he or she is given a secret code number for all future calls. If a felony is solved as the result of a tip, the caller is rewarded up to $1,000. In any event, Crimestoppers asked me to publicize my case by appearing in a short television clip. I didn't know what to expect, but said I'd do it.

I was driven downtown to the Federal Building and escorted to an upper-floor office, where I met the Crimestopper spokesperson from the police department. "Good morning, Mrs. Rogers," she said. "We appreciate your interest in helping us present your case. This airing will be a sixty-second spot. Now, we just want you to take a seat on this stool, relax, and tell us what occurred on 10 March."

I was watching the technician focus the camcorder. "I'd rather not have my face shown. Can you block it out?" Afterwards I realized how silly my request was, since my picture had been front-page news. "Are you going to ask me questions or what?"

"Just tell us your feelings and the message you want the public to hear. Okay, we'll start filming when you're ready."

I turned toward the camera, took a deep breath, and began talking.

"My life has been threatened, that of my family has been threatened. I've lost my job, I can't go back to my home. And my life has completely done a turnaround." I described the explosion, my escape from the van, and how I'd been helped to the nearby truck. "And I sat there and watched my van burn."

I paused to collect my thoughts, then continued. "We don't know who did it . . . someone is out there who committed a very cowardly act, and together as a community we have to find out who it is, so that it doesn't happen to anybody else. It was me last week. It could be you tomorrow."

I turned to the man who was filming. "I guess that's all."

"Good job. Would you like to see it? We'll replay it on the monitor."

Shortly after the piece aired, an anonymous benefactor donated $25,000 to my case, the Vincennes crew donated $1,000, and additional money began to flow in from other sources around the country. Very shortly the total rose to more than $40,000, the most ever collected for a single Crimestoppers case in the San Diego area.

Two weeks after the bombing, a friend arranged a meeting of the lower-school teachers at a popular downtown restaurant. They were very solicitous, asking how I was and bringing me small gifts. I shared with them some of the good wishes and support we were receiving daily from all over the world. They began to tell me behind-the-scene stories.

"Sharon, parents were threatening to pull out their children if you weren't immediately terminated."

Another remarked, "One parent whose child wasn't even in your class held a service of thanksgiving that he'd been spared."

Then more bits and pieces: "And you know that ——— has been pulled out. When she met with the school's scout troop last week, she wasn't allowed to cross the street to the school grounds."

"You heard about the bomb threat on the fourteenth. The bomb squad was called in accompanied by their dog, Blast. He didn't find any bombs but did locate a tennis ball in one of the desks. The children loved him. Can you believe we weren't even alerted to the threat?"

"A psychologist was brought in to help the children come to grips with their fears. The telling thing was that they weren't afraid, but just kept asking when you were returning."

Despite the chatter, I could sense that my friends were more than aware of the bodyguards. In fact they had been interrogated by the FBI several times, asked how long they had known me, if I had any enemies to their knowledge, if Will and I were happily married, how often they socialized with us—that sort of thing. The questions had made them uncomfortable, nervous, and more than a little irritated.

Even with all the upsetting table talk, we laughed a lot too. It was good being with close friends again. And I had another reunion to look forward to: Bill was arriving from New York that evening.

Both the FBI and the NIS were devoting enormous effort to the case. Every scrap of physical evidence that could be recovered had been meticulously catalogued and shipped to the FBI lab for analysis. Parked next to the van, our sedan was "tented" in plastic and, using a technique involving fumes from the substance found in Crazy Glue, latent prints were developed. The technician explained that they hoped to come up with strange finger or palm marks. To this day there is still a lump of glue on the fender.

Our entire neighborhood, the Country Day faculty, and members of the *Vincennes* crew were interviewed. Psychological profiles of the type of individual likely to employ pipe bombs were developed. Eyewitnesses to the explosion were thoroughly checked out, and everything they had seen was being run to ground. Was there an individual near the intersection with a remote triggering device? What color and make were the vehicles close to the van? How many explosions had been heard—one, two? If two, was the second another bomb or simply the gas tank exploding? A close neighbor who had reported being approached some time earlier by an individual asking where I lived underwent hypnosis. The agents hoped that some subconscious scrap of information might be recalled.

One of the senior NIS agents commented that they needed to move quickly while interest was keen, but that we shouldn't hope for a quick solution. "When things move on and upper-level interest dies, the dog workers on the case will need all this."

Meanwhile, our situation at the BOQ was growing intolerable. Sharon and I were bumping into each other. The lobby of the building had to be cleared every time we passed through it, and Bill was due in for spring break. I discussed this with the NIS agent in charge of personal security, Cliff Link, a dapper individual with a ready smile and a terrific sense of humor. His flexibility and understanding helped us over a number of rough spots as we tried to adjust to our new existence.

Link came up with the option of moving to the BOQ at the North Island Naval Air Station. Built by the army during the 1920s, it was configured like a single-story motel, Bill would have his own private room, and access could be controlled without us having to stop the world. This proposal looked as though it would work, and preceded by the now-familiar security screen, we moved.

Bill was scheduled to arrive from New York on Good Friday, 24 March, accompanied by his NIS escort. His plane didn't arrive until well after midnight, and by the time the traveling road show returned to North Island we were beat.

At six the next morning, Sharon and I were startled by an incessant pounding on the door and shouts of "Get out! Get out!" I pulled on a pair of pants, jerked open the door, and a disheveled agent yelled, "Get out now! There's a device under your window!"

Sharon was frantic. "Get Bill out, get Bill out!"

Unable to locate the key to his room, the agents were pounding on his door, screaming "Wake up, wake up! Outside! Outside!" The racket finally got his attention and we were hustled across the court and into the lobby. The agents were pretty agitated, as we had refused to budge until Bill was out of his room.

The security team cordoned off the wing and called the bomb squad. They must have been camped on the lawn; it seemed to be only minutes before they arrived. In the meantime, Sharon, Bill, and I were huddled in the lobby with our hair in our eyes. The doors swung open and an imperious figure, hair up in curlers, swept by with her husband in tow.

"I know what's going on. I know who she is. Get me out of this place."

Her husband, obviously embarrassed and following in close trail formation, was muttering, "Now, now, everything's all right."

Almost simultaneously, the lead agent stuck his head through the doors and reported that the device was a discarded hydraulic oil can.

Bill looked at me and shook his head. "Dad, the inmates are running the asylum."

Though the case was receiving widespread attention, we were still surprised when the newspapers reported White House interest. Marlin Fitzwater, President Bush's press secretary, told reporters in Washington in reference to my dismissal, ". . . [I]t's very disturbing to have anyone have their job affected by something that happens to them through these kinds of outside forces. We have to do everything possible to prevent terrorism. We need to be understanding about individuals. President Bush has deep concern for Mrs. Rogers."

In the middle of all this furor, we'd been looking forward to a traditional Easter Sunday with services in our church. But at the last minute I said, "Will, I can't do it. Too much has happened, we're too visible, and I can't imagine disturbing that beautiful service with rows of armed agents and all eyes on us. I don't know who considers me a threat and who doesn't. What if people get up and leave the service?"

Will, trying to reason with me, countered with a suggestion. "Let's attend the base chapel. How does that sound?"

The service was quiet and lovely and we were thankful to be

together. When it was over, we tried to leave unobtrusively, but practically the entire congregation approached and offered us their best wishes.

I had started talking frequently with the parents of my fourth-graders. After receiving my letter, they realized it was not my choice to leave the school. They also realized that in wanting me to stay on, they were in the minority. They drafted a letter of support anyway and sent it to Tim and the board.

> The undersigned parents of children in Sharon Rogers' fourth-grade class at La Jolla Country Day School find that the decision to dismiss Sharon was unconscionable for the following reasons:
>
> —The loss experienced by Sharon's students and the impact of this major discontinuity in their fourth-grade education was not taken into account. The fact that this institution, which our children believe protects and nurtures them, removed a respected and loved teacher for convenience, rather than supporting her in her time of need, is a poor lesson in ethics.
>
> —The full group of parents of children in the class was not consulted. Rather, it appears that only those parents who were vocal immediately were represented in the decision process, whereas those demonstrating a more circumspect and restrained response to the panic of the events were excluded.
>
> —The dismissal is grossly unfair to Sharon and caused her to pay a second, and even worse, lifelong price for the tragedy.
>
> —The widespread community and national ridicule suffered by our school, of which we were all extremely proud until last week, has caused more real danger to the school and our children than the Rogers' van bombing itself.
>
> —We believe that this hasty decision should be rescinded and that Sharon Rogers should be immediately reinstated as a faculty member at the La Jolla Country Day School.
>
> Special arrangements allowing Sharon to carry out her duties as a fourth-grade teacher at the school should be discussed and implemented to comply with Sharon's security requirements and the concerns of the parents for the safety of their children.

With this letter, the line was drawn.

17

——◇◇◇——

SETTLEMENT

Steady of heart, and stout of hand.
—Sir Walter Scott, *The Lay of the Last Minstrel*, 1805

Country Day was under fire from the media, the public, even Washington. In an attempt to mend fences, the school hired Richard Roth, a Los Angeles public relations specialist, and invited the parents and media to an evening forum. The gymnasium was packed with parents sitting on folding chairs and in bleachers. Local television crews arrived to film the event, hoping to get sound bites to the newsroom by their eleven o'clock deadline. Mr. Roth was guiding the agenda.

Among the first people to speak was a parent of one of my fourth-graders. At the microphone he asked, "What is the danger to the school if Sharon Rogers is on campus?"

Tim Burns was standing behind a podium with several members of the parents' association seated on either side of him. "The danger is an implied one, probably," he said. "That in itself was probably manifested most dramatically to me by the fact that Sharon had driven that van to school before. It wasn't as if it [10 March] was the only day she drove it.

"And when in fact a very dramatic situation took place the day before. She had students in the van and I was dismayed when that reached the press as quickly as it did, almost within a couple of hours of the accident itself. Those two situations led me to think the children could be at risk." He was referring to a field trip I had taken the children on.

Another questioner, unknown to me, talked for several minutes at the microphone. "If this incident had nothing to do with Sharon, why did the navy move the Rogers to a navy base? . . . I'm upset that the media says she was fired when we said we'd pay her for the rest of the year. . . . I'm upset that Congressman Lowery would say she's been fired. Well, elections come around every two years and we can always go to the polls. . . . And all this name calling is counterproductive.

"I haven't heard the press say let America stand up to terrorism, just that Country Day should stand up to it. When are America and the press going to stand up to it? . . . I'm not embarrassed by the decision and the way the school's handled it. The government's told Sharon Rogers, 'Better not go home, better go the BOQ, better have guards'—until the government can assure us substantial safety, we've done the right thing."

The first questioner was given the floor for one more comment. "Isn't it a fact that Sharon has complete mobility? She can go home every day. And, in fact, the only place in San Diego County where she can't go is La Jolla Country Day School where she's been teaching for twelve years."

Tim responded, "It's not what security she has attached to her person, but what we can provide for the 700 students and 100 faculty and staff when we're together on campus."

The meeting had been in session for almost an hour when someone I knew took the microphone and described the following scenario to the parents. "I drove into the parking lot of the neighborhood pharmacy when I saw a very strange man watching me and looking at my license plate. Once inside the store, my daughter ran to me and said Sharon Rogers was at the checkout stand. Well, my son had been taught by her in first grade and he's in the fourth grade this year so I wasn't just going to avoid her. So I walked up to her. But having three men and a woman in suits in the pharmacy, it's not natural, it's not normal, it's awkward and tension producing.

"My children were practically shivering, and I must admit I was frightened myself. . . . Everything she was telling me—she apparently was wearing some kind of monitor they were listening to. You know that when I was talking to her the entire place cleared out. Obviously people knew who she was and everyone backed away."

A friend of mine videotaped most of the meeting and right afterward delivered the cassette to the house. I began watching it. Fear, it seems, causes intelligent people to distort the truth and say outrageous things. Tim's reference to the "very dramatic situation" that took place the day before the bombing left me puzzled. Nothing dramatic had occurred on the field trip. Nor had people cleared out of the pharmacy the day I ran into the parent and her children. I was not hooked up to a transmitter. And I was beginning to worry about voter backlash against our friend, Congressman Bill Lowery, who had stuck his neck out to support me.

Right or wrong, the school continued to be the focus of the media. Even with the hiring of the PR specialist, it seemed their every decision backfired.

Yellow ribbons had become a symbol of the American public's support for hostages and service personnel missing in action. Someone hung yellow ribbons on thirty to forty trees on the school campus and attached them to the sign in front of the main gate. A picture appeared in the local newspapers. The school's maintenance staff was instructed to take the ribbons down before classes began. When questioned by a reporter, one landscaper replied, "My boss told me to clean it up." But the message was clear: Somebody who supported me had taken the time to tell the community that not everyone on campus agreed with my dismissal.

"Above average," the senior inspector commented as he briefed me on the results of the Vincennes's OPPE re-exam. Those were sweet words. The inspection team schedule had been too tight for an immediate second attempt, and we had labored through several days of unpleasant anticipation. Icing on the day's cake was a message we received as we returned to San Diego scheduling the ship for a mid-May visit to Portland, Oregon. The city was hosting a Say No to Drugs festival and had asked the navy to send a ship to participate in the activities. Portland was one of the crew's favorite ports and I wanted Sharon to fly up to meet us. It would be my last underway period before the change of command and an opportunity to divert her attention from the events surrounding her dismissal from Country Day.

It was well into the evening before I was able to wrap up and leave the ship. As I climbed into the car with my NIS shadows, one of them remarked, "Mrs. Rogers is at Las Vegas with Fluffy." Las Vegas was the current code word used by the agents for our home. Since the bombing, any radio reference to Sharon, me or our location was made with randomly changed cover words. Initially they had used Duke, Duchess, Fluffy (for the dog) and Castle (for the house). With Bill's arrival for Easter we had shifted to King, Queen, and Joker. For some reason Paddock was stuck with Fluffy.

The agent continued, "Her school had some sort of parents' meeting and it was videotaped. She went to your home to use the VCR."

This was a new development. When I arrived Sharon was engrossed in the tape and I could see the frustration and hurt in her expression. At that instant, as the TV flickered with angry images of people we had known for years and tears welled up in Sharon's eyes, I realized that somehow this school issue had to be resolved. Our silence and inactivity were costing too much.

Sitting alone one morning in the BOQ, I received a call from Tim Burns. "Sharon, some members of the board of trustees want to meet with you tomorrow at five in the law office of one of our members. Can you be there?"

"I'll get back to you. What's the address of the law office?"

"It's close to the school."

"By the way," he said, "have you been listening to the local radio talk show? They're calling me a fascist pig!"

I hadn't been listening to the radio. "I'll try to make it to the meeting, Tim. Thank you for the call." The local and national publicity was beginning to take its toll on him and the board members.

I had no idea what my legal rights were regarding my dismissal. Will was out at sea, and I was reluctant to meet with a lawyer and the executive board without knowing my rights. After consulting with friends whose advice I respected, I asked Patrick Shea, a lawyer with a local firm, to represent me at the meeting.

"Mr. Shea, I'm a teacher. That's the profession I've trained and studied for. I've been doing it my entire adult life and I'm good at what I do. I want my profession returned to me. I want to continue teaching. I also want to know if Country Day can legally dismiss me on the grounds they stated in their press release."

"I'll meet with the board and listen to what they have to say. Tell me about your contract."

"We're all on yearly contracts. They used to run five years, but that was changed."

"Sharon, with all this publicity, it could be three to four years before anyone feels comfortable hiring you again."

"Well, I know that some people at Country Day feel I should leave the profession, and I've been told by Tim Burns that if he can't hire me, who could?"

"There's a possibility that in view of your potential loss of income, we can work out a settlement for you."

That was an alternative I wanted to avoid, I explained. I didn't want to put a financial burden on the parent body.

"I'm sure they have insurance coverage for this sort of thing," he said.

"In that case, it's all right with me if we have to pursue that avenue. But my first choice is to teach."

I felt comfortable with Pat. Tall, slim, impeccably dressed, he looked the picture of a successful attorney. And he seemed to be genuinely interested in my situation. As I listened to him talk, it was apparent that he was quick and knew his business.

"Okay, Sharon. I'll meet with the board at five tomorrow. We'll see where we go from there."

After leaving the office, as the NIS drove me back to the BOQ, I stared out the window at the passing landscape thinking, How had it come to this? How had my relationship with the school I loved taken such a turn?

Amid all the hysteria, name calling, and ugliness, there were eighteen people, my class parents less two, who vocalized their support and attempted to have me reinstated. There was also one board member who resigned on the spot the morning the dismissal was announced, and another who followed his lead.

A family of one of my students had earlier set the stage for a series of reunions. One Sunday afternoon the children were invited to their home. The children didn't expect me to be there, only the parents knew. Hugs exchanged, we sat around the den catching up on school news. Some questioned me about the bomb, and I explained to them briefly what had occurred. This seemed to satisfy them. Shortly the conversation turned to chitchat. We ate pizza, then walked out on the patio where the NIS were standing guard. The children fired questions at them, and before long the agents had loaned their walkie-talkies to the enthusiastic group. The children played G-men, dashing behind bushes and sending imaginary radio messages to one another.

Even though we'd talked by telephone, nothing could have been more reassuring to them than to see and touch someone who had been erased from their lives so quickly and dramatically. The children now knew for sure that Mrs. Rogers was "okay."

This first reunion meant a great deal to me. I sent a lily to our hosts and on the accompanying card wrote, "You've brought peace of mind to a teacher and her class. Thank you."

While Sharon and her class were engaged in a spirited game of catch, I met with the parents in the living room. They were naturally concerned for their children, but also for Sharon and me. I spent considerable time explaining the security aspects of our situation and answering their questions. We were absolutely safe, I assured them, and felt confident that no matter how long it took, the FBI, NIS, and myriad other agencies kicking over every rock in the country would arrest and prosecute the bombers. They were interested in the investigation but at the same time sensitive to the fact that we were not free to discuss the effort in detail.

I pointed out that despite the presence of the NIS we could go anywhere and do anything and had every intention of shortly moving back into our home. They were all surprised at this, for the rumor mill had us moving in the dead of night to randomly sited safehouses. I quashed this and other flights of heated imagination, including one that had me being transported around the base in an armored vehicle.

The most important thing on their minds was finding a place where the children could be reunited with their teacher. I didn't have much to offer in the way of sound suggestions, so we resolved to keep pursuing the matter. From the look on the faces of those parents, it seemed certain that someone would eventually come up with an idea.

The whole affair was a success, a welcome change for everyone, and the catalyst that would ultimately bond a group of acquaintances into steadfast, lifelong friends.

The parents were adamant about reuniting their children with me in a classroom environment. They had been exploring ideas such as having me teach through closed-circuit TV, leasing a trailer, renting a room in the police substation or the civic center, meeting in parents' homes. Much effort and many hours were expended in pursuit of this goal. In view of all this, I wasn't surprised when a parent called me and said arrangements had been made so that in a few days I could meet with my class. A parent who owned a nearby restaurant had loaned us a conference room.

Immediately, I began preparing plans for our two-hour session. The parents were serious about recreating a genuine classroom atmosphere, and I wanted to deliver a lesson that would meet their expectations.

Pat Shea, who was continuing negotiations with the school, consulted with me on a regular basis. "Sharon, they've offered you two contracts, neither of which puts you back into the classroom. Is this what you want?"

The first contract stated that I could continue an educational relationship with the school if the FBI, NIS, and local police would guarantee 100 percent safety for the children, faculty, and staff. Naturally, that was impossible. The second one called for "substantial" safety and added vaguely that my responsibilities might include working on the school yearbook, working with alumni, or helping other teachers prepare lesson plans. I recalled Tim Burns sitting at our breakfast table with Will and me. "Tim, neither of these contracts is viable," I had said. "I'm a trained teacher and I want to return to a classroom next fall." Looking surprised, he replied, "Well, I didn't know that was what you wanted."

"Sharon," Pat continued, and I tuned back into our conversation, "why would you want to be a part of an organization that doesn't want you? You've been hurt enough, and I recommend we proceed toward a settlement so you can reach closure, put this behind you, and get on with your life."

"I agree with you. I don't see any other way. Let's proceed."

So Pat drafted a letter to the school:

Mrs. Rogers's attitude toward La Jolla Country Day remains one of deep affection and overwhelming consideration for its students, teachers, staff and extended family.

[She] is very concerned and sympathetic with the awkward . . . position in which the school . . . finds itself. She has struggled with the issues presented as a result of the actions already taken by the school in an effort to craft a resolution which will be fair to her and the school. The following issues are:

1. How to ensure the health and safety of the school community;

2. How to protect the school from the perceived threat of a terrorist act [while protecting her career]. . . .

4. Separate from her career satisfaction, Mrs. Rogers's job plays an important economic role in the life of her family. . . .

Keeping the above in mind, the two alternative teaching agreements are completely inadequate. Her present contract clearly identifies her as a full-time fourth-grade teacher. . . . The new agreements do not preserve for her that position, and it is impossible to determine from the agreements what exact position she would hold. . . .

After several additional meetings, the school and I reached the following agreement:

—. . . [T]he issue of potential danger resulting from Mrs. Rogers's continued presence on campus is difficult to quantify. The School has decided that the most appropriate resolution is to no longer have Mrs. Rogers . . . on the School campus.

—Both the School and Mrs. Rogers are committed to the . . . safety of everyone in the School community.

—Despite their differences, Mrs. Rogers continues to care deeply about the La Jolla Country Day School community and considers it an excellent school.

—The School enters into this Agreement in recognition of Mrs. Rogers's outstanding contribution to the quality of its program.

—Mrs. Rogers and the School agree as follows:

1. Mrs. Rogers will resign her employment with the School;

2. The School shall pay Mrs. Rogers the sum of $135,000 as separate consideration in satisfaction of all and any claims against the School for physical and emotional distress . . . and all other claims she may have of every source and type.

There were pages and pages of additional legalese, but essentially the settlement had been reached.

I learned later that the parents had continued meetings with Tim Burns to come to an agreement regarding regular off-campus teaching.

I met with the children as a class only once again, in a nearby hotel meeting room.

The school's attorney, Robert Bell, quashed any further meetings when he wrote to the parents: "I do not think it is appropriate for Mrs. Rogers to continue in a teaching relationship with current students . . . regardless of where the teaching takes place. . . ."

Pat Shea wrote the following reply:

> . . . My understanding is that the parents desire these meetings in hopes of transitioning their children from the unpleasantness of the earlier dispute to a more normal relationship with Sharon's substitute and a better relationship with the school.
>
> The parents have advised Sharon that they are prepared to do anything to continue these weekly visits, including having their children excused from class for personal unexplained reasons. Sharon does not desire this, and in fact is most insistent that this program be one which is not disruptive to the children and not adversarial. We are looking at maybe four more meetings. . . . Sharon is not willing to fight the school, if the school actively opposes the program.

Mr. Bell's response was short: "The School adamantly opposes the program referred to in your letter. In our view Mrs. Rogers's conduct as well as that of the parents of the fourth-grade kids is disruptive. . . . Although they may be well meaning, their actions are in fact educationally counterproductive."

On that note, the sessions stopped.

Because the press had taken such an interest in my story and daily articles continued to be written, we decided a press conference was the most effective way to close this whole affair. The NIS drove Will and me to a local hotel where the conference was to take place. As we entered, we could see dozens of reporters, TV cameras, radio hookups, and microphones. We were seated at a long table, Will on my right and Pat Shea on my left.

A statement had been prepared, and I had rehearsed it numerous times so as to deliver it in a controlled manner. However, when I reached these words I choked up and, momentarily, was unable to continue: "I will miss my relationship with the school. But most of all I will miss my students and their courageous and thoughtful parents."

Will reached over and squeezed my arm. "Many people have asked if I am angry at the way I have been treated by the school. I must say that over the past weeks I have felt many different emotions, but today I am simply disappointed, more disappointed than I can possibly express."

With the conclusion of my remarks, the reporters seemed sympathetic, for their questions reflected sensitivity and understanding.

18

EMERGENCE

We shall breathe the air again . . . in our own beloved home.
—George Frederick Root, *Tramp! Tramp! Tramp!*, 1862

Sharon and I were sorting through a pile of laundry in the BOQ when she suddenly turned to me. "We have to get back into the house. I need to be at home."

"The NIS is gearing up to get us back by the change of command, Sharon."

She walked to the window and stared at the agent standing in the courtyard. "No, Will, I mean now. I can't wait four to six weeks, even if it means a move without NIS."

"I'll see what I can do," but as I walked outside to talk to the team leader I knew what he would say. The investigation was ongoing and media interest intense, particularly following Sharon's press conference. As I expected, he was less than excited over the prospect but agreed to do what he could. Flexible as always, in a couple of days the team developed what they felt was a workable solution. They told me it would take about a week. This news jump-started our mood several notches.

We realized with the return home that we'd have to increase our own personal security, upgrading the alarm system in the house and installing sophisticated warning devices in the cars. Our shrinking savings account, never large, evaporated with these blows. Regardless, the expense was secondary to our desire to reestablish a normal routine.

One facet of the security bubble that gave us pause was whether to acquire weapons. The deadliest item in our house was an old rusty shotgun, a relic of my boyhood. After much discussion we sought the advice of an NIS weapons expert on what to buy and how to go about it. Nine-millimeter and .380 semiautomatics were ordered and permits arranged. Since Sharon had never so much as held a handgun and my experience was limited, professional instruction and practice were a must. Again, the NIS agreed to help and we were duly driven to the San Diego County sheriff's outdoor range.

As we stood in the middle of the firing flats listening to the instructor—"in a developing situation, you may not have time to chamber a cartridge. . . . Wherever you keep the weapons, rounds should be chambered with the safety on"—I was struck by how foreign this was to both of us. The image of Sharon, the gentlest person I have ever known, standing in the swirling dust listening intently while she held this lethal weapon in her hand reminded me of a third-rate TV movie. Unfortunately, it couldn't just be switched off.

When the moment came for live firing, the agent lectured, "If you have to use these weapons in a situation, don't try to wound. Shoot for the body mass, you want to put him down." He turned to Sharon and asked, "Mrs. Rogers, if you're faced with a situation in your home, do you think you could do that?"

She didn't say a word, but faced downrange and after struggling briefly with the cocking slide emptied the seven-round clip into the black portion of the target.

The agent, silent for a moment, remarked, "I think I have my answer." So did I.

During our absence the security team occupying the house had recorded a number of anonymous phone calls. The caller never spoke, but it was obvious to the agents that someone was on the line. After a week or so these stopped. Then a few days after our return the "breather" calls resumed. We reported this to the FBI, and they asked to install a voice-triggered tape recorder on the line. We agreed. Eager to do something that would get results, Sharon and I perversely hoped the crank calls would continue. We weren't disappointed. During each call we engaged the recorder, noted the time, and forwarded the tape to the FBI. Somebody was out there and we had high hopes the Feds would run him down.

Several tapes had been collected when the calls abruptly ceased. After a few days I contacted the bureau asking if any headway had been made. "Captain, I'm embarrassed to tell you this, but we didn't follow up quickly enough and the phone company purged their calling records."

I was stunned and angry. "In other words, somebody sat on this and a lead was blown?"

The agent responded, "I'm afraid that's right. Between you and me there are too many fingers in the pie. Things are getting stepped on."

Despite this setback, every conceivable lead was being pursued. The FBI had called in a team to assist in developing a psychological profile of the type of individual who would employ a pipe bomb. Hundreds of vehicle license numbers were being checked out and leads generated from the remains of the bomb tracked down. One avenue receiving a lot of attention involved a query directed to a close neighbor by two men who had appeared to be of Middle Eastern descent. Shortly before the bombing our neighbor was standing in his front yard when these two characters pulled up to the curb and said, "Where does the captain live?" But Sharon and I had to remind ourselves continually of the early FBI and NIS comment: Don't hope for a quick solution.

The NIS, good to its word, had built a security net around our home and neighborhood in only a few days. They placed sensing devices around the perimeter of the yard and parked a large trailer-van above our house in the shopping-center parking lot. This vehicle served as a command post and housed about a half dozen NIS agents. Additionally, there was always a manned car sitting in our cul de sac. It was still good to be home.

Whenever NIS agents were driving me around they purposely avoided the intersection of Genesee and La Jolla Village Drive where the bombing had occurred. I appreciated their concern. Now, however, the FBI had a request. They had borrowed a 1984 Toyota van similar to mine and asked me to drive it along the same route I'd taken on the morning of 10 March. They wanted to measure the rise in engine temperature, hoping the information would shed some light on the type of explosive device used to detonate the bomb. They were also monitoring how heavy or light my foot was on the gas pedal, how many times I stopped, and the speed at which I drove.

This was the first time I had driven since the explosion. Climbing into the van's cab, I tried to remain as calm as possible. I wondered if I would ever again put the key into the ignition without thinking twice.

Several people rode in the van with me, examining every move I made and taking notes. We drove to the spot and stopped. Traffic was light, there was no one behind me. For the first time I saw the large blackened area burned into the concrete. My mind flashed back to 10 March and the days following when I'd watch the news and see passersby standing on the curb taking pictures or just staring at the charred area. As I drove the van back to the house, I overheard the FBI people comparing notes and puzzling over their discoveries.

The investigation was not limited to San Diego. We learned that our friends next door, who were traveling in Africa, had been located and interviewed.

My sister and brother-in-law in Fort Worth were asked if during their February visit they had noticed any Mideastern faces in the neighborhood. They thought they had. The FBI spent one day with them developing an artist's composite. The agents were amused when the drawing turned out to be an exact replica of our neighbor's handyman.

Time and distance obviously weren't going to hinder the investigation.

Will's approaching change of command was never far from my mind. I was busy planning for the deluge of relatives and out-of-town friends who would be arriving for the ceremony. Hoping for a typical southern California day, we had decided to host a reception in the backyard the afternoon following the ceremony. The first thing on my agenda was to spruce up the space with more plants and flowers. I decided to buy some clay pots at the navy exchange. When I discussed this plan with the NIS, I sensed hesitation. However, they drove me to the base and we parked in back of the garden shop.

We hadn't been there long when one of the agents approached me. "Mrs. Rogers, we've been asked by the manager to leave."

"What's the matter?"

"We don't have navy IDs and aren't allowed in the exchange."

"You've got to be kidding!"

Standing with a pot in each hand, I put them down and left.

As we drove off the driver grumbled, "We never know what the manager's attitude is going to be."

I grumbled, too, because I didn't have my pots.

As the day approached for the *Vincennes*'s departure for Oregon, the development of security measures for the trip occupied a good deal of the personal security detachment's attention. I wanted the effort to be kept low profile, but there was no way. The security people were worried about the large number of guests scheduled to make the trip up the Columbia River from Astoria to Portland. They were also concerned about crowds surrounding us during the visit. Initially, they wanted to cancel the guest cruise up the river, an action I adamantly refused to consider.

"Captain, we don't feel we can cover you and Mrs. Rogers—too many spaces and passages."

I explained that my movements would be confined to the bridge since the ship would be proceeding in restricted waters during the entire passage.

"I'm not going to move past the wings and pilothouse. Keeping an eye on us shouldn't be that tough. Besides, Sharon and I will be as secure with the Portland folks as we are riding around in the cavalcade. They just aren't stocking-over-the-face types."

The issue was put to bed, but I could see they were still nervous about the trip.

Two agents escorted me on the flight to Oregon while Will sailed with the *Vincennes*. During a stopover in San Jose I was sitting in the lounge waiting for the NIS to process our tickets. One of the agents at the counter was informing the airline that she and her partner were carrying firearms. It was a long discussion and all the while the airline clerk stared at me. She thought that I was a prisoner in custody. We chuckled about this for the remainder of the trip.

Upon arrival I was driven to a Hilton Hotel. The NIS and the Portland police cooperated on tight security; agents swarmed over our wing.

I was looking forward to the early-morning drive to the small coastal town of Astoria. We were to meet the *Vincennes* after she crossed the bar and entered the Columbia River. Despite my nagging concern for the publicity Will and the ship would receive in Portland, the trip upriver was refreshing. In Will's command chair on the bridge, I whiled away hours spotting eagles in the treetops and soaring through the sky. An osprey with young perched on her nest in the middle of a range mark in the river. The passing scenery and the power of the Columbia began to peel away some of my anxieties.

The transit took six to seven hours. Once in Portland, the *Vincennes* moored alongside the quay wall at Marine Park, almost in the center of the city. The ship was the backdrop for the antidrug festival's kickoff ceremony. Dozens of school buses had brought hundreds of children from surrounding areas to the park. Bands, clowns, mimes, and jugglers entertained them. A large portable stage had been erected and Will was scheduled to speak there. I was watching the crowd as carefully as the NIS was. At one point I alerted an agent to keep an eye on one man whose actions looked peculiar.

Will's speech received an enthusiastic reception. I was glad when he was off the stage and out of the surge of people pressing forward to shake his hand.

My request for low-profile security had, as expected, gone by the board. We were on the Portland police department's turf, and they weren't taking any chances. A big, friendly, but businesslike sergeant of detectives was assigned to augment the security detail and act as liaison between the police and the NIS. As soon as we arrived he remarked, "Captain, anything you and Mrs. Rogers want to do or see while you're here, just let me know."

We quickly found out the result of any request. We were scheduled to speak at a Navy League dinner and the trip from the hotel had every trapping of a presidential motorcade: five police cruisers with NIS vehicles sandwiched between, cops on motorcycles roaring ahead to block off approaching intersections, lights flashing, sirens screaming, gaping pedestrians. Sharon and I slumped down in the back seat, laughing self-consciously. As we passed a large group of people waving excitedly, I commented between stifled laughs, "Wave, they think it's the queen."

19

CHANGE OF COMMAND

To yield with a grace to reason
And bow and accept the end. . . .

—Robert Frost, *Reluctance*, 1913

As the last line was made fast to the pier, "Moored, shift colors" blared from the announcing system. I passed the final orders to the helm: "All stop, finished with engines and rudders." Nick Gee's comment to me, just before I relieved him, passed through my mind: "When you know it's the last time you'll tie her up, the last time you'll ever do something you've done your whole adult life . . . it's tough." We were back from Portland, my relief was on board, the change of command was only a few days away, and Nick was right, I couldn't escape a feeling of bittersweet finality.

From the moment the date of the turnover had been established, everyone on board wanted to welcome the new commanding officer in style. The ceremony in which the responsibility of naval command is passed from one individual to another has been performed virtually unchanged for hundreds of years. Great effort is always expended to make it a memorable occasion. We were determined to make this one a benchmark.

Responsibility for administrative duties had long since been divided up. There were two issues on which we were spending a lot of time. The first was the expected size of the crowd. Normally, unless the ceremony marks the shift of a carrier or senior flag-officer command, the guest list numbers around two hundred. With RSVPs still pouring in we were well past a thousand, and that number didn't include the families of the crew, most of which were expected. So the audience would have to be seated on the pier, not on board. We simply didn't have the deck space.

The other problem, not anticipated when planning started, was the level of security called for by the NIS. The initial plan, which Executive Officer Doug McDonald and I jokingly referred to as Festung San Diego, was more than I was prepared to accept. It would turn the ceremony into visiting day at the penitentiary. After much discussion and compromise among the team leader of the personal security detachment, Doug, and myself, an acceptable plan had been hammered out. Doug and I had our fingers crossed that some fool wouldn't call in a bomb threat. That would have sent the paranoia and security coverage soaring.

Vice Admiral Kihune had agreed to act as the principal speaker, Ted Atwood was going to deliver one of the stem-winder invocations and benedictions for which he was famous, and the ship was blessed with the finest mess specialist I had ever served with, Master Chief Petty Officer Jon Lodi. He and his galley troops had promised a reception tour de force. Doug had managed to secure the Marine Band, we had acquired bunting, the flags were washed, and the crew had spent a lot of extra effort during the Portland transit to spit-shine the Lady.

Since the audience would be on the pier, we decided to conduct the ceremony on the foredeck, sandwiched between the forward missile launcher and mount 51. The crowd would have a good view. I was determined to have the turnover occur onboard. We wanted to have the reception there too and decided if the crowd kept moving, we could use the flight deck and hangar bay. The guest list continued to grow. I hoped we wouldn't be forced out of this plan. The crew wanted to apply some extra touches that wouldn't work anywhere else.

The date for the change of command that my relief, Captain Robert Lynch, and I had agreed on was 27 May. For me the few days remaining seemed to fly by, but in Bob's case I'm sure the reverse was true. Saying farewell to a crew with whom so much had been shared would be difficult. Over the weeks I had visited every space repeatedly, trying to develop a lasting image of the ship's every nook and cranny.

One advantage of the turnover that Sharon and I were both looking forward to was a reduction in the security. After considerable discussion it had been agreed that following the ceremony, except for background surveillance, the NIS team would be released. It was made abundantly clear that should future developments warrant, we would see them again—instantly.

The move from the BOQ back home had been a big morale boost. We more than appreciated what the security team had done for us and had established genuine friendships with its members. They made going to the theater at the last moment or getting seats in a crowded restaurant a piece of cake. Still, the vigilant phalanx was a constant reminder of 10 March and our loss of personal freedom. From this standpoint, its imminent departure was welcome.

Despite my reluctance, I couldn't hold back the clock. The crew and ship had been inspected, most logs and records signed, my personal gear removed. For all intents and purposes, command of the *Vincennes* was now in the hands of the new commanding officer. When my final full day as skipper drew to a close I kept finding reasons to remain on board. Finally, having exhausted even the most remote excuses, I left. As I stepped onto the pier I paused to look at the ship draped in her ceremonial bunting. She was ready; I wasn't.

Weather in San Diego is for the most part good, but 27 May arrived cloaked in late-spring unpredictability, one of those days the Chamber of Commerce doesn't advertise. A low gray marine layer accompanied by chill winds wasn't exactly what Bob Lynch and I had envisioned. The weather wasn't going to stop the show, but as I left the house, at about six o'clock, I crossed my fingers for a midmorning break.

The final logs and records needed to be signed and several safe combinations and key bundles turned over to Bob. But the real reason for my early arrival was a desire to walk the ship one last time. I had just laid out my dress uniform and was headed for the cabin door when Doug McDonald stuck his head in. "How about a cup of coffee, Skipper?" I started to reach for my cup and thought better. "Doug, I want to see how the ship looks and what the crew is up to. Why don't you come with me?"

It was still chilly with a steady wind across the deck, but like a good executive officer he appeared eager to join me. As we moved toward the flight deck he asked, hesitantly, "Captain, how does it feel to give her up?" I could tell he wasn't making idle conversation. I told him what Nick Gee had said to me, then added, "Doug, without my saying it, I'm sure you understand that command of this ship has been a mixture of tremendous highs and some pretty bottomless lows. I'd be lying if I told you I wouldn't trade a day. I can think of more than a few I'd pass in a New York minute. However, the officers, crew, and the ship herself will always be a part of me and I wouldn't trade that for anything. I'll regret my final departure, but I had my opportunity. It's time for someone else to sit in the righthand bridge chair."

Until that moment I had not been fully able to sort out my feelings, but as I pondered what I had said my remarks didn't seem far off.

The ceremony was scheduled to start at ten o'clock, but by nine the guests were already starting to stream down the pier, which was secured to all but those assigned to ships alongside. A metal detector and sniffer dog were positioned at the pier entrance, and the *Vincennes* had been swept by a bomb team. Waterside security was being handled by a SEAL team from the Special Warfare Command on Coronado. This blanket was augmented by members of the personal security detachment, who mixed with the crowd. They were trying to blend in, but that was impossible because they were carrying slim black briefcases and whispering down their sleeves.

Bob and I had decided to host a small preceremony reception in the wardroom for our families and close friends. Shortly before nine— we had just wrapped up the last administrative detail—the quarterdeck watch called. "Skipper, your family and Captain Lynch's have arrived. The boatswain has his people helping with your brother's wheelchair and the officer of the deck said to tell you that Admiral Kihune's aide called. The admiral's delayed and won't make the wardroom reception. He passed the admiral's regrets."

That was a disappointment; I'd hoped to introduce Admiral and Hope Kihune to my family before the crush of the big reception. But I wasn't surprised. Kihune was famous for his tight schedule.

I was in bed watching Will pin his full dress medals to his high-necked whites and thinking that this would be an emotional day for him.

"It's early, Will. Don't you want a cup of coffee before you leave?"

"I'll get one on the ship. I want to look over the speech one more time. And Sharon, be sure to arrive by nine. Admiral Kihune and the guests will be showing up and I'd like you to be in the wardroom with me."

After he left, I heard the rest of the family stirring. It was a half-hour drive to 32nd Street, and we had arranged for the NIS to pick us up by eight-thirty. As I looked at my new dress hanging on the door, I thought about the day I'd bought it. My female escort wasn't available and two men were on duty. I felt uncomfortable dragging these guys through women's departments, but time was running out and I needed something special for Will's ceremony. Following me about, they tried to look inconspicuous, these two tall agents in business suits. This was another outing that made the personal column in the evening *Tribune*.

The NIS rang the doorbell right on time. It was blustery and cold and I was dressed for a spring day in a short-sleeved cotton dress. But it was too late to turn around and change.

At the main gate of the base, posted signs gave directions to the *Vincennes*'s change of command ceremony. Cars were already beginning to fill the parking lot across from the pier and I was relieved that we could easily drive through the heavy security and up to the ship. We wouldn't be late.

State flags, buffeted and whipped by the wind, stood in rows out-lining the ship. The sound reminded me of sails when they begin to luff. Hundreds of chairs were lined up one behind the other under two enormous white tents. Climbing the gangway I could see the quarterdeck ringed in white McNamara's lace, a fancy macramé the sailors had knotted from shredded canvas. The officers were in full dress, replete with swords, and the crew was lined up in white jumpers.

One of the officers escorted us to Will's cabin. He was alone.

"Everything okay, Will?"

He was standing with his back to us, looking contemplatively out the porthole. Then, turning toward us, he walked over and hugged me. "Are you ready to get this show on the road?"

Chief Lodi and his men had put together a beautiful brunch of sweet rolls, fresh fruit, coffee, and juice. The *Vincennes*'s presentation silver shone and fresh flowers surrounded the centerpiece, a small ice sculpture of the ship's crest.

Many of the Texas family had flown in. It was nice to be able to visit with them before the ceremony began. The room thinned out as people were being escorted to their seats on the pier. It's customary for the commanding officer's family to be among the last seated. Presently an officer led me to my reserved seat. No sooner had I sat down than the first of my fourth-graders ran over to me. Before I knew it I was exchanging hugs with at least a dozen former students. Our reunion was postponed when Doug McDonald approached the microphone. "Ladies and gentlemen," he announced, "please rise for the arrival of the official party."

A few minutes before ten, six strokes of the quarterdeck bell announced the arrival of Vice Admiral Kihune. Smiling and upbeat as usual, he snapped on his ceremonial sword, offered his congratulations to Bob Lynch and me, and commented, "Will, Team 49 has turned in their usual magnificent effort. The ship looks great. I know one of you is ready, and it looks like most of San Diego is on the pier. Let's not keep them waiting." As we stepped into the passageway, Kihune squeezed my shoulder. "Will, you did a helluva job. Remember that and keep smiling."

Bob and I proceeded to the elevated podium. The admiral paused at the weather break, then joined us as the band played the "Admiral's March" followed by "Ruffles and Flourishes." Ted Atwood stood and delivered a moving and pointed invocation.

> O Eternal Lord God, as we gather this morning for this change of command, we recognize, in sorrow, that terrorism has been to our shores. Our first utterance is a prayer of thanksgiving that Sharon, the victim, survived.
>
> Never in all of naval history has any other naval officer been challenged to make so many judgments in so brief a period of time to protect and preserve both his ship and his crew. While there is a burden he will bear forever, this captain does not look back, confident he had no other option. The sadness with which we bid farewell to Will is tempered by our gratitude for your grace which galvanized him. . . .
>
> It is our abiding prayer that the officers and men of the United States ship *Vincennes*, who serve under their new captain . . . will continue to demonstrate such fidelity and intrepidity that the carillons of peace will so displace the thunder of battle that never again will the sons of our land have to go forth into combat and offer themselves on the altar of peace.
>
> This we humbly ask in your most holy name. Amen.

Vice Admiral Kihune followed Ted. The admiral's concern for people and his desire publicly to recognize their contributions are well known. Although his comments embraced me personally, more importantly he addressed the crew as a superb team. "Tried by events of enormous magnitude," he said, "they never wavered, emerging from the center of the storm with bonds forged that will last their lifetime." Kihune's remarks stole some of my intended thunder, but I considered them just right coming from a man who never pays lip service to anything.

Sharon's parting words to me as she started to her seat had been, "Don't get emotional." I certainly didn't intend to "hang crepe," nor did I plan to dwell on events of 3 July. But during these last few moments of command, with a microphone and captive audience, there was a point or two I wanted to make. First I acknowledged the guests and members of the press and extended our appreciation for their attendance. Then I paused, silently praying that the drafts and redrafts of my speech had produced the right choice of words.

Cruiser: the name combines two things that have always fascinated Americans, speed and power. A salvo from her main battery can hurl tons of streamlined metal forty miles high and far over the horizon at speeds faster than a rifle bullet, with pinpoint and deadly accuracy. Her turbines can send the strength of 80,000 horses pounding into her propellers. Almost two football fields in length, but with the form of a racing scull . . . she was born to battle a rising sea as fiercely as a determined enemy. This superb product of American technology was designed, from her keel up, to go anywhere in her country's interest, to stand in harm's way if she must . . . and win!

Much verbiage has been uttered in debate over the performance and value of this ship and her sisters. The truth is the Aegis cruiser, by orders of magnitude, represents the most capable air-defense and battle-management platform in the world. She has repeatedly demonstrated her ability to successfully engage multiple targets approaching at several times the speed of sound. Tested exhaustively in every conceivable scenario, her reliability and redundancy are second to none. She has the agility and speed of a ballet dancer coupled with the firepower equivalency of a task force of World War II vintage. She and her kind are truly masterpieces of American technology and ingenuity.

I paused again as I prepared to pay my tribute to the young men who had sailed with me and given me their loyalty and support, not for dramatic effect but rather a mental boost. The next part was going to be tough to get through.

Emperor Charlemagne, when faced with a particularly difficult and fractious problem in maintaining the security of his kingdom, invariably summoned his most capable knight—Paladin. Contained within the crest on Paladin's shield was a representation of the black knight of the chessboard. This symbol has been adopted by Team 49.

The warship exists as an instrument of national will, and it takes hundreds of men to enable her to execute that will and to spend the thousands of hours of training . . . to be ready to do so. These people are the heart and soul of the ship. Walking about her, I hear the echoes of the past mingle with the sights and sounds of the present. There is certain knowledge that the men who have dwelled here and dwell here now are the essence of United States cruiser *Vincennes*. These men and their families are fiercely proud of themselves, their ship, and all that they have accomplished—truly a band of brothers.

Whether hosting heads of state, entertaining a kindergarten class, reroofing an orphanage, or rising to any operational or administrative task, they have done it right, with class and aplomb. And perhaps the ultimate accolade: when called upon in the violent and confused crucible of combat, they performed precisely as the situation dictated— with courage and without hesitation. I am most proud of them!

I turned and saluted the crew drawn up in ranks on the pier. Every bit of respect I had went into that salute and I hoped each man in those crisp white ranks understood that. The most difficult part was over. I smiled at Sharon in the front row, and although I had not shared any of my remarks with her before, I could see her relax.

In today's world of violent peace, there exists an active, subterranean, and shadowy war—a war which does not employ the sophistication of complex weaponry or the clash of large forces. Rather, it is a conflict that pits rabid ideology against the soft underbelly of irrational fear, preys on a lack of courage and enlists the unwitting support of those without moral fiber or conviction. This of course is the war of terrorism.

Although victory over this threat to our freedoms may require, at times, force of arms, the most effective weapon is the strength and dedication of a united people. In this struggle there are no noncombatants and we must avoid the lack of commitment illustrated by these lines of Shakespeare:

But I remember, when the fight was done,
When I was dry with rage and extreme toil,
Breathless and faint, leaning upon my sword,
Came there a certain lord, neat, and trimly dressed,
Fresh as a bridegroom; and his chin new reaped . . .
. . . he made me mad
To see him shine so brisk, and smell so sweet,
And talk so like a waiting-gentlewoman
Of guns and drums and wounds,—God save the mark!—
And telling me . . .
. . . but for these vile guns,
He would himself have been a soldier.

I turned again to the crew and commented, "She's a proud horse, manned by a proud crew who represent a proud navy. Never, ever rein her in." The wind gusted through the signal halyards, causing the hoists to crack and snap. The crowd was momentarily silent. Then a wave of applause broke out and I was conscious of the crew clapping and cheering.

The clock had run out. I read my detaching orders, turned to Captain Lynch, saluted, and spoke the words that would sever me from command of the *Vincennes*. "I'm ready to be relieved, sir." Bob responded with, "I relieve you, sir."

He made some brief remarks, and as he concluded the ship's senior enlisted adviser, Master Chief D. G. Bryan, stepped forward to make the traditional presentation to the departing commanding officer of a national ensign that has flown over the ship. The flag was beautifully cased in dark walnut and as Bryan cradled the open box in his arms I noticed the folded colors were faded, torn, and stained. I could just make out the inscription on a brass plate fixed to the backing: "This ensign flew over USS *Vincennes* (CG 49) during her combat engagement in the Persian Gulf on 3 July 1988."

As the chief saluted and shook my hand, I could barely respond.

If this had been first on the agenda, I would have been pressed to make it through with a straight face.

Will's speech, filled with spirit, seemed to touch an emotional chord in the crowd. Proud of his reserve, I was also relieved that this portion of the ceremony was over.

With the navy hymn playing softly in the background, our good friend Ted Atwood offered the benediction:

> Eternal Father, strong to save, when the waves caress our shores—
> With the tide that ends and wanes—
> May they ever serve as a reminder of Sharon who was spared
>   and Will who never waned.
> Eternal Father, strong to save, whose arm hath bound the restless
> Wave, O hear us when we cry to thee
> For those in peril on the sea. Amen.

As the final notes of the hymn faded, Doug McDonald invited the guests to a reception on the flight deck.

Sitting to my right, Hope Kihune leaned over, hugged me, and whispered, "That was a wonderful and moving ceremony, Sharon. Bob and I are very proud of you and Will."

Just as the ceremony concluded and the guests began to stream toward the after brow for the reception, the gray overcast parted, the sun broke through, the wind dropped, and the temperature rose. Master Chief Lodi and the crew had outdone themselves. A large white tent spanned the flight deck and the vertical safety nets were draped with signal flags. Inside the hangar bay, more signal flags and the ship's house flag with its black chess knight hung from the overhead and the bulkheads.

Long tables arrayed in a U shape were covered with an endless train of appetizers. The centerpiece was an enormous chess knight sculpted from an ice block. On a smaller table in the center of the bay was a meticulously detailed seven-foot-long model of the *Vincennes*. This creation was the handiwork of a crewman who had invested several years and thousands of dollars in its construction. At the bow and stern of the model were two large, intricately decorated cakes. From the grins on the faces of the crew, it was obvious they had created the desired effect. First cabin!

I had lost Sharon somewhere in the crush, and it was ten or fifteen minutes before I caught sight of the tall NIS escort accompanying her. She was backed up against the helo fueling pit surrounded by her fourth grade, their parents, and a gaggle of our friends. She wouldn't be doing much in the way of circulating.

Several members of the press whom I recognized were clustered at the bottom of the brow. I caught their attention, exchanged a thumbs up, and waved them on board. They had been on the scene since well before eight and looked as if they might enjoy a cup of coffee.

Master Chief Bryan touched my sleeve. "Skipper, please let me or the exec know about fifteen minutes before you and Mrs. Rogers are ready to leave. The mess wants to join the wardroom in saying good-bye."

I responded, "Master, we've about done it. As soon as I can free up Sharon and say goodbye to Captain Lynch, we'll be ready. Do me a favor—run down the boatswain and tell him the rest of my family is ready to leave."

By the time I had found Doug and Bob and gently worked Sharon free of her circle, the master chief's fifteen minutes were easily up. As

We share a moment with crewmen after the change-of-command ceremony on the USS *Vincennes*, 27 May 1989. (Photo by Marjo Rogers)

Vincennes crewmen line up on the pier to bid individual goodbyes to us as I'm relieved of command, 27 May 1989. (Photograph by Marjo Rogers)

Sharon and I emerged on the quarterdeck, I glanced at the pier and pulled her back inside the skin of the ship. I needed a moment to compose myself. Waiting on the pier were not only the wardroom and chief's mess but the entire crew as well, assembled in a long white line.

As the ship's bell sounded the four strokes announcing my final departure, the chief boatswain trilled a long call on his pipe and we started down the line. Salutes, handshakes, hugs, quick private words passed between us and every man in that line. Finally at the end of the pier, we turned, waved, and entered the waiting sedan. Both of us were quiet during the drive home, touched by this outpouring of affection.

As we pulled up to the curb in our cul de sac, the NIS agents got out of their cars and those who had remained at the house collected in the driveway. We shook hands and thanked them for all they had done. "I hope this is the last time we meet like this," everyone was saying. As Sharon and I stood and watched them drive away I wondered if we'd ever need them again.

20

NEW HORIZONS

For this is wisdom: to love, to live,
To take what Fate, or the Gods, may give.
—Laurence Hope, *The Teak Forest*

As I maneuvered through stop-and-go freeway traffic on the way to visit friends, I remarked to Sharon, "It's good to just get in the car and go without having to file a parade permit." No sooner were these words out of my mouth than a synthesized electronic voice bellowed, "Warning, warning, you are too close to the car, step back! Warning, you are too close to the car, five . . . four . . . three . . . two . . . one!" At this point the car horn began to sound repeatedly, joined by a wailing siren and repeated flashing of lights. Our exotic auto alarm system had faulted and was screaming at drivers on the freeway. It seemed like miles before we could exit and silence the stupid thing. Even our car, it seemed, wanted to remind us to keep our eyes open.

We were on our way to the home of one of my students. After graduating from Country Day children leave lower school and enter middle school, or fifth grade, an important passage for them. Although a graduation exercise had already been held, the parents and children wanted a second one so that Will and I could take part. As we approached the house we could see brightly colored balloons marking the occasion. Children, parents, and teachers mingled outside and in, where there were banners and more balloons, and the sweet excitement of children permeated the air. The boys were all dressed in coat and tie and the girls wore their party best. The ceremony began with the children standing on a winding staircase singing a song they had composed for me.

I had made awards and commendations with individual messages for all of the children. Handing these out and giving hugs allowed me to recognize each child in a special way. Will, dressed in his open-necked whites, delivered a short "commencement" address. I had managed to control my emotions up to this point. The parents had presented me with several beautiful gifts and I was deeply moved. But when my room mother unveiled a large photo montage of scenes of the children and me taken during the school year, my reserve crumbled. All the wonderful memories came flooding back, and I had to stop and ask for a handkerchief. All of us had been through so much; we sensed that this afternoon was a time for healing. Later that night I received a phone call advising me to tune in a local TV channel. One of the parents had provided the station with a videotape of the party. This replay gave us a chance to relive the day.

I presented awards to my fourth-grade students during the special graduation exercise.

Shortly after the "graduation," we received a call from the navy's office of legislative affairs asking if we would meet with Senator Arlen Specter, chairman of the Senate Intelligence Committee. Senator Specter wanted to hear first hand about the bombing and my subsequent dismissal from Country Day. He was in the process of writing a bill that would establish a federal program to provide rewards to individuals who furnish information about acts of terrorism against American citizens or property.

The senator had entered a *New York Times* story about the bombing into the *Congressional Record* with this comment: "Mr. President, when I read this account I feel very sad for Mrs. Rogers, very sad for the community, very sad for the school, and very sad for what has resulted. If we are to stand up to terrorism, if we are to have men serving in the navy, and if we are to have relatives, wives of such military heroes subjected to terrorist attacks and then to have them let down by their fellow members of their community and schools, I think it is a very sad day for this country and it really undercuts our efforts to fight terrorism."

So we went to D.C. The morning after our arrival we drove straight to the senator's office in the new Rayburn Building. After introductions, Will and I settled into comfortable leather chairs facing his desk. I thanked him for his interest in my problem and for bringing it to the attention of the Congress.

He leaned forward, hands crossed on his desk. "Tell me about the bombing."

I recounted the whole scenario of 10 March. He seemed sympathetic and discussed his proposed legislation. Half an hour later we said our goodbyes. I was impressed by his sincerity and commitment to halting terrorism. And his efforts paid off: His bill passed the House and the Senate.

The flurry of events associated with the change of command was behind us. In July I had relieved an old friend, Captain Todd Barthold, of command of the Tactical Training Group and was thoroughly enjoying what Sharon and I agreed would be my last tour. The school was responsible for introducing deploying units and afloat staffs to the latest high-level tactical doctrine. There was a lot to learn and I was spending considerable time getting myself comfortable with the operation.

Sharon had decided to test the waters, sending her resume around and substitute teaching. The phone was ringing regularly with fill-in requests and she was puttting miles on the car responding to these. We felt ourselves fading into welcome obscurity.

We were going to spend Christmas with our families in Texas and intended to drive, since we anticipated having a full load of packages and luggage. As the holidays grew closer our excitement rose. Then, just before Thanksgiving, a breaking headline invaded the cocoon we thought we had spun: "Iranian Parliament Vows to Place *Vincennes* Skipper on Trial."

I walked into the house and found Sharon standing in the family room, newspaper in hand. "Will, have you seen this? What does it mean? Should we call the NIS? What now?" I hadn't seen the article, but Harry Stovall had called me at work and given me a rundown. "Harry told us to try not to worry. They don't think it's necessary to resume the personal security detachment. But they're going to increase surveillance." He was good to his word; the familiar gray Ford was already parked at the end of the street.

As the days passed there was no additional chest pounding on the part of the Iranian government. We had planned to leave on 19 December. At noon on the eighteenth, the phone rang at my desk.

"Captain, this is Stovall. I can't go into much detail on the phone, but we've received source information that there may be an attempt on the part of an Iranian fundamentalist group to kidnap you. We don't assign a lot of credibility to the info, but no one is ready to dismiss it either. What are your plans for the holidays? Have they changed?" We had faithfully kept the NIS apprised of our movements.

"No change, Harry, and no one but you and the family know what they are. You guys aren't planning to run in the security detachment, are you?" I thought to myself, No way! We're going to disappear quietly. I can't deal with all that overpowering security and I sure as hell don't want to tell Sharon to kiss this Christmas goodbye, too.

Stovall hadn't received any order to put the security detachment in place, but he did say he was getting pressure from well above his pay scale.

About an hour later I left to get the car washed. As the car was drying I glanced across the street into the faces of NIS agents Ed Swee-ney and Ed Jex, seated in their car. Both were active in the bombing investigation. Sharon and I knew them well. I walked over and stuck my head in the window. "I already know the answer, but I hope I'm wrong." Sweeney grinned, " 'Fraid so, Skipper. We were detailed to find you and provide trail until you get to the house and the security detachment arrives." The picture of the Rogers family trapped on an endless carousel haunted me all the way home.

The phone was ringing as I walked into the house. It was Stovall. "Captain, sorry, but the VCNO [Vice Chief of Naval Operations Admiral Leon Edney] put it out that there would be no chances taken with your and Sharon's safety. Arrangements are being made to fly you and the family to Texas. I'll send someone out to the house with the details as soon as possible."

"Harry, see if you can get this reevaluated daily. This is going to be tough to deal with and it's sure going to screw up the security team's Christmas." He hung up with a promise to see what he could do, but remarked, "Don't worry about the team. This is their job."

As I hung up, Sharon and Bill walked in. No explanations were necessary. The crowd of agents and vehicles in front of the house was enough.

The evening was consumed with cryptic phone calls to Texas attempting to explain the change of plans in a roundabout way. Early the next morning we were taken to North Island Naval Air Station for the flight to Fort Worth. Sharon has never been a fan of small aircraft. "Do you think it's going to be little?" she kept asking. As we passed the boarding gate I could see she had nothing to be concerned about. Sitting on the tarmac, its aft boarding ramp lowered, was a DC-9. Sharon was relieved. "Where should we sit?" she said when we entered the cabin. It looked as though there were seats for a hundred, and with the exception of accompanying agents, Sharon, Bill, and I were the load. I laughed. "I don't think it makes any difference."

The aircraft belonged to VR 60, a reserve logistic squadron from Memphis. The cockpit crew had been notified of the Rogers airlift mission the night before. Despite what must have been a great deal of personal upheaval, they were a cheerful bunch. Under normal circumstances they flew for American Airlines and they did everything to make the trip pleasant, even inviting Bill to the flight deck. The crew chief was the equal of any airline flight attendant. In addition to his other duties he took the role of handing out coffee and snacks seriously, although his baggy green flight suit fell short of commercial standards.

When we landed at Carswell Air Force Base in Fort Worth, there was a delay in taxiing instructions. It wasn't long before the reason became apparent. As the plane rolled onto the hardstand, Sharon nudged me. "I thought this whole thing was supposed to be quiet. Look out the window." Lined up alongside the fence were about ten cars, a large strip of red carpet was being rolled out, and several air force officers stood by saluting the aircraft. We had been watching the weather reports, and Texas was gripped by the coldest December in eighty years. I slid down in the seat. "This is embarrassing," I said. "Those people out there are in class A uniforms. We're bundled up like a bunch of pilgrims and there's no way out." As we started toward the door, Sharon poked me in the back and whispered, "I think the air force wanted to show the navy a class act."

It was too cold to stand in the raw wind for long, but we took the time to thank the base commander and protocol officer for Carswell's hospitality and got into the center vehicle of the caravan. As we sped through the base, every side road was blocked and air police rigidly saluted. Sharon smiled. "Someone from Portland must have phoned ahead."

The advance NIS team had rented a small RV and parked it in front of my brother-in-law's house. Except for brief forays the agents kept their thin San Diego blood inside the vehicle. My sister-in-law kept up a steady flow of coffee, but not even that could keep the chill out of their metal box. I kept pressing the team leader to stay in touch with Stovall, hoping the decision would be made to stand the effort down.

On the morning of 23 December welcome news came. The implied threat to our safety had been reassessed as minimal and once we had been delivered to San Antonio on Christmas Eve, the security detachment would leave. Everybody was happy with this decision. As soon as we arrived at my parents' home, we were on our own. But there was no escaping the realization that at any time, without warning, we might find ourselves sequestered under the NIS umbrella once again.

QUESTIONS LINGER. Does my husband remain the number one target of the Iranian Republic, as stated by the Twelve-Member Council of

Guardians, a constitutional watchdog body? It approved a law giving Iran power to arrest Americans anywhere and put them on trial. Tehran's radical newspaper *Abrar Daily* wrote, "Will Rogers III, commander of the missile cruiser *Vincennes*, should be the first person brought to trial under the new law." That is a sobering threat to live with.

What was happening in the cockpit of Flight 655? Were the voices of the *Vincennes*'s crew being recorded? Why wasn't the flight recorder ever recovered, submerged as it was beneath shallow and accessible water? Why did Iran delay so long in providing the flight's manifest? Certainly the airline had a record of the plane's passengers. Why didn't the aircraft respond to repeated radio warnings? One Iran Air pilot, Amir Razvani, was quoted by the wire services as saying, "We never responded; we ignored calls from American warships." I continue to wonder who the intended victim was of the pipe bomb. Someone was obviously monitoring our house, aware of our morning routine. Is it a coincidence that the first and only night the van was left outside, a bomb was attached to its undercarriage?

These questions and many others aside, I will never stop grieving for the victims of the Airbus and their families. I will feel that day's impact for the rest of my life, and it will forever be a reminder to me of the senselessness of war.

Through our close encounter with terrorism I have learned that it is all too easy for understandable fear to turn into ugly rumor mongering, hurtful gossip, and hatred. The strongest weapon people can employ against terrorism is to stand solidly together, seek intelligent solutions, and not abandon the victim.

People have often asked me how I coped. My family's unfailing encouragement, humor, and love enabled me to press on. The navy community backed us 100 percent. My colleagues' support never wavered. The love of my students was always evident and the courage of their parents saved my sanity. The general outpouring of friendship was a great comfort.

When you come as close to death as I did, life takes on sharper meaning. I welcome each day and treat it as a gift.

Within the family we repeatedly and in great detail rehashed the event that precipitated everything—the shootdown of Flight 655 on 3 July 1989. Certainly in those few minutes, errors were made. We played the "what if" scenario hundreds of times trying to find a crucial, missing piece of the puzzle. Finally we came to accept the views of Admirals Trost and Crowe. In a statement to the press Trost noted: "As the *Vincennes* investigation shows, there were in fact errors made by the crew. But neither the crew nor the ship failed as some have suggested. In fact, it was shown that the ship and crew performed well. The crew was involved in numerous combat engagements and was processing and synthesizing a voluminous amount of information in a very compressed time. That's typical in the heat of a combat situation." And in his remarks summarizing the results of the board of inquiry, Crowe wrote that "taken individually, the mistakes were not crucial to the decision to fire two standard missiles at the Airbus. Even cumulatively, they do not change the picture in a decisive way. Our past experience in the Gulf, the intelligence available to the ship, and the rules of engagement all supported such a judgment by the ship's captain. Captain Rogers did what his nation expected of him in defense of his ship and crew." Certainly their statements are appreciated. But the burden remains with me. As long as questions linger, this chapter will not be closed.

When the first anniversary of the van bombing approached, the principal agents held a meeting with Sharon and me. We wanted a verbal review of where things stood, and all of us felt that the anniversary might trigger renewed interest in the case and create new leads. The senior FBI agent recapped the investigation. "We've covered a lot of ground and accumulated a great deal of physical evidence," he said. "What we don't have at this point are workable suspects."

Following considerable discussion, the lead investigator concluded, in an emphatic tone, "Captain and Mrs. Rogers, I want you to know that this case will be pursued until it's solved—no matter how long it taskes."

"Someone, somewhere," one of the NIS agents added, "is going to make a remark or drop their guard. When that happens, we'll be there."

March came and went, then April, then May. Once again we began to push the past aside. Although the memories remained, a black jumble of sorrow, fear, anger, and confusion, we felt that time would dim if not erase those dark riders.

Like most people, we had read or heard that life-altering or -threatening circumstances transform life into something more vivid and precious. We have found this phenomenon to be dramatically true. New priorities emerged for us, along with a deepened appreciation for one another. We have slowed the pace of our lives in order to seize the moment and examine, critically, what yesterday seemed to be important goals.

As a family and as individuals, fused and tempered by the events of the past, we feel stronger. We are determined never, ever, to give in, and continually to look for the next horizon.

EPILOGUE

The past must not be used as an anvil for beating out the
present and the future.

—Paul-Emile Borduas

The events of 3 July 1988 and 10 March 1989 that form the centerpiece
of this book are behind Sharon and me. In the context of the drama
that has since occupied the world stage, most of the circumstances
surrounding these two days are minuscule historical footnotes. Nevertheless, numerous people caught in the vortex resulting from the
destruction of Iran Air Flight 655 found the direction of their lives
instantly and permanently altered. Others, less dramatically affected,
nonetheless played pivotal roles in this story. All, regardless of their
degree of involvement, have been distanced by time and other events
from the center of this particular storm.

Rear Admiral Anthony Less, USN, a masterful diplomat and naval
officer who successfully managed the navy's role in the Persian Gulf
tinderbox during the volatile 1988–89 period, was subsequently promoted to vice admiral. As of this writing he is commander, Naval Air
Forces, Atlantic. Rear Admiral Bob Kihune was promoted to vice admiral and after completion of his tour as commander, Naval Surface
Forces, Pacific, became deputy chief of naval operations for surface
warfare. Rear Admiral William Fogarty relieved Rear Admiral Less as
commander, Joint Task Force, Middle East, and held that post through
the violent days of Operations Desert Shield and Desert Storm.

Vic Guillory and Scott Lustig were selected for promotion to full
commander, and both later completed successful executive-officer
tours aboard new-construction Aegis cruisers. Ted Atwood retired

from the navy in 1989 and is currently the assistant rector of an Episcopal church in San Diego. Transfers and retirements have dispersed those who made up the crew of the *Vincennes* during the period covered here, but our ties to these men and their families remain intact and we hope they never fade.

After the 1989–90 school year, Dr. Tim Burns resigned as headmaster of La Jolla Country Day, accepting the head position at a private school on the East Coast. The Country Day faculty, concerned with the course taken by the school after the van bombing, began unionizing. This effort was later set aside following good-faith assurances by the school administration to redress faculty grievances.

After retirement from the navy in 1991, I accepted a position with a San Diego firm specializing in leading-edge technical solutions to military and civilian problems. Sharon, having completed a year of substitute teaching and working on a task force to redefine the direction of California elementary education, returned full time to the classroom. Our son Bill graduated from Colgate in the spring of 1991.

Index

The **Naval Institute Press** is the book-publishing arm of the U.S. Naval Institute, a private, nonprofit society for sea service professionals and others who share an interest in naval and maritime affairs. Established in 1873 at the U.S. Naval Academy in Annapolis, Maryland, where its offices remain, today the Naval Institute has more than 100,000 members worldwide.

Members of the Naval Institute receive the influential monthly magazine *Proceedings* and discounts on fine nautical prints, ship and aircraft photos, and subscriptions to the quarterly *Naval History* magazine. They also have access to the transcripts of the Institute's Oral History Program and get discounted admission to any of the Institute-sponsored seminars offered around the country.

The Naval Institute's book-publishing program, begun in 1898 with basic guides to naval practices, has broadened its scope in recent years to include books of more general interest. Now the Naval Institute Press publishes more than sixty titles each year, ranging from how-to books on boating and navigation to battle histories, biographies, ship and aircraft guides, and novels. Institute members receive discounts on the Press's nearly 400 books in print.

Full-time students are eligible for special half-price membership rates. Life memberships are also available.

For a free catalog describing Naval Institute Press books currently available, and for further information about U.S. Naval Institute membership, please write to:

Membership & Communications Department
U.S. Naval Institute
118 Maryland Avenue
Annapolis, Maryland 21402-5035

Or call, toll-free (800) 233-USNI.

THE NAVAL INSTITUTE PRESS

STORM CENTER

The USS *Vincennes* and Iran Air Flight 655

Designed by Karen L. White

Set in Joanna
by JDL Composition Services, Inc.
Baltimore, Maryland

Printed on 55-lb. Glatfelter antique cream
and bound in Holliston Kingston natural and Rainbow linen
by The Maple-Vail Book Manufacturing Group
York, Pennsylvania